Managing Crisis

Managing Crisis

Crisis

PRESIDENTIAL DISABILITY AND THE TWENTY-FIFTH AMENDMENT

Edited by

ROBERT E. GILBERT

Fordham University Press
New York
2000

Library of Congress Cataloging-in-Publication Data

Managing crisis : presidential disability and the twenty-fifth amendment / edited by
Robert E. Gilbert.
    p. cm.
  Includes bibliographical references and index.
  ISBN 0-8232-2086-9 (hardcover)—ISBN 0-8232-2087-7 (pbk.)
    1. Presidents—United States—Succession. 2. United States. Constitution.
25th Amendment. I. Gilbert, Robert E.
  KF5082.M36 2000
  342.73′062—dc21   00-041104

Printed in the United States of America
00 01 02 03 04 5 4 3 2 1
First Edition

To my father

CONTENTS

ACKNOWLEDGMENTS

Projects of this type always depend for their completion on many individuals. Although in our respective chapters, several other contributors and I have thanked various individuals for their help, I would like to express my appreciation here to those who played key roles in expediting the entire process. To the contributing authors, of course, I am particularly grateful. Working with each of them has educated me in aspects of this topic that previously I had not considered fully or at all. Also, I am grateful to others who have helped in various ways, especially Joseph M. Azam, Amilcar Antonio Barreto, Duane Brown, Barbara McIntosh Chin, Brandon Dillon, Janet-Louise Joseph, W. D. Kay, Richard Olender, and Jong Wai Tommee.

To the Center for the Study of the Presidency, which awarded me a research grant that enabled me to find the time necessary to bring this work to completion, I am grateful indeed. In particular, I thank Ted Buerger, Chairman of the Center's Board of Trustees, for his encouragement and support. Also, I wish to acknowledge Kathleen Hall Jamieson, Dean of the Annenberg School, for co-sponsoring (with the Center for the Study of the Presidency) the Symposium on Presidential Disability in October 1998 that led to the writing of this book. Her support is very much appreciated.

Finally, I thank those associated with Fordham University Press who helped in the process of preparing this work for publication, especially Mary Beatrice Schulte and Loomis Mayer. Their advice has been sound, their input has been helpful, and their many efforts are gratefully acknowledged. Also, to those reviewers who read the manuscript prior to publication, offering comments that were both perceptive and constructive, I offer a special word of appreciation.

Robert E. Gilbert
Boston
February, 2000

EDITOR'S INTRODUCTION

It was late September, and the president of the United States was vacationing in Colorado. His normal routine was to spend the mornings working in his office at Lowry Air Force Base and then play golf in the afternoons. On September 23, he followed his usual routine, but this time his golf game was badly disrupted by official business. Dwight D. Eisenhower later described his frustrating experience that day. He had hardly started playing when:

> word came that Washington was calling on the telephone. At the clubhouse I learned that Secretary [of State] Dulles wanted to talk to me, but by the time I could answer, I was informed that the Secretary was en route to an engagement, and that he would call again in an hour. At the appointed time I was back at the clubhouse only to be told there was difficulty on the lines. I would be notified as soon as the circuits were ready for us. When word came again that my call was waiting, I went back to the clubhouse once more and this time talked with the Secretary. . . .[1]

After resuming his golf game, the president was called back to the telephone still again. Eisenhower had been annoyed at these interruptions, because he felt they were unnecessary, and, as they mounted, his mood deteriorated rapidly. His White House Physician, Howard Snyder, recalled that the president's anger became so intense that "his veins stood out on his forehead like whipcords."[2] Although he attempted to resume his golf game, the president soon experienced symptoms of indigestion and departed for his mother-in-law's home, where he had been staying.

Most cardiologists on the case later agreed that Eisenhower probably had suffered a heart attack on the golf course that afternoon rather than on the following day when it was officially diagnosed. On September 24, the nation was informed that the president was suffering from indigestion, but soon the White House admitted that he had suffered a heart attack. The repercussions were immediate. For example, the Dow Jones Index fell by thirty points, and the value of stocks was reduced by some twelve billion dollars, the most serious decline since the Depression of 1929.[3]

Eisenhower recuperated at Fitzsimmons Army Hospital until the middle of November and then traveled east for additional recovery time at his farm in Gettysburg, Pennsylvania. He returned to the White House a few days before Christmas, although his doctors insisted that he modify his work schedule so that excessive fatigue would be avoided.

During his lengthy hospitalization, the president was deeply troubled about what incapacity would mean in the case of the president of the United States. Worried that his ill health might put the nation at risk, Eisenhower instructed his attorney general, Herbert Brownell, to draw up a constitutional amendment to deal with instances of presidential disability. The Brownell Amendment was submitted to Congress in early 1957. It was similar to, but not identical with, the present disability amendment, reading as follows:

> Section 1: In case of the removal of the President from office, or of his death or resignation, the Vice President shall become President for the unexpired portion of the then current term.
>
> Section 2: If the President shall declare in writing that he is unable to discharge the powers and duties of his office, such powers and duties shall be discharged by the Vice President as Acting President.
>
> Section 3: If the President does not so declare, the Vice President, if satisfied with the President's inability, and upon approval in writing of a majority of the heads of executive departments who are members of the President's Cabinet, shall discharge the powers and duties of the office as Acting President.
>
> Section 4: Whenever the President declares in writing that his inability is terminated, the President shall forthwith discharge the powers and duties of his office.[4]

Interestingly, the Brownell Amendment gave no clear role whatsoever to Congress in matters of presidential disability. It did not specify that the president's letter indicating his inability to discharge the powers and duties of his office should be addressed to congressional leaders; it did not give Congress the power to establish a "body" other than the cabinet in the determination of presidential disability;

it did not give Congress the power to resolve disputes between a president and an acting president over whether the president is able to resume the powers and duties of his office.

Neither the Democratic nor the Republican leaders in Congress were particularly supportive of the amendment. House Speaker Sam Rayburn argued that the proposal would shock the country, because it would be viewed as an indication that the president was about to turn over his duties to the vice president. Senate Majority Leader Lyndon Johnson noted the need for extensive study and deliberation before any congressional action could be taken. Senator William Knowland, the Republican Senate leader, was convinced that a president's disability should be determined by a committee that had significant congressional representation. Since the congressional leadership was unenthusiastic and far from being of one mind about the Brownell Amendment, Congress took no action on it. Instead, Eisenhower drafted and sent a letter of understanding to Vice President Nixon, outlining procedures to be followed in the event of the president's inability. Dated February 5, 1958, that letter contained language significantly different from that of the March 3, 1958, press release on the subject, which is quoted in chapter 1 by John Feerick. Therefore, it is cited here in full:

1. In any instance in which I could clearly recognize my own inability to discharge the powers and duties of the presidency, I would, of course, so inform you and you would act accordingly.

2. With the exception of this one kind of case, you will be the individual explicitly and exclusively responsible for determining whether there is any inability of mine that makes it necessary for you to discharge the powers and duties of the presidency, and you will decide the exact timing of the devolution of this responsibility on you. I would hope that you would consult with the Secretary of State, Governor Adams [the Chief of Staff], and General Heaton [one of Eisenhower's doctors], and if possible, with medical experts assembled by him, but the decision will be yours alone.

3. I will be the one to determine if and when it is proper for me to resume the powers and duties of the Presidency.

4. If any disability of mine should, in the judgment of any group of distinguished medical authorities that you might assemble, finally become of a permanent character, I will, of course, accept their decision

and promptly resign my position. But if I were not able to do so, and the same group of consultants would so state, then you would take over not only the powers and duties but the perquisites of the Presidency including the White House itself.

5. In temporary cases of my inability, we agree that you should act for the necessary period in your capacity as Vice President and additionally as Acting President.[5]

Eisenhower's letter of understanding stood as the operative document on presidential disability until he left office in 1961. Even though the constitutional legitimacy of such a letter is in some doubt, a similar letter of understanding was written by President Kennedy to Vice President Johnson and was in effect during the 1961–63 period. When Lyndon Johnson became president after the assassination of John Kennedy, he entered into a similar agreement with House Speaker John McCormack, next in line of succession to the presidency since the vice presidency was then vacant.[6] Shortly after being elected to a term in his own right, President Johnson entered into a similar arrangement with the country's new vice president, Hubert Humphrey. This arrangement was in effect for two years and, as Dr. James M. Young describes later in this volume, was actually implemented during the period of Johnson's gall bladder surgery in September 1965.

Finally, with President Johnson's strong support, Congress passed a presidential disability amendment as the Twenty-Fifth Amendment to the Constitution in July 1965. After being ratified by the requisite number of states, it was formally added to the Constitution in February 1967. The text of the Amendment is included in the Appendix, so will not be detailed here. However, it is worth noting at the outset that by 1985, eighteen years after its adoption, the Amendment's first three sections had already been implemented. This means, of course, that only the fourth section has yet to be invoked.

A SYMPOSIUM

During the years since its ratification, the Twenty-Fifth Amendment has received occasional attention. In October 1998, a Symposium on Presidential Disability and the Twenty-Fifth Amendment was held at the Brookings Institution in Washington, D.C., co-sponsored by the Center for the Study of the Presidency and the Annenberg School of Communications. The participants were John D. Feerick, Dean of the Fordham University School of Law; James M. Young, M.D., White House Physician to Presidents Kennedy and Johnson; Lawrence C. Mohr, M.D., White House Physician to Presidents Reagan and Bush; Robert S. Robins, a political scientist at Tulane University; and Robert E. Gilbert, a political scientist at Northeastern University.

This book project developed out of the symposium. Rather than simply publish the five papers given at Brookings, the decision was made to invite additional papers from other relevant authors and publish the entire collection as something of a retrospective on the Twenty-Fifth Amendment as the country enters a new millennium. The history and politics of the American presidency—and of the country—have been affected dramatically by the frequent illnesses suffered by presidents and, at times, by the concealment of those illnesses. The language of the Constitution has now been changed to confront this reality, but in a manner that carefully protects the essential principles on which the American political system is constructed.

THINGS TO CONSIDER

It is important to remember that the framers of the Constitution established a political framework based, first and foremost, on the doctrine of separation of powers. Thus, there would be three distinct branches of the national government, each with its own prerogatives and responsibilities. However, the framers also wanted to incorporate checks and balances into the new system and deliberately created overlapping powers among the branches so that the ensuing rivalries and conflicts would keep the government from becoming oppressive.

The drafters of the Twenty-Fifth Amendment were careful to respect the intentions of the Constitution's original framers. They conferred on *executive branch* officials (the vice president and cabinet) the prerogative of separating a *chief executive* from his powers and duties and excluded Congress from playing any dominant role, ex-

cept in one narrow and rather remote instance, as will be discussed
later by several authors. At the same time, the Amendment's drafters
showed respect for the checks-and-balances concept in various ways,
especially, perhaps, when they gave the *legislative branch* the power
to approve presidential nominations to a vacant vice presidency. Just
as the Senate must approve presidential appointments to the cabinet,
a key element of the checks-and-balances system, the Twenty-Fifth
Amendment now gives this prerogative to *both* houses of Congress
when presidential appointments to the vice-presidential office are to
be made. So, as several authors discuss here, the provisions related
to presidential disability and succession as set forth in the Twenty-
Fifth Amendment are consistent with, and faithful to, the fundamental intentions of the Founding Fathers. For this reason, they reinforce
rather than threaten the delicate balance of the constitutional system.

This book should be of interest to historians, presidency scholars,
political psychologists, those interested in politics and the life sciences, constitutional lawyers, and other scholars of the Constitution.
Ten of the chapters explore different topics related to the Twenty-
Fifth Amendment from the particular perspective of the author. The
authors' backgrounds are quite varied and include medicine, law,
political science, government, psychology, and journalism. Several
authors offer standard academic analyses of issues related to the
Amendment; several are practitioners who worked for, or opposed,
congressional enactment of the Amendment in the 1960s; several are
presidential physicians who reflect on their unique experiences in
the administrations of several different presidents and discuss issues
related to presidential disability and the usefulness of the Twenty-
Fifth Amendment from their own particular vantage point.

Given the very different backgrounds of the authors and the widely
varying approaches they take here toward issues relating to presidential disability and the Twenty-Fifth Amendment, this book is an unusual one. Therefore, it should not be approached as standard
academic fare. Anecdotal as well as scholarly, practical as well as
theoretical, the chapters included here offer a spectrum of opinion
relating to different, but interrelated, aspects of the topic. At first
glance, they may appear to be somewhat disjointed; on reflection,
they will be seen as a more comprehensive examination of the
Twenty-Fifth Amendment than standard academic analysis could

provide, precisely because of their multidimensional nature. Occasionally, they may even seem somewhat repetitious, but this is only because certain events and certain presidencies are so central to an examination of issues related to the Twenty-Fifth Amendment. Although an effort has been made to minimize the incidence of such repetition, it seems important for each author to be able to offer his or her "take" on the subject as he or she thought most appropriate.

Readers will find that the authors sometimes disagree, which is not surprising in light of the complexity of the subjects being discussed. For example, some argue that Section 3 of the Amendment already has been invoked; one argues that it has not been. One writes that consideration should be given to invoking the Amendment whenever a president is in mourning over the death of a loved one; another argues that such invocation would be ineffectual and pointless. One states that Woodrow Wilson—the very prototype of a disabled president—was aware of his severe illness; another writes that he was not aware, an important point when studying possible scenarios involving the disability provisions of the Amendment. The occasional differences in opinion and in interpretation of events should strengthen, rather than weaken, the volume, since they provide readers with a variety of informed viewpoints.

Although none of the authors see the Twenty-Fifth Amendment as perfect or as resolving all issues related to the disability of presidents, there is something of a consensus that the Amendment is a very effective and important addition to the Constitution and that structural changes to it are unnecessary. Within the existing language of the Amendment, however, several facilitating mechanisms might well be helpful, and several of these are suggested in various chapters.

One common point of reference here is that, for the Amendment to work as it was intended, medical input on a continuing basis is essential in assessing the president's health and ability to serve. Some critics, however, see the need for a decisive change in the way this input is achieved. To this end, a dramatic and far-reaching proposal has been made from time to time and is still being advanced by its defenders, although they often differ on the details. This probably represents the principal "reform" proposal made with regard to the Twenty-Fifth Amendment since it was added to the Constitution more than thirty years ago, and it is a controversial one.

A Persistent Proposal

In 1999 Dr. Herbert Abrams suggested that a "system should be enacted that ensures the vice president, the Cabinet, and the public of objective, independent and accurate assessments of the president's health" and then went on to urge the creation of a medical advisory committee to achieve these goals. Abrams argued that the surgeon general should choose the members of this committee from a list prepared by the president of the Institute of Medicine of the National Academy of Science and that such members should have overlapping terms of six years. The committee would include "a reasonable mix of Democrats and Republicans," and its final composition would be "subject to the approval of the secretary of Health and Human Services." Members of the committee could not be removed at the whim of the president and would serve as a "powerful antidote to the White House cover-ups of the past." Indeed, Abrams concludes, "the independence, breadth of expertise, lack of conflict of interest, availability, and credibility of the committee would assure the public of an objective appraisal and would preclude inaction by the executive branch in the face of disability."[7]

Eleven years earlier, Dr. Bert Park had made a similar proposal, but his "medical committee" was somewhat different from, and less bureaucratized, than Abrams's. Park wrote then that:

> the Twenty-Fifth Amendment has been hailed as a far-reaching statement covering virtually every contingency likely to be faced in future cases of presidential inability. Yet precisely where the vice president and cabinet are to obtain the data to judge a prospective case should the president fail to certify his or her own disability was all but ignored by the Amendment's sponsors. They chose instead to bow to dubious precedent of depending on presidential physicians as the single most important future source of information. Moreover, if these physicians have occasionally misled us, it is now rather naïvely assumed that the media will not.[8]

In order to deal effectively with the problem of medical cover-ups perpetrated by "presidential physicians," Park suggested that a "Presidential Disability Commission, staffed at least in part by physicians skilled in disability determination and chosen or appointed by a president before the inception of the new administration," would represent an important contribution. This disability commission would not have the power to "depose the president" since the Amendment leaves that matter to the vice president and cabinet. Rather, Park explains, "the Commission's task would be restricted only to gathering the medical facts to assist the vice president in making a meaningful decision should the question of inability arise."[9]

In 1995, Park reintroduced his proposal. This time he wrote that "the findings of an independent medical panel with no political axe to grind would be of immeasurable benefit to a vice president, who might otherwise be accused of usurping power for personal gain." He went on to argue that organized medicine has now "established in practice a clear and useful distinction between the terms 'impairment' and 'disability.'" "Insofar as such a distinction has proved enduring and practical in determining disability among corporate CEOs and the like," he asked, "why not extend such methodology to future alleged instances of impairment and consequently disability in the nation's chief executive?"[10]

Park's question is a good one and clearly deserves an answer. A number of authors in this volume provide several. Not surprisingly, the answers are disparate, ranging from the theoretical to the practical, but consistently they are negative. Once again, the widely varying backgrounds of the authors enriches the discussion. In this particular instance, the insights of the "practitioners" are reinforced by the analyses presented by those with a more "academic" orientation.

The Book's Content

Apart from this issue and on a broader level, each of the volume's contributing authors offers a variety of insights related to the Twenty-Fifth Amendment, its history and development, strengths and weaknesses. For example, as a member of the task force that helped develop the Amendment, John D. Feerick provides an insider's account of its legislative history and subsequent development. He also reviews the various presidential succession laws passed by Congress at various points in history. Feerick's overall conclusion is that the Amendment has served the nation well and that its perceived weaknesses are, in fact, its strengths: it protects the president from being ousted precipitately, respects both separation of powers and checks and balances, ensures stability in the event of succession, and protects the interests of the American people.

After surveying instances of presidential illness and medical cover-ups that have occurred throughout American history, Robert E. Gilbert emphasizes the particular strength of the Twenty-Fifth Amendment in providing for cases of presidential disability while protecting the institution of the presidency. Such protection is a major contribution to a political system that is grounded on separation of powers and checks and balances and in which a sick presidency would pose far graver risks than a sick president. Gilbert argues that remedies offered to address the Amendment's perceived weaknesses often overlook this central fact.

Former senator Birch Bayh, a leading force behind congressional enactment of the Twenty-Fifth Amendment, writes that the Amendment is intended to ensure that, in instances of presidential disability, the national interest will always come first. Although he believes that it is becoming increasingly likely that the Amendment will be followed in future instances of presidential disability, Bayh recommends a number of steps to facilitate implementation, including possible passage by Congress of a new, and quite controversial, law. He also calls for a national dialogue about presidential disability so that the public will understand the mechanisms that are in place to deal with it.

In the next three chapters, three White House Physicians (James M. Young, M.D., E. Connie Mariano, M.D., and Lawrence C. Mohr, M.D.), who collectively cared for five different presidents, offer their observations not only on the Twenty-Fifth Amendment but also on such subjects as the dramatic evolution of the White House Medical Unit, the type of medical care provided to presidents and members of their families (and staffs), the close but professional relationship existing between presidents and their physicians, doctor–patient confidentiality, and the important differences between medical impairment and political disability. Additionally, the responsibilities of White House Physicians, the importance of outside medical specialists in the care of the president, the role of White House Physicians in the Washington power structure and the need to enhance that role, particularly with regard to possible invocation of the Twenty-Fifth Amendment, are all addressed. Since the opinions of these authors derive from their experiences as members of the "inner circle," they are particularly informative.

Jerrold M. Post explains that acute disability poses fewer problems for the political system than disability that is subtle. He examines the unique difficulties posed at several levels of political life by psychiatric illness and substance abuse, both of which may impair a leader's mental and emotional reactions. Relating these difficulties to the area of presidential disability, he suggests several conditions that should automatically trigger active consideration of the Twenty-Fifth Amendment's invocation, including significant use of psychoactive drugs and the diagnosis of any progressive, mentally disabling condition.

Beginning with the provocative proposition that health care for presidents can be "bad, even disastrous," Robert S. Robins studies the role played by five different types of first lady (protector, manager, adviser, supporter, and partner) in their husbands' administrations and assesses the likely role of each type in instances when invocations of the Twenty-Fifth Amendment's disability provisions are being contemplated. Evaluating Edith Wilson, Florence Harding, Eleanor Roosevelt, Mamie Eisenhower, and Lady Bird Johnson, Robins emphasizes the view that, although the president's spouse does not act very differently from other members of the inner circle, his or her role in invocations of the Amendment is likely to be pivotal.

Joel K. Goldstein's focus is the relationship between the Amendment and the vice presidency, a subject that rarely gets sustained attention but clearly should. He points out that the vice presidency is the "star" of the Amendment, and that the Amendment would not have been possible without the development of the vice-presidential office that occurred during the past half-century. As Goldstein relates, the Founding Fathers' ambivalent feelings toward the vice presidency made it difficult for them to deal with issues of presidential disability. With the subsequent transformation of the vice presidency, however, the way was paved toward enactment of the Twenty-Fifth Amendment, and the office and Amendment now enjoy a mutually reinforcing relationship.

Tom Wicker provides something of a conclusion to the volume. He reminds us that he opposed the Twenty-Fifth Amendment when it was being considered by Congress in the 1960s, in large part because he saw it as a new and dangerous means by which presidents could be removed from office unfairly. His thinking has evolved, however, and he now concludes that it serves a number of useful and very important purposes. Among these, Wicker sees the Amendment as contributing over time to better vice presidents and providing the American people with a greater voice in filling vice-presidential vacancies than they have in the selection of the vice-presidential candidates at the nominating conventions.

It was precisely to assess fears of arbitrary usurpation as well as other criticisms outlined in the Wicker chapter that led both the Miller Center Commission (1980s) and the Working Group on Presidential Disability (1990s) to revisit the Twenty-Fifth Amendment in detail. Since these two groups systematically and over a lengthy period of time dissected the various provisions of the Amendment, it is important that their conclusions be included here, particularly since they are based on the inputs of many individuals with expertise in relevant areas and contribute so strongly to the historical record. Therefore, edited versions of the reports of both groups follow the Wicker critique and are, in a very real sense, a response to it and to other concerns that have been expressed about the Amendment. Particularly interesting is the fact that the findings and recommendations of both groups are quite similar, even though separated in time by some eight years. The Miller Center Commission Report is edited here by Kenneth W. Thompson; the Working Group Report, by Robert J. Joynt, M.D., and James F. Toole, M.D. In both instances, the editors also provide an introductory commentary.

The Authors' Objective

The issue of presidential disability is an extremely important one since it is intricately intertwined with the health of the nation. The hope of all contributing authors is to increase understanding of both the issue and the importance and usefulness of the Twenty-Fifth Amendment in resolving problems related to it. It should be recognized, however, that no law or constitutional provision can solve once for all the problems springing from the central fact that all human beings, including all presidents, are mortal. The Twenty-Fifth Amendment is designed not to solve such problems but rather to make them manageable. It is within this context that this book should be read.

NOTES

1. Dwight D. Eisenhower, *Mandate for Change* (Garden City, N.Y.: Doubleday, 1963), p. 536.

2. Howard McCrum Snyder, Papers, Box 11, "Draft on DDE's Heart Attack," Dwight D. Eisenhower Library, Abilene, Kans., p. 4.

3. Piers Brendon, *Ike* (New York: Harper & Row, 1986), p. 313.

4. Dwight D. Eisenhower, Papers as President of the United States, Administration Series, Box 8, "Herbert Brownell, Jr.," 1957 (3), Dwight D. Eisenhower Library, Abilene, Kans., pp. 3–4.

5. Eisenhower Papers, Administration Series, Box 32, "Rogers, William P.," 1958 (5).

6. John W. McCormack, Oral History, September 23, 1968, John F. Kennedy Library, Boston, Mass., p. 33.

7. Herbert L. Abrams, "Can the Twenty-Fifth Amendment Deal with a Disabled President? Preventing Future White House Cover-Ups," *Presidential Studies Quarterly*, 29, No. 1 (Winter 1999), 118, 129.

8. Bert E. Park, "Presidential Disability: Past Experiences and Future Implications," *Politics and the Life Sciences*, 7, No. 1 (August 1988), 56.

9. Ibid., 57.

10. Bert E. Park, "Resuscitating the 25th Amendment: A Second Opinion Regarding Presidential Disability," *Political Psychology*, 16, No. 4 (December 1995), 826, 831.

1

The Twenty-Fifth Amendment: Its Origins and History

John D. Feerick

The legislative history of the Twenty-Fifth Amendment has its origins in the early state constitutions that were familiar to the framers. That history is examined here, as are the several presidential succession laws passed by Congress before the Amendment was added to the U.S. Constitution in 1967. This chapter acknowledges that the Amendment has become an item of popular discussion as evidenced by its use in such movies as Dave *and* Air Force One. *It concludes that the Amendment has served the nation well, filling gaps that had long existed. At the same time, it respects the presidency and ensures stability in the event of succession.*

> Wise and constructive solutions must rest on historical knowledge, an appreciation of the constitutional possibilities, and a feel for the political processes in a government of separated powers functioning in a time of crisis.
>
> —Paul Freund

Upon its adoption in February 1967, the Twenty-Fifth Amendment repaired "geological faults in our governmental structure that under pressure could produce upheaval and grave disorder."[1] One involved the inability of a president: more specifically, who had the power to determine the existence and termination of an inability and what was the status of a vice president in such a case? No answers were pro-

I acknowledge with great appreciation the diligent assistance of Matthew Friedman, a recent graduate of Fordham Law School. His help left nothing to be desired.

vided by the Constitution as adopted, though the presence of ambiguities in the area of inability was noted at the Convention of 1787.
A second "fault" involved the lack of any provision for filling a vacancy in the vice presidency caused by the death, resignation, or
removal of a vice president. This is not surprising since the office of
vice president was an afterthought, created late in the Convention;
and, in any event, the Constitution provided for the contingency of
no president and vice president by empowering Congress to establish a line of succession by statute.

The deaths and inabilities of presidents and vacancies in the vice
presidency that had occurred prior to the Amendment made the need
for provisions and procedures to deal with these contingencies a constitutional imperative. The Twenty-Fifth Amendment responded to
that need. When it took its place in the Constitution, it became the
third amendment to deal directly with the subject of presidential
succession. The chapters in this book address many subjects that bear
on the Twenty-Fifth Amendment. This chapter deals with the background to the Amendment, its long legislative history, and the historical events and considerable thought that shaped its provisions and
approach. The chapter concludes with some comments on recent efforts to facilitate the Amendment's implementation.

THE BACKGROUND: THE FRAMING OF THE
ORIGINAL SUCCESSION PROVISION

When the Founding Fathers met in the summer of 1787, they were
not oblivious to issues of succession, as they had encountered instances of death and disability by governors under the colonial char-
ters and the first state constitutions. All the early state constitutions
contained succession provisions. For instance, the New York State
Constitution of 1777 provided in Article XX:

> And in case of the impeachment of the governor, or his removal from
> office, death, resignation, or absence from the state, the lieutenant gov-
> ernor shall exercise all the power and authority appertaining to the
> office of governor, until another be chosen, or the governor absent, or
> impeached, shall return, or be acquitted.

Article XXI added:

> And if, during such vacancy of the office of governor, the lieutenant governor shall be impeached, displaced, resign, die, or be absent from the state, the president of the senate shall, in like manner as the lieutenant governor, administer the government, until others shall be elected by the suffrage of the people, at the succeeding election.

At the Constitutional Convention of 1787, a provision on executive succession appeared in the August 6th draft of the Constitution submitted by a Committee on Detail. When the provision was discussed on August 27th, note was made of its failure to explain either the reach of the term "disability" or the identity of the person or persons to determine it.[2] In September 1787, as the Convention rushed to a conclusion, the framers created an office of vice president and reworked the provision on presidential succession, but not without leaving a number of gaps for the future. It is interesting to note the development of the provision in the first month of September.

As it went to the Committee on Style on September 8, 1787:

> Sec. 2: [I]n case of his removal as aforesaid, death, absence, resignation or inability to discharge the powers or duties of his office the Vice President shall exercise those powers and duties until another President be chosen, or until the inability of the President be removed.

> Sec. 1: The Legislature may declare by law what officer of the United States shall act as President in case of the death, resignation, or disability of the President and Vice President; and such Officer shall act accordingly, until such disability be removed, or a President shall be elected.[3]

As it returned on September 12, 1787:

> In case of the removal of the president from office, or of his death, resignation, or inability to discharge the powers and duties of the said office, the same shall devolve on the vice-president, and the Congress may by law provide for the case of removal, death, resignation or inability, both of the president and vice-president, declaring what officer shall then act as president and such officer shall act accordingly until the disability be removed, *or the period for chusing another president arrive.*[4]

The italicized expression was subsequently changed at the Convention to "or a President shall be elected" as originally suggested by

James Madison. With this amendment, the returned draft provision became Article II, section 1, clause 6 of the Constitution. Left unclear, among other things, was what "devolved" on a vice president in a case of succession and whether a succeeding vice president served for the rest of the term, until the removal of an inability, or until a new election was called. These were no small matters, as history would reveal.

IMPLEMENTING THE CONSTITUTION

In the first Congress, steps were taken to implement the Constitution in many areas, including that of presidential succession. The members of that Congress debated who should act as president in the event of a vacancy in both the presidency and the vice presidency. They did so with an eye on the personalities of the people then serving in the offices proposed for the line of succession. One member of the first Congress said that the Senate was intent on keeping Thomas Jefferson, then secretary of state, from being held up "as King of the Romans."[5]

Proposals favoring a cabinet line of succession, a line involving the leaders of Congress, and succession by the chief justice were introduced and debated in the first Congress. Indeed, some thought that the subject was too academic and that succession would be a rare occurrence. No consensus emerged, and the subject was revisited in the second Congress. After extensive debate, during which the House of Representatives favored succession by the secretary of state and the Senate by its President pro tempore, Congress passed the country's first succession law, running the line of succession to the President pro tempore and the Speaker. James Madison and others questioned whether legislative leaders were "officers" within the meaning of the Constitution's succession provision.[6] Since the law was never to be applied, the issue became one for constitutional scholars.

THE DEATH OF A PRESIDENT

Upon the death in office of President William Harrison in 1841, considerable debate ensued as to the assertion by his vice president,

John Tyler, that he had become president, formally taking the title of president and serving out the president's term. Former president John Quincy Adams, then a member of Congress, said in his diary for April 16, 1841:

> I paid a visit this morning to Mr. Tyler, who styles himself President of the United States, and not Vice-President, acting as President, which would be the correct style. But it is a construction in direct violation both of the grammar and context of the Constitution, which confers upon the Vice-President, on the decease of the President, not the office, but the powers and duties of said Office.[7]

Some believed Tyler was correct, while others expressed concern over the precedent that was being created. If the vice president became president, they felt, a recovered president would not be able to reclaim his powers and duties in a case of inability, since the Constitution did not distinguish among the various contingencies it specified. One senator, William Allen of Ohio, raised the specter of a president who had been disabled but recovered only to find the vice president claiming to be president. "What would become of the office?" he asked. "Was it to vibrate between the two claimants?" He warned that, if the "office" of president devolved in a succession event, "the most fearful convulsions might follow."[8] Still others viewed the matter as academic, because there was a permanent vacancy in the presidential office. There was no possibility of a president who had died, resigned, or was removed seeking to recover his "office" or "powers and duties." Despite the controversy over his status, Tyler's claim to the presidency was accepted by the country at large, and the precedent he set was later followed by other vice presidents when presidents died in office.[9]

THE INABILITY OF A PRESIDENT

The case of "inability" hypothesized by some at the time of Harrison's death became a real occurrence on the morning of July 2, 1881, when President James A. Garfield was shot in the back as he was leaving Washington, D.C., for a tour of New England. For eighty days he hovered between life and death, dying on the night of September 19, 1881. During the period of his inability, the cabinet sought to discharge the responsibilities of their departments while Vice President Chester A. Arthur hesitated to take any affirmative steps lest he be labeled a usurper. The cabinet debated what the Constitution contemplated in a case of inability and sought unsuccessfully to engage Arthur in the business of the government. It is reported that a majority of the cabinet was of the view that if Arthur did assume the duties of president, he would become president for the remainder of the term. Others outside the cabinet were also of that view, though there were still others who were of the view that a vice president acted only temporarily in a case of inability and that Congress had the power to declare an inability or, at a minimum, to establish a procedure for making such a pronouncement.[10]

After his assumption of the office of president upon Garfield's death, Arthur pressed Congress to address the inadequacy of the country's succession laws, stating:

> Is the inability limited in its nature to long-continued intellectual incapacity, or has it a broader import?
>
> What must be its extent and duration?
>
> How must its existence be established?
>
> Has the President whose inability is the subject of inquiry any voice in determining whether or not it exists, or is the decision of that momentous and delicate question confided to the Vice-President, or is it contemplated by the Constitution that Congress should provide by law precisely what should constitute inability, and how and by what tribunal or authority it should be ascertained?
>
> If the inability proves to be temporary in nature, and during its continuance the Vice-President lawfully exercises the functions of the Executive, by what tenure does he hold his office?
>
> Does he continue as President for the remainder of the four years' term?
>
> Or would the elected President, if his inability should cease in the interval, be empowered to resume his office?
>
> And if, having such lawful authority, he should exercise it, would the Vice-President be thereupon empowered to resume his powers and duties as such?[11]

No answer to any of these questions was forthcoming, with the result that the country would go through another inability crisis when President Woodrow Wilson suffered a stroke in 1919. Then the affairs of the country and world were more urgent than in 1881. Yet the uncertainties that surrounded the succession provision operated as a disincentive to Vice President Thomas Marshall's exercising any presidential authority and caused a problem for the cabinet. As in 1881, the cabinet sought to fill the leadership vacuum, but not without receiving a strong negative reaction from a disabled president, who requested the cabinet's leader, the secretary of state, to resign his office for usurping presidential authority.[12]

THE SECOND SUCCESSION LAW

Although Garfield's assassination produced no response from Congress on the issue of presidential inability, it did lead to a change in the line of succession beyond the vice presidency. When Arthur assumed the presidency upon Garfield's death, there was then, because of legislative practices in use at the time, no President pro tempore or Speaker of the House of Representatives. Had anything happened to him during that period, a crisis of epic proportions could have confronted the country. Fearful of that, Arthur prepared a secret proclamation convening an immediate session of Congress to elect a President pro tempore.[13]

Four years later, when Vice President Thomas Hendricks died in office, there was again neither a President pro tempore nor a Speaker. As a consequence, President Cleveland did not attend Hendricks's funeral so as to avoid "even the remote chance of accident, incident to travel."[14]

These incidents, together with the risk of the opposition party to that of an elected president being in control of Congress at the time of a presidential succession event, led Congress in 1886 to replace the legislative leaders in the line of succession with the members of the cabinet, in the order in which the different departments were created. It was felt that with a cabinet line of succession, there would be continuity of administration and policy, and no question about their status as constitutional "officers."[15]

LEGISLATIVE EFFORTS TO CLOSE SUCCESSION GAPS

The Succession Law of July 18, 1947

Following the death of President Roosevelt, President Truman urged Congress to revisit the line of succession, declaring that a president should not have the power to choose his successor, as would be the case with a cabinet line of succession. He said that the office of president "should be filled by an elective officer," stating that the Speaker of the House "is the official in the Federal Government whose selection, next to that of the President and Vice-President, can be most accurately said to stem from the people themselves."[16] A period of debate and discussion ensued, at the conclusion of which Congress placed the Speaker and President pro tempore, respectively, ahead of the cabinet in the line of succession. A proposal for a special presidential election whenever the legislative leaders and cabinet were called upon to serve as president was rejected, though urged by President Truman. Instead, Congress provided in the 1947 statute for a legislative successor to serve for the balance of the term except in a case of inability or failure to qualify. A member of the cabinet so serving would be superseded by a new Speaker or President pro tempore.

Like its predecessors, the Succession Law of 1947 has never been implemented, with serious issues remaining unresolved as to its constitutionality and wisdom. Foremost among the constitutional questions is whether having the Speaker of the House or the President pro tempore of the Senate assume the presidency, if a vacancy in the office should occur between elections, violates the separation of powers principle, one of the most fundamental in our system. Also, like the Succession Act of 1792, this law could effect a political transfer of a current administration when a majority of Congress, or either House, is in the hands of the opposing party. However, the existence of Section 2 of the Twenty-Fifth Amendment, providing for a new vice president, makes this risk a remote one.

Efforts During the Eisenhower Years

Prior to the Eisenhower Administration, the issue of presidential inability received limited attention in Congress. In 1920, a number of proposals were introduced in Congress, some calling for the Supreme Court to decide a president's inability, and others, the cabinet. Hearings were held, then the subject faded from public consciousness, to return once again in the mid-1950s.

During his eight years as president, Eisenhower suffered a heart attack, an attack of ileitis, and a stroke that temporarily affected his speech. In the period following his heart attack, the cabinet met regularly, and the vice president presided at its meetings and performed other duties of the president. Said Vice President Nixon: "[The committee system] worked during the period of President Eisenhower's heart attack mainly because . . . there was no serious international crisis at that time. But had there been a serious international crisis requiring Presidential decisions, then . . . the committee system might not have worked."[17]

Shortly before the president's heart attack in September 1955, the House Judiciary Committee opened a study of the problem of presidential inability, widely distributing a questionnaire, which asked, among other things, the following questions:

> What was intended by the term "inability" as used in . . . the Constitution? Shall a definition be enacted into law? Who shall initiate the question of the President's inability to discharge the powers and duties of his office? Once raised, who shall make the determination of inability? If temporary, who raises the question that the disability has ceased to exist? Once raised, who shall make the determination of cessation? In the event of a finding of temporary disability, does the Vice-President succeed to the powers and duties of the office or to the office itself? Does Congress have the authority to enact legislation to resolve any and all of these questions, or will a constitutional amendment or amendments be necessary?[18]

Following the responses to this questionnaire, the Committee placed a number of proposals into legislative drafts. Some gave a decisive role to the vice president in the determination of an inability; others, the cabinet, Supreme Court, or a medical panel appointed by the chief justice. All permitted the president to declare his own inability and, most of them, the end of his inability. Hearings were held before the House Judiciary Committee in 1956 and 1957 without any consensus being reached. Attorney General Brownell presented on behalf of the administration a proposal under which the president could determine his own inability or, alternatively, the vice president could determine the existence of an inability with the concurrence of a majority of the cabinet. In either case, the vice president would only act as president, and the president could reclaim his powers and duties upon his declaration of recovery.

In reply to the criticism that the administration's approach would permit a ping-pong sort of dispute between the president and the vice president (that is, repeated declarations of inability and recovery), Brownell said that whoever was wrong might be subject to the remedy of impeachment.[19] Brownell's successor, William Rogers, suggested that in a case of disagreement between a president, on the one hand, and a vice president and cabinet, on the other, Congress should have the power to resolve the dispute.

Other proposals on the subject of inability were also advanced. Senator Frederick Payne of Maine put forth a proposal under which the chief justice of the Supreme Court would, upon the suspicion of the vice president of a presidential inability, appoint a panel of civilian experts to evaluate the president.[20] Those opposed to Senator Payne's recommendation felt that this would place the type of extrajudicial function upon the Supreme Court that it had usually rejected in the past.[21] There was also at that time a concern for leaving a presidential inability determination in the hands of medical experts. Professor Joseph E. Kallenbach of the University of Michigan stated that, "the panel of medical experts would be entrusted with making a kind of decision which would actually lie beyond their competence."[22] He went on to explain that the determination of whether a physical or mental condition is such that the public interest might seriously be affected if executive powers were to remain in the president's hands involves factors far beyond a doctor's diagnosis of a particular patient's condition. At the 1958 Hearings before the Subcommittee on Constitutional Amendments of the Senate Judiciary Committee, chaired by Senator Estes Kefauver of Tennessee, Attorney General Rogers gave strong testimony against the use of any medical commission, stating:

> Some have suggested that the commission be empowered to employ physicians and require the President to submit to physical and mental examinations, and there have been different proposals for the commission and the vote of the commission and so forth. We think these plans should be rejected for a number of reasons.
>
> First, it seems unwise to establish elaborate legal machinery for giving the President physical and mental examinations. This would give a hostile commission power to harass the President constantly, and risk danger of irresponsible demands for commission action. Not only would provision for such physical and mental examination be an affront to a President's personal dignity but it would also degrade the presidential office itself.

Second, it seems ill advised to establish complicated procedures which would prevent immediate action in case of an emergency, because there is a need for continuity in the exercise of Executive power and leadership—especially in time of crisis. Investigations, hearings, findings, and votes of a commission could drag on for days or weeks and result in a governmental crisis, during which no one would have a clear right to exercise Presidential power.

Third, such a commission would be totally unnecessary except where there was a dispute between the President and the Vice President in the executive branch itself.[23]

Other proposals included suggestions that a commission be set up comprising representatives of the executive, legislative, and judicial branches of government. In opposition to such an idea, Rogers stated that "it would appear to be a violation of the doctrine of separation of powers for officials in Congress to participate in any initial decision of Presidential inability."[24] He went on to say that "in effect, it would enable Congressional leaders to put the President out of office, and to keep him out, by declaring that he lacks the ability to perform his duties."[25] At the same time, however, Eisenhower himself seemed to favor the idea of a commission consisting of the chief justice and medical personnel. He also favored a cabinet line of succession beyond the vice presidency. Former president Truman suggested a commission of the vice president, chief justice, Speaker, and the majority and minority leaders of each House. The commission would have the power to select a group of medical authorities. If these authorities found the president "incapacitated," Congress would be so informed and empowered by a two-thirds vote to have the vice president become president for the remainder of the term.[26]

Despite the earnestness of the effort, neither House of Congress was able to reach agreement on any of these proposals, though the Senate Subcommittee on Constitutional Amendments favorably reported the Brownell approach, as modified by Rogers.

INFORMAL ARRANGEMENTS TO ADDRESS THE INABILITY PROBLEM

As Congress sought unsuccessfully to solve the problem of presidential inability, Eisenhower put his own hand to work and developed

an inability policy for his own administration, a summary of which
was released to the press on March 3, 1958:

> The President and the Vice President have agreed that the following
> procedures are in accord with the purposes and provisions of Article
> 2, Section 1, of the Constitution, dealing with Presidential inability.
> They believe that these procedures, which are intended to apply to
> themselves only, are in no sense outside or contrary to the Constitution
> but are consistent with its present provisions and implement its clear
> intent.
>
> 1. In the event of inability the President would—if possible—so
> inform the Vice President, and the Vice President would serve as Act-
> ing President, exercising the powers and duties of the office until the
> inability had ended.
>
> 2. In the event of an inability which would prevent the President
> from so communicating with the Vice President, the Vice President,
> after such consultation as seems to him appropriate under the circum-
> stances, would decide upon the devolution of the powers and duties of
> the Office and would serve as Acting President until the inability had
> ended.
>
> 3. The President, in either event, would determine when the inabil-
> ity had ended and at that time would resume the full exercise of the
> powers and duties of the Office.[27]

At the outset of the Kennedy administration, Attorney General
Robert Kennedy issued an opinion providing support for this type of
arrangement, stating, "there is no question that the Vice President
acts as President in the event of the President's inability and acts in
that capacity 'until the disability be removed.'" He said that "there
is no substantial question that it is the Vice President who determines
the President's inability if the President is unable to do so." He concluded by endorsing the agreement reached by President Eisenhower and Vice President Nixon, declaring that he was "of the
opinion that the understanding between the President and the Vice
President which I have approved of above is clearly constitutional
and as close to spelling out a practical solution to the problem as is
possible."[28]

THE ARRIVING AT A CONSENSUS

In June 1963, under the leadership of Senator Kefauver, the Senate
Subcommittee on Constitutional Amendments favorably reported the

Brownell/Rogers approach for resolving the problem of presidential inability. Kefauver's sudden death in August, however, halted progress, but the assassination of President Kennedy in November jolted Congress into a realization that it must find a solution. Had Kennedy survived the assassin's bullets, his condition undoubtedly would have confronted the nation with another case of presidential inability.

Under the leadership of Birch Bayh of Indiana in the Senate and Emanuel Celler of New York in the House of Representatives, Congress turned its attention to the subject of presidential inability in 1964 as well as to the related issue of vice-presidential vacancy. It was joined in the effort by a blue ribbon commission of the American Bar Association. The commission met in January 1964 and recommended that the Constitution be amended to provide:

1. . . . [I]n the event of the inability of the President, the powers and duties, but not the office, shall devolve upon the Vice President or person next in line of succession for the duration of the inability of the President or until expiration of his term of office.

2. . . . [In] the event of the death, resignation or removal of the President, the Vice President or the person next in line of succession shall succeed to the office for the unexpired term.

3. . . . [T]he inability of the President may be established by declaration in writing of the President. In the event that the President does not make known his inability, it may be established by action of the Vice President or person next in line of succession with concurrence of a majority of the Cabinet or by action of such other body as the Congress may by law provide.

4. . . . [T]he ability of the President to resume the powers and duties of his office shall be established by his declaration in writing. In the event that the Vice President and a majority of the Cabinet or such other body as Congress may by law provide shall not concur in the declaration of the President, the continuing inability of the President may then be determined by the vote of two-thirds of the elected members of each House of the Congress.

5. . . . [W]hen a vacancy occurs in the office of Vice President, the President shall nominate a person who, upon approval by a majority of the elected members of Congress meeting in joint session, shall then become Vice President for the unexpired term.[29]

A great deal of debate took place during the proceedings of the commission on the wisdom of spelling out a mechanism in the Constitution itself rather than setting forth a general power authorizing Congress to legislate on the subject of inability, its commencement and termination. To place a specific method in the Constitution, it was reasoned, would make the process self-executing and be consistent with other parts of the Constitution involving the presidency, which contain much specificity, such as in the case of impeachment. However, the commission ultimately included a provision enabling Congress to change the cabinet as the body to function with the vice president were it to prove to be unworkable.

In the final analysis, the ABA commission favored a constitutional amendment for a number of reasons. Some thought that Congress had no power to legislate in this area, believing that the Constitution entrusted the vice president with the decision-making authority. It also was felt that to avoid a constitutional amendment and proceed by statute could invite a constitutional challenge at a time of an inability crisis. Members of the commission were additionally of the view that an amendment was required in order to make certain the status of a vice president who assumed presidential authority during a period of inability.

As for the recommendation that the vice president be involved in a determination of inability, the commission believed that he should not be forced to act in a situation where he thought it was inappropriate. This would be ensured by requiring the concurrence of the vice president. On the other hand, since he would be an interested party, there was a possibility that he might be too reluctant to act when it was imperative that he do so. Therefore, the assistance of the cabinet was considered important and helpful, given the close relationship they would have with the president and their familiarity with the facts and circumstances. On balance, it was felt that the use of both the cabinet and the vice president would generate public confidence in any joint decision and be compatible with the principle of separation of powers.

The possibility that a president might prematurely declare that he was "able" led to the inclusion of a provision that the vice president and cabinet could prevent the president from continuing to serve while Congress resolved the issue. The vice president would serve in the interval so that there would be no question about the capacity of the person acting as president. A two-thirds vote of Congress was made a requirement for preventing the president from resuming his powers and duties in order to give every benefit of the doubt to the elected president.

The recommendations of the ABA were presented to Congress in early 1964 and wide support coalesced around them, although there were some who pressed other approaches, including Eisenhower who said in a letter dated March 2, 1964: "Many systems have been proposed but each seems to be so cumbersome in character as to preclude prompt action in emergency. My personal conclusion is that the matter should be left strictly to the two individuals concerned, the President and the Vice-President, subject possibly to a concurring majority opinion of the President's Cabinet."[30] For a disagreement between the president and vice president, Eisenhower favored a referral to a commission, which would have included in its membership four medical persons. The findings of the commission would have to be submitted to Congress for approval. At the hearings there were also many proposals for dealing with a vice-presidential vacancy: Congress alone to fill the vacancy; provide for the election of two vice presidents; reconvene the last electoral college to select a new vice president, with the president's recommendation; and create a statutory office of First Secretary or Deputy President.[31]

In September 1964, the Senate unanimously approved the approach reflected in the ABA recommendations. However, the House took no action, wanting to do nothing that could be viewed as an affront to its popular Speaker, John McCormack, who then stood next in line of succession.

In 1965, both Houses of Congress reached agreement on this approach, but not without adding a number of important details. No subject received more attention than the time period for congressional action. The differences at times were so great that it appeared the proposed amendment would fail.[32] Eventually, however, both Houses agreed on the three-week period specified in Section 4. No time period for congressional action on filling a vacant vice presidency was included in Section 2.

Agreement was also reached that the term "inability" should deliberately be left vague so as to give the decision-makers maximum flexibility in a time of crisis. It was decided that an attempt to define "inability" could unintentionally omit situations in which the Amendment should in fact be invoked. Further, a detailed definition could lead to debates of interpretation, slowing down a transfer of power at a time when the country could least afford such controversy. There-fore, the framers of the Amendment concluded that the best solution would be to leave the term open and flexible. The legislative history does, however, offer guidance. Among the cases referred to in the debates were when the president had to undergo surgery, or was rendered unconscious by an accident, or was physically or mentally ill, or was kidnapped or could not be located.

Remarks made by Senator Bayh during Senate debates in Febru-ary 1965 are significant: "The word 'inability' and the word 'unable' as used in [Section 4] . . . , which refer to an impairment of the President's faculties, mean that he is unable either to make or com-municate his decisions as to his own competency to execute the pow-ers and duties of his office. I should like for the RECORD to include that as my definition of the words 'inability' and 'unable.'"[33]

As Senate discussion continued, Senator Bayh and Senator Robert Kennedy of New York examined in greater detail the problems of physical and mental inability. On June 30, they engaged in this im-portant exchange:

> SENATOR KENNEDY. Is it not true that the inability to which we are referring in the proposed amendment is total inability to exercise the powers and duties of the office?

> SENATOR BAYH. The inability that we deal with here is described sev-eral times in the amendment itself as the inability of the President to perform the powers and duties of office. It is conceivable that a Presi-dent might be able to walk, for example, and thus, by the definition of some people, might be physically able, but at the same time he might not possess the mental capacity to make a decision and perform the powers and duties of his office. We are talking about inability to per-form the constitutional duties of the office of President.

> SENATOR KENNEDY. And that has to be total disability to perform the powers and duties of the office.

> SENATOR BAYH. The Senator is correct. We are not getting into a position, through the pending measure, in which when a President makes an unpopular decision, he would immediately be rendered un-able to perform the duties of his office.

> SENATOR KENNEDY. Is it limited to mental inability to make or com-municate his decision regarding his capacity and mental inability to perform the powers and duties prescribed by law?

SENATOR BAYH. I do not believe that we should limit it to mental disability. It is conceivable that the President might fall into the hands of the enemy, for example.

SENATOR KENNEDY. It involves physical or mental inability to make or communicate his decision regarding his capacity and physical or mental inability to exercise the powers and duties of his office.

SENATOR BAYH. The Senator is correct. That is very important. I would refer the Senator back to the definition which I read into the RECORD at the time the Senate passed this measure earlier this year.

SENATOR KENNEDY. It was that definition that I was seeking to reemphasize. May I ask one other question? Is it not true that the inability referred to must be expected to be of long duration or at least one whose duration is uncertain and might persist?

SENATOR BAYH. Here again I think one of the advantages of this particular amendment is the leeway it gives us. We are not talking about the kind of inability in which a President went to the dentist and was under anesthesia. It is not that type of inability we are talking about, but the Cabinet, as well as the Vice President and Congress, are going to have to judge the severity of the inability and the problems that face our country.

SENATOR KENNEDY. Is it not true that what we are talking about here as far as inability is concerned, is not a brief or temporary inability?

SENATOR BAYH. We are talking about one that would seriously impair the President's ability to perform the powers and duties of his office.

SENATOR KENNEDY. Could a President have such an inability for a short period of time?

SENATOR BAYH. A President who was unconscious for 30 minutes when missiles were flying toward this country might only be disabled temporarily, but it would be of severe consequence when viewed in the light of the problems facing the country. So at that time, even for that short duration, someone would have to make a decision. But a disability which has persisted for only a short time would ordinarily be excluded. If a President were unable to make an Executive decision which might have severe consequences for the country, I think we would be better off under the conditions of the amendment.[34]

Just as several types of "inability" were described as falling within the intent of the amendment, so too several types of "inability" were excluded. Unpopularity, poor judgment, and laziness are examples. As for a president's stepping aside during an impeachment inquiry in order to defend himself, no mention was made of such a case. Since Section 3 is quite broad in what it permits, such a use of the Amendment would seem possible.[35]

The president was given the power to declare both his own inability and when he had recovered. In a situation where a disabled president did not or was unable to declare his own inability, the Amendment pinned the decision-making responsibility on the vice president and cabinet. On the off-chance that the cabinet proved unworkable, the Amendment gave Congress the power to change the body that would function with the vice president. For the case where a president disagreed with a determination of inability, Congress was empowered to resolve the controversy within a period of time not to exceed twenty-one days.[36] During the period of resolution, the vice president would continue to act as president.

In addition to its inability provisions, the Amendment established in Section 1 that "In case of the removal of the President from office or of his death or resignation, the Vice President shall become President." In Section 2, it established the procedure that "Whenever there is a vacancy in the office of the Vice President, the President shall nominate a Vice President who shall take office upon confirmation by a majority vote of both Houses of Congress." The vice president so chosen would have all the powers and duties of a vice president elected by the people. The Amendment gave a decisive role to the president in order to ensure that there was an effective working relationship between the two and in recognition of the role played by a presidential candidate in the choosing of a running mate.

Throughout the crafting of the Amendment, suggestions to cover other contingencies were made, carefully considered, and then rejected, to some extent because it was feared that the Amendment would become cumbersome and complex and perhaps fail to gain a congressional majority.[37] Walter Lippmann captured the sentiment of the time when he said that the Amendment "is a great deal better than an endless search . . . for the absolutely perfect solution . . . which will never be found, and . . . is not necessary."[38]

RECOMMENDATIONS TO IMPROVE THE AMENDMENT

Since passage of the Amendment in 1967, many recommendations have been made concerning it. Some call for another constitutional

amendment; others, for statutory changes; and still others, for a congressional streamlining of the process of selecting a vice president
and for presidential guidelines that would facilitate the use of the
inability procedures in an appropriate case.[39] The failure of President
Reagan to use the Amendment in 1981 when he underwent surgery
after being shot, and his disclaimer of having used it in 1985 when
he had surgery for removal of a polyp, prompted criticisms of the
Amendment and led to its review by important groups of citizens.

In 1985, the White Burkett Miller Center of Public Affairs at the
University of Virginia appointed a Commission on Presidential Disability to review the nation's past experiences with the Amendment
and, if necessary, recommend proposals for its change. Ultimately,
the commission determined that a stronger assumption of duties by
the White House itself was a better solution to any questions than
further legislation would be, offering several suggestions to ensure
the Amendment's success in the future.[40] These are included later in
this volume, but it is worth noting here that one of its suggestions
has, in large part, already been implemented. Specifically, the commission recommended that between election day and inauguration,
the president-elect, the vice president-elect, the White House physi-
cian-designate, the president's counsel-designate, and the president-
elect's spouse discuss the Twenty-Fifth Amendment and devise plans
of action designed to meet all medical contingencies.[41] The Bush administration, ninety days into the president's term, held such a meeting in the Oval Office to discuss the procedures involved in any use
of the Twenty-Fifth Amendment and to ensure that everyone involved understood his or her role. The Clinton administration did
essentially the same.

In 1997, another group, the Working Group on Presidential Disability, which included some fifty of the nation's leading physicians,
attorneys, historians, political scientists, journalists, and others familiar with the Amendment's adoption process and which was assisted
by former Presidents Carter and Ford, published its own set of recommendations.[42] These, too, are presented later in this volume and
so, with but one exception, will not be mentioned here. To this one,
I must raise objections.

A CRITICAL PERSPECTIVE

The Working Group's recommendations have great merit except, as
I see it, its fourth recommendation concerning a medical determina-

tion of presidential impairment. The recommendation reads as follows: "Determination of presidential impairment is a medical
judgment based upon evaluation and tests. Close associates, family,
and consultants can provide valuable information which contribute
to this medical judgment."[43] The existence of a determination of presidential "impairment" separate and apart from the determination of
presidential "inability" implies that a two-threshold determination
must take place when, in fact, the Constitution speaks of only one.
By bifurcating the test of competency, we would run a grave risk of
complicating the Twenty-Fifth Amendment. After a physician has
made a decision in which he or she declares the president "impaired," what role, if any, is left as a practical matter to those responsible under the Constitution for determining a president's inability?
The legislative history and debates of the Twenty-Fifth Amendment
leave no doubt that only those specific constitutional decision-makers
are entrusted with the determination of presidential inability. When
the Amendment was adopted, it was decided by Congress and the
states that Section 4 would grant only those accountable to the public
the responsibility of making such a decision as to the president's competency.

In my opinion, a formal determination of presidential impairment
would convey an inaccurate picture of the proper role of medical
advice in decisions under Sections 3 and 4 of the Amendment. The
proposal implies that the medical role will be limited to a single determination when in most circumstances the appropriate doctors will
be involved continually in a less formal but advisory function, offering medical advice to the decision-makers and responding to questions on a continuing basis. In fact, the legislative history surrounding
the Amendment makes clear that the framers intended that the constitutional decision-makers solicit expert medical opinion.[44] Decisions regarding the exercise of executive power under the
Amendment, however, should be made by accountable constitutional
officials, not by doctors, attorneys, or others who have not been
elected by the people or confirmed by their representatives.

Perhaps the biggest potential harm a two-prong system could produce is public confusion. It is not uncommon, especially today with
the ever-expanding growth in media coverage, that confidential information from the White House might be leaked. What would happen
if a physician's finding that the president is impaired was leaked to

the public prematurely? At best, this could create public confusion and distrust and would make it nearly impossible for a president to carry out his duties if either he, or the vice president and cabinet (or other body as provided by Congress), disagreed with the physician's findings or took some time to reach a decision.[45]

CONCLUSION

The Twenty-Fifth Amendment has become a popular subject of discussion, as evidenced by its use in such movies as *Dave* and *Air Force One*, to say nothing of works of fiction. It also was a topic of discussion during the impeachment inquiries concerning the conduct of Presidents Clinton and Nixon and in the controversy surrounding President Reagan's arms shipment to Iran in 1985, shortly after having major intestinal surgery. While the contexts involving the Amendment have been varied, the events that solidified its strength were the Watergate-related crises of 1973–74. President Reagan's hesitation to use the Amendment in 1981 and 1985 was unfortunate, but it may have operated to strengthen the Amendment by virtue of the criticisms he received and the steps taken by subsequent administrations to understand the Amendment and put contingency plans into effect.

When all is considered, the Twenty-Fifth Amendment has served the nation well, first when it was faced with the resignation of both a president and a vice president, and second by filling gaps that had left the nation vulnerable for almost 180 years. In 1973, when he became vice president following the resignation of Spiro Agnew, Gerald R. Ford called attention to this fact by remarking: "Together we have made history here today. For the first time we have carried out the command of the 25th Amendment. In exactly 8 weeks, we have demonstrated to the world that our great republic stands solid, stands strong upon the bedrock of the Constitution."[46]

The Amendment is now positioned to be a crucial tool should the country again confront a case of presidential inability. As for the weaknesses said to exist in it, I suggest that they are its strengths. The Amendment respects the presidency by making it difficult to oust a president from exercising his powers and duties, giving a decisive role to those likely to protect the president, and embodying

checks and balances at every point of the process. It avoids a definition of the term "inability" so as to provide the decision-makers with
flexibility and avoid the legalisms such a definition could cause in a
time of political crisis. The Amendment deals with the subjects it
covers practically, in a manner consistent with the principle of separation of powers, and in a way that ensures stability and continuity in
the event of succession. And, it should be added, the Amendment
involves only persons who have been elected by the people or approved by their chosen representatives. It is a product of enlightened
self-government, a constitutional milestone.

NOTES

1. John D. Feerick, *From Failing Hands: The Story of Presidential Suc-cession* (New York: Fordham University Press, 1965), p. x.
2. *The Records of the Federal Convention of 1787*, ed. Max Farrand, vol. 2 (New Haven, Conn.: Yale University Press, 1911; repr. 1937), p. 626.
3. Ibid., pp. 573, 575.
4. Ibid., pp. 598–99 (emphasis added).
5. *The Works of Fisher Ames*, ed. Seth Ames, vol. 1 (Boston: Little Brown, 1854), p. 114.
6. See Feerick, *From Failing Hands*, p. 61; *Writings of James Madison*, ed. Guillard Hunt, vol. 6 (New York: G. P. Putnam's Sons, 1906), p. 95 and n. 1.
7. *The Memoirs of John Quincy Adams*, ed. C. F. Adams, vol. 10 (Phila-delphia: J. B. Lippincott, 1874), pp. 463–64.
8. Congressional Globe, 27th Cong., 1st sess., 1841, p. 5.
9. Vice Presidents Millard Fillmore, Andrew Johnson, Chester A. Ar-thur, Theodore Roosevelt, Calvin Coolidge, Harry S. Truman, and Lyndon B. Johnson all acted under the Tyler precedent.
10. See Symposium—"Presidential Inability," *North American Review*, 133 (1881), 442–43; *New York Times*, October 22, 1881, p. 4.
11. *The Messages and Papers of the Presidents, 1789–1897*, ed. James D. Richardson, vol. 8 (Washington, 1897), pp. 24–25.
12. See Gene Smith, *When the Cheering Stopped: The Last Years of Woodrow Wilson* (New York: William Morrow, 1964).
13. See George F. Howe, *Chester A. Arthur* (New York: F. Ungar, 1957), p. 154.
14. Ibid., p. 141; *New York Herald*, November 26, 1885, p. 3.
15. See Feerick, *From Failing Hands*, pp. 140–46.

16. See *Congressional Record*, 91st Cong., 1945, p. 6272.

17. CBS Reports, The Crisis of Presidential Succession (January 8, 1964).

18. See Staff of the House Committee on the Judiciary, 84th Cong., 2d Sess., *Presidential Inability* 1956, Committee Print.

19. Hearing Before the Special Subcommittee on Study of Presidential Inability of the House Judiciary Committee, 85th Cong., 1st sess., 1957.

20. Presidential Inability: Hearings Before Special Subcommittee to Study Presidential Inability of the House Committee on the Judiciary, 84th Cong., 2d Sess., 1956.

21. Any support for the Supreme Court being involved ended when Senator Kenneth B. Keating released a letter from Chief Justice Earl Warren concerning the undesirability of having the court participate in the determination of a president's inability: "It has been the belief of all of us that because of the separation of powers in our Government, the nature of the judicial process, the possibility of a controversy of this character coming to the Court, and the danger of disqualification which might result in lack of quorum, it would be inadvisable for any member of the Court to serve on such a Commission." Hearings on Presidential Inability Before Subcommittee on Constitutional Amendments of the Senate Committee on the Judiciary, 85th Cong., 2d sess., 1958, p. 14.

22. Presidential Inability: Hearings, p. 85.

23. Presidential Inability: Hearings Before the Subcommittee on Constitutional Amendments of the Senate Committee on the Judiciary, 85th Cong., 2d sess. (1958), p. 165 (hereinafter 1958 Senate Hearings).

24. 1958 Senate Hearings, 85th Cong. 2d sess., p.14.

25. 1958 Senate Hearings.

26. Harry S. Truman, "Truman Proposes a Panel on a President's Disability," *New York Times*, June 27, 1956, p. 1.

27. See John D. Feerick, *The Twenty-Fifth Amendment: Its Complete History and Applications* (New York: Fordham University Press, 1976; repr. 1992), pp. 83–107.

28. See 42 Op. Att'y Gen. 69 (1961–1974), (providing an official statement on the proper role of the vice president during a period of presidential inability).

29. Feerick, *From Failing Hands*, pp. 60–61, Appendix D.

30. Hearings Before the Subcommittee on Constitutional Amendments of the Senate Judiciary Committee, 88th Cong., 2d sess., 1964, p. 232.

31. Feerick, *Twenty-Fifth Amendment*, pp. 66–73.

32. The politics of the Amendment are admirably treated in Birch Bayh, *One Heartbeat Away* (Indianapolis: Bobbs-Merrill, 1968).

33. *Congressional Record*, 111 (1965), p. 3282.

34. Ibid., p. 15381.

35. See Feerick, *From Failing Hands*, pp. 197–203.

36. See Feerick, *Twenty-Fifth Amendment*, pp. 83–107.

37. Some of the contingencies not addressed by the Amendment are: the inability of a vice president or a person in line of succession when acting as president, in the event of simultaneous inabilities of the president and vice president. At the request of Representative Richard Poff of Virginia, who played a key role in the development of the Amendment in the House of Representatives, this author drafted suggested provisions for some of these contingencies, but they were not formally considered during the House debates.

38. Walter Lippmann, *New York Herald Tribune*, June 9, 1964, p. 20.

39. See Feerick, *Twenty-Fifth Amendment*, pp. xix–xxvii, 193–207.

40. *Papers on Presidential Disability and the Twenty-Fifth Amendment*, ed. Kenneth Thompson (Lanham, Md.: University Press of America, 1988), p. 59.

41. Ibid., p. xxi.

42. See Working Group on Disability in U.S. Presidents, *Disability in U.S. Presidents: Report: Recommendations and Commentaries by the Working Group* (Winston-Salem: Bowman Gray Scientific Press, 1997). For articles and essays authored by several members of the Working Group on Presidential Disability on the potential merits and weaknesses of the Twenty-Fifth Amendment, see *Wake Forest Law Review* (Fall 1995).

43. See *Disability in U.S. Presidents, Report*, Recommendation Four, p. 14.

44. See, for example, Staff of the House Committee on the Judiciary, *Report on Inability* 1, 84th Cong., 2d sess., 1956, Committee Print, p. 4 (reply of Stephen K. Bailey, Princeton University) (replying to Celler's questionnaire and proposing a panel to include "at least 2 men of outstanding reputation in medicine and psychiatry"); p. 5 (reply of Everett S. Brown, University of Michigan) (proposing a panel to include "proper medical experts"); 1958 Senate Hearings, note 22 at p. 37 (statement of Frederick A. Payne) (proposing that the chief justice appoint a panel of qualified medical experts).

45. See, also, *Disability in U.S. Presidents, Report*, Appendix 1, pp. 20–21.

46. Congressional Record 119 (1973), 39926.

2

The Genius of the Twenty-Fifth Amendment: Guarding Against Presidential Disability but Safeguarding the Presidency

Robert E. Gilbert

In 1967, the Twenty-Fifth Amendment, sometimes referred to as the presidential disability amendment, was added to the Constitution of the United States. Its overriding objectives are that presidential transitions will be smooth and orderly and that the powers of the presidency will always reside in a person physically and mentally capable of exercising them. Although the amendment is sometimes criticized for alleged imperfections, its greatest—and yet most unheralded—virtue is that it provides for the disability of presidents without disabling the institution of the presidency. In a very real sense, this is the genius of the Twenty-Fifth Amendment.

The subjects of presidential illness and presidential disability, until recently, have received relatively little attention. Since so many illnesses suffered by presidents of the United States have either been downplayed in their seriousness or concealed altogether by the White House, this lack of attention has been understandable. However, the history of the American presidency makes clear that presidential health and presidential disability should be seen as serious

Many thanks to Robert S. Robins of Tulane University and Michael C. Tolley of Northeastern University for their helpful comments and suggestions on an earlier draft of this chapter.

and ongoing concerns. Of the forty-one men who have served as president, eight have died in office, either by assassination (Lincoln, Garfield, McKinley, and Kennedy) or by natural causes (W. H. Harrison, Taylor, Harding, and F. D. Roosevelt). This means, of course, that some 20 percent of presidents have died in office, a statistic that, in itself, supports the contention that the presidency is a killing position.

Although the deaths of the eight sitting presidents cited above are well known, it is not so well known that some of these presidents were ill for considerable periods of time before their deaths. Nor is it common knowledge that a startlingly large number of presidents who survived their terms in office suffered serious ailments while serving as the nation's chief executive. A cursory tour through American history reveals both the frequent occurrence of serious illness among presidents and the frequent medical concealments:

- In 1798, President John Adams showed signs of emotional instability and was described by one of his own Cabinet members as "actually insane." Trying to lessen the tensions of office and avoid a complete collapse, the President absented himself from the capital for more than six months, which provoked criticism that he was neglecting his duties. The cause of his erratic behavior recently was ascribed to hyperthyroidism, a malady related to stress.[1]
- In 1813, President Madison suffered for three weeks from a high fever that apparently led to some delirium. He was unable to carry out his responsibilities fully during this period, and a number of his visitors came away convinced that the President was deranged.[2]
- In 1841, President William Henry Harrison caught a cold at his inauguration which developed into the pneumonia that, in conjunction with hepatitis, ended his life within thirty days.[3] For much of his one month as president, then, Harrison was seriously ill.
- In 1889, President Cleveland underwent two surgeries for cancer of the jaw. Because he did not want to complicate his relationship with Congress, the president insisted on complete secrecy, and both procedures were performed not in a hospital but on board a yacht traveling slowly up the Hudson River. A portion of Cleveland's upper jaw was removed, and he was fitted with an artificial rubber jaw to fill up the cavity created by the surgery and improve his speech. The White House announced simply that the president had had a bad tooth extracted and denied that anything more serious had occurred. It was not until 1928, twenty years after Cleveland's death, that we

learned definitively of these major and very intricate medical procedures from one of the participating physicians.[4]

- In 1919, President Wilson's stroke, although severe, was initially concealed from the nation. His White House Physician announced that "The President has exerted himself so constantly and has been under such a strain during the last year and has spent himself without reserve on this trip that it has brought on a serious reaction in his digestive organs." A second announcement informed the country that Wilson's "trouble dates back to an attack of influenza last April in Paris from which he never really recovered. The President's activities on this trip have overtaxed his strength and he is suffering from nervous exhaustion. His condition is not alarming."[5] In truth, Wilson was completely paralyzed on the left side, and his vision was permanently damaged, making it impossible for him to read with any accuracy. His speech was labored and indistinct, and he would burst into tears without apparent cause.[6] Indeed, the president was so ill that he was wholly incapacitated for several months and partially incapacitated for the remainder of his life.

- In 1923, President Harding became very ill while traveling from Alaska to California. Even before this journey, the president had to sleep propped up on pillows, because he could not breathe if he lay flat, and complained of shortness of breath when he played golf. A White House physician who examined him after he was stricken on the trip to California was alarmed to find that the "left border of his heart was well to the left of normal. The heart sounds were muffled with irregularity. The President had a dilated heart."[7] Another White House physician subsequently announced to the press that there was nothing serious about the President's condition and that he was only suffering from a violent case of ptomaine poisoning. Harding was bedridden for several days before dying "unexpectedly" of cardiovascular disease. During his final days of life, the President was too ill and too depleted to carry out his responsibilities.

- In 1924, President Coolidge showed distinct signs of clinical depression following the death of his sixteen-year-old son from blood poisoning.[8] He lost interest in politics and the presidency after the boy died, spent about twelve of every twenty-four hours asleep, and withdrew sharply from interaction with Congress and even with his own cabinet.

- In 1944, medical examinations revealed that President Franklin Roosevelt suffered from moderately severe and advanced hypertension, obstructive pulmonary disease, and congestive heart failure. A cardiologist found that Roosevelt's heart was grossly enlarged, that the mitral valve was not closing properly, and that excessive pressure was being exerted on the aortic valve. He felt that the president might die at any moment but that with proper treatment he might live on for months, maybe even a year or two. The White House Physician announced simply to the press that "the check-up is satisfactory. When we got through, we decided that for a man of sixty-two, we have very little to argue about."[9] A year later, after winning a fourth term, Roosevelt was dead.

- In 1955, President Eisenhower's massive heart attack was described initially to the press as a "mild coronary thrombosis," then as being of only "moderate" severity. When the president suffered a stroke in 1957, White House medical bulletins maintained that it was wholly unrelated to his 1955 heart attack. However, one of the eminent cardiologists who treated Eisenhower was convinced that the 1957 stroke had been caused by a ventricular aneurysm that he had detected at the time of the coronary thrombosis but that had never been revealed to the public.[10]

- In 1961, a president was inaugurated who suffered from Addison's disease, which involves a failure of the adrenal glands. This condition, which made President Kennedy wholly reliant on medication, was never disclosed to the nation and was strongly denied by the president, not only to the public but even to one of his own doctors.[11] Only after Kennedy's death was his condition acknowledged by those close to him.[12]

- In 1965, President Lyndon Johnson underwent gall bladder surgery at Bethesda Naval Hospital. Initial medical reports marveled at how "beautifully" he had come through surgery and how he had "unusual recuperative powers."[13] Later, however, Johnson's press secretary admitted that his recuperation was going quite slowly. Also, years after Johnson's death, we learned from Dr. James Young, one of his White House physicians and a contributing author to this volume, that during this surgery the president had developed a potentially dangerous cardiac condition that he and a colleague detected and managed to bring under control.[14]

- In 1981, news bulletins concerning President Reagan's gunshot wound were misleading and incomplete. His surgeon later disclosed that when the president arrived at George Washington University Medical Center, he had lost almost half his body's blood supply, his left lung had collapsed, and he had no recordable blood pressure.[15] Although the president's condition was clearly serious, the White House did all it could to accentuate the positive. Press releases told of the jokes Reagan had shared with his doctors; the Reagan children were instructed not to rush to the airport in California, because this might communicate to the press that there was cause for alarm; and the first lady decided not to spend the first evening at the hospital because "I'd be sending out a message to the world that Ronnie's condition was critical. It was, of course, but at that moment I didn't want people to know."[16]

In light of the frequency of presidential illness and death throughout American history, it is unfortunate that the original Constitution of the United States spoke so little and so ambiguously about such issues. Article II, section 1, is clear on only one point: the order of presidential succession beyond the vice presidency is for Congress to determine. On everything else, it is vague and raises more questions than it answers.

Specifically, it points out that in cases of the death, resignation, or inability of the president to discharge the powers and duties of his office, "the same" shall pass to the vice president. It does not make clear whether "the same" refers to the presidential office itself or to its powers and duties, an important distinction since the former would result in the vice president's becoming president while the latter would not.[17] However, it would certainly appear that the framers of the Constitution intended the latter reading: when a president died, was impeached, resigned, or became disabled, the powers and duties of the presidency, not the office itself, would devolve on the vice president, who would then serve as acting president.[18]

Also unclear from a reading of the Constitution and the debates surrounding it is the meaning of the word "inability," the method by which it was to be ascertained, and, perhaps even more important, the process, if any, by which a president could regain either the office or the powers and duties of the office when said "inability" ended. The latter was a particularly glaring omission, because it made it very unlikely that any president would admit to any inability since, to do so, might well mean permanent forfeiture of the office and/or its powers.

A CONSTITUTIONAL AMENDMENT

Because of these Constitutional ambiguities as well as the serious illnesses he faced as president,[19] Dwight D. Eisenhower proposed in 1957 that a presidential disability amendment be added to the Constitution. Such an amendment, Eisenhower believed, would clarify and improve the Constitution's language from the vantage point provided by almost two hundred years of experience. Congress, however, took no action on the proposed amendment during either the remainder of Eisenhower's Administration or the Kennedy Administration that followed.

The Kennedy assassination in 1963 played an important role in moving the amendment to adoption. Not only did it vividly teach the lesson that youth is no impediment to death, but also Lyndon Johnson, the new president, had suffered a serious heart attack in 1955 and was very sensitive to the issues of presidential health and incapacity. Moreover, when Johnson was elevated to the presidency, the vice presidency became vacant and would remain vacant until after the next election and inauguration of a new vice president. This caused some concern in the administration since it meant that, under the Presidential Succession Law of 1947,[20] Johnson would be succeeded—if he left office or became disabled before the next election and inauguration—by the Speaker of the House, seventy-two-year-old John McCormack of Massachusetts. More troubling was that if McCormack should leave office or become disabled before the next election and inauguration, he would be succeeded by the President pro tempore of the Senate, eighty-six-year-old Carl Hayden of Arizona, a member of Congress since Arizona had become a state in 1912. Johnson decided, then, to urge enactment of a presidential disability amendment, very similar to that proposed by Eisenhower some eight years earlier, as the Twenty-Fifth Amendment to the Constitution, but out of deference to McCormack and Hayden, he refrained from doing so until he was inaugurated in January 1965 to a term in his own right and after Hubert Humphrey took office as the new vice president. Two years later, in February 1967, the presidential disability amendment was added to the Constitution.

The Twenty-Fifth Amendment, the full text of which is found in the Appendix, introduces several important changes in American constitutional law. First, by making clear that, despite the intentions of the Constitution's original framers, the vice president becomes president, not acting president, of the United States whenever the president dies, is removed, or resigns, Section 1 of the Amendment formally enshrines the Tyler precedent in the Constitution.[21] In 1974, when Gerald Ford replaced Richard Nixon as president, Section 1 of the Amendment was implemented for the first time.

Second, by establishing in Section 2 a procedure for filling a vacant vice presidency, the Amendment in effect ends presidential succession at the vice president and, under ordinary circumstances, prevents it from actually reaching congressional leaders or members of the cabinet. This feature of the Amendment has already become operative on two occasions: in 1973 when President Nixon chose Gerald Ford as his new vice president following the resignation of Spiro Agnew; and in 1974, when President Ford chose Nelson Rockefeller as the new vice president after Ford succeeded Nixon in the White House. If the Twenty-Fifth Amendment had not been added to the Constitution, and if the intentions of the original framers had been respected, Speaker of the House Carl Albert, a Democrat, would have become acting president of the United States in 1973, bringing about a change in party control of the executive branch, and there would have been no vice president in office until one was inaugurated on January 20, 1977. Since the vice presidency has been vacant on eighteen occasions in American history,[22] Section 2 of the Amendment is a useful and important addition to the fundamental law of the land.

The third and fourth sections of the Twenty-Fifth Amendment address directly the issues of presidential disability and succession. Neither Section 3 nor Section 4 defines precisely what is meant by disability. This is understandable since disability (or inability) can come in many forms and a rigid constitutional definition would surely lead to confusion and conflict. Nevertheless, presidential illness, physical or psychological, temporary or permanent, stands at the center of both sections, though Section 4 even extends to such extraordinary occurrences as the kidnapping of presidents or their capture in war.[23]

Section 3 applies to instances in which a president decides to transfer voluntarily the powers and duties of the presidency to the vice president because he is, or is about to become, unable to function as president. This may be due to such factors as illness, intense grief over the loss of a loved one, or perhaps even severe distraction caused by a protracted impeachment proceeding.[24] He need simply inform congressional leaders in writing of his intention to transfer his powers and, at the moment he specifies, the vice president becomes acting president. The consent of Congress is not required. Under Section 3, the president remains president at all times, and the vice president simply acts in his place, relieving him of his powers and responsibilities until the president chooses to reclaim them. After the president informs congressional leaders in writing that he is reclaiming his powers and duties, the transfer is automatic, not requiring congressional consent, and the vice president resumes vice-presidential responsibilities.

Section 3 clearly should be invoked when the president is about to be rendered unconscious for a lengthy period of time, as, for example, during major surgery. It should have been invoked, but was not, when President Reagan underwent a three-hour operation under general anesthesia following the 1981 attempt on his life by John Hinckley. Section 3 almost certainly would have been invoked during the Bush Administration, making Vice President Quayle acting president, if the president's sudden episode of atrial fibrillation in May 1991 had necessitated the administration of electrical shocks to his heart. Dr. Lawrence Mohr, a White House physician at the time and a contributing author to this volume, indicates, however, that when medication satisfactorily stabilized Bush's heartbeat, invocation of Section 3 became moot.[25] In 1997, the Clinton Administration decided not to invoke Section 3 when the president underwent a two-hour operation to repair his badly torn quadriceps tendon, because he had received only a local anesthetic which did not affect his central nervous system or render him unconscious or unable to communicate.[26]

Although some scholars argue that Section 3 has never been invoked,[27] I agree with those who maintain that it has been invoked on one occasion—in 1985, prior to President Reagan's surgery for colon cancer.[28] Although Reagan's letter to congressional leaders at the time indicated his belief that Section 3 was not intended for "such brief and temporary periods of incapacity," the president still informed them that, commencing with the administration of anesthesia, he was passing on his powers and duties to Vice President Bush, who was to act in his place. Some eight hours later, Reagan reclaimed his powers and duties by writing to congressional leaders and informing them that "I am able to resume the discharge of the Constitutional powers and duties of the Office of President of the United States" and "have informed the Vice President of my determination and my resumption of these powers and duties."[29]

If Section 3 was not invoked in this instance and *if* presidential power was passed on legitimately to the vice president and then retaken legitimately by the president several hours later, Section 3 of the Amendment would have no real purpose and be wholly unnecessary. However, since Section 3 provides the only clear constitutional means by which a president can *transfer and then reclaim* his powers and duties, I believe that it *had* to have been invoked by Reagan in 1985, despite his apparent reluctance to do so. President Reagan later came to the same conclusion. In his 1990 autobiography, he writes: "Before they wheeled me into the operating room, I signed a letter invoking the Twenty-Fifth Amendment, making George Bush acting president during the time I was incapacitated under anesthesia."[30]

Section 4 of the Twenty-Fifth Amendment represents a major constitutional problem area, since its language conjures up images of governmental overthrows and coups d'état. In the event a disabled or seriously impaired president is unable or unwilling to transfer his powers and duties to the vice president, Section 4 allows the vice president to supplant him and become acting president, provided a majority of the cabinet (or some other body created for the purpose by Congress) gives its assent. Under the complex provisions of Section 4, the president may regain his powers and duties by informing congressional leaders that an inability no longer exists. However, the vice president and a majority of the cabinet (or congressionally created body) may challenge the president in his determination to regain his powers and duties. In this terrible confrontation, Congress is given the power to decide within a specified period whether the president shall regain, or the acting president shall retain, the powers and duties of the presidential office. At least a two-thirds vote in each house of Congress is required for the vice president to prevail.

Prior to adoption of the Twenty-Fifth Amendment, the only mechanism by which a disabled but, for whatever reason, uncooperative president could be separated from his powers was impeachment. But this mechanism is inherently flawed since ill health does not constitute treason or bribery, nor is it another high crime or misdemeanor. Section 4 establishes a procedure much preferable to impeachment since it provides for the temporary or even permanent separation of a president from his powers and duties, without his concurrence and possibly even over his strong objections, for reasons other than the impeachable offenses cited in Article II, section 4 of the Constitution.

Without doubt, however, Section 4 provides a procedure that is complex and potentially very painful. It requires strong action on the part of the vice president, an official who owes his high office not only to the voters but also to the president he would be moving to supplant. Vice presidents tend to be politically deferential individuals since they have very little independent power and fear public condemnation for untoward aggressiveness or excessive ambition.[31] They also may fear retribution by the president who is, after all, *their* leader as well as the country's.

Section 4, therefore, presents potential problems for the vice president and is unlikely to be invoked except in the most serious of situations. If, for example, a president suddenly and unexpectedly loses consciousness for a lengthy period of time, the vice president might well be forced to invoke Section 4, even though with considerable distaste and unease. On the other hand, in instances when a president is to receive general anesthesia during a surgical procedure but chooses not to invoke Section 3 of the Amendment, it would be unlikely, absent a crisis, that the vice president would invoke Section 4. All high-level political figures undoubtedly remember the experience of Secretary of State Alexander Haig in 1981. After the assassination attempt against President Reagan, Haig announced to the press that "as of now, I am in control here at the White House. . . ."[32] Regardless of how well intentioned Haig may have been, his words were interpreted as a bold grab for power. Reagan himself later complained that on the day he was wounded, "George Bush was out of town and Haig immediately came to the White House and claimed he was in charge of the country."[33] This sad episode marked the beginning of the end of the political career of Alexander Haig. Within fifteen months, he had returned to private life.

But if circumstances are such that the vice president does decide to invoke Section 4, the consent of a majority of the cabinet is necessary. Here, too, the process is likely to be painful. Like the vice president, cabinet members also owe their high political positions to the president. They are members of the president's official family and understandably would be reluctant to appear disloyal to him. Although individual cabinet members may have occasional policy or personal conflicts with the president, the cabinet as a whole is unlikely to develop a high level of institutional autonomy.[34] This does not mean, of course, that cabinet members will be impervious to the national interest or that they will not act when the national interest is clearly threatened. A critic of the present constitutional arrangement writes that "one can hardly imagine a more politically charged event than disagreement between the vice president and the cabinet over presidential disability."[35] This is surely true, but it is not clear why a disagreement between the vice president and any other group would not be "politically charged" under the circumstances. After all, separation of a president from his powers and duties is a political act and will always be "politically charged." It could hardly be otherwise.

Some "Other Body" or an "Impairment Panel"?

The Twenty-Fifth Amendment authorizes Congress, if it so chooses, to set up another "body" as a replacement for the cabinet in the determination of presidential disability. The composition of such an alternative body would be for Congress to determine, but, in making this determination, Congress would have to consider carefully whether this body would enjoy wide public acceptance, a crucial consideration in itself.

One possible suggestion might be for Congress to replace the cabinet in the process of presidential displacement outlined in Section 4 with a body composed of physicians and give that body the power to vote to remove or retain the president in conjunction with a recommendation by the vice president. Such a plan is extremely unwise. It would invest unwarranted power in the hands of a body unaccountable to the public and is unlikely to win public support or the support of the president's allies in Congress, particularly given the long and well-known involvement in partisan causes by medical groups, such as the American Medical Association.[36] Moreover, this proposal would transform a decision that is political into one that is medical. Determining presidential impairment is a medical judgment; deciding whether to separate the president from his powers is a political one. Each is important, and one may be related to the other, but they must not be confused.

Despite the weaknesses of this particular proposal, medical consultation must be an integral part of most invocations of the disability provisions of the Twenty-Fifth Amendment. The Senior White

House Physician, chosen by the president without the consent of the Senate, must play a vital role in caring for the president and in assembling groups of medical consultants, as necessary and appropriate, to assist in that care. Moreover, the Senior White House Physician should play a key role whenever consideration is given to any invocation of Section 3 or 4 of the Twenty-Fifth Amendment for reasons of ill health. To this end, this physician should perhaps be given the additional title of Special Assistant or Counselor to the President so that his or her important place in the process will be more clearly understood by other White House aides and high-level officials.[37] The Senior White House Physician, and the medical consultants gathered by him or her, should give to the vice president and members of the cabinet, in private and as warranted by the circumstances, information relevant to the president's medical condition. On the basis of this information, these political officers should take whatever action they deem appropriate under the Twenty-Fifth Amendment to protect the national interest.

It is important to remember that, at times, the national interest demands that political considerations take precedence over medical ones. For example, according to one account, Franklin D. Roosevelt "would have been objectively rated from 5–15 percent impaired by March 1944."[38] Even if accurate, this could well be interpreted as meaning that Roosevelt was between 85 percent and 95 percent *unimpaired* in March 1944 and, therefore, could safely run for re-election that fall, particularly since the war was entering its final stages and a change in Commanders-in-Chief could be harmful. In this instance, the demands of politics almost certainly would have taken precedence over medical "facts" and estimates.

Although medical input is vital in any determination of presidential disability, it does not seem necessary or wise either to add a detailed medical consultation clause to the Twenty-Fifth Amendment or to establish by statute or concurrent resolution, as has been suggested, a standing group of medical consultants at the beginning of every presidential administration to "screen" the president's health. Despite the variations that exist in such proposals, one prominent but seriously flawed prototype is that a Presidential Impairment Panel should be established by the president before his or her inauguration and that such a panel, equally divided by party, should monitor the president's health on a yearly basis and report its findings to the vice president.[39]

This proposal has some merit in that it tries to bring informed medical information to the vice president, but it suffers from the fact that it does so by creating a formal, institutional structure that is, for several reasons, highly problematical. It is unclear, for example, how a formal annual report to the vice president would not become public knowledge, particularly given the aggressive American media and the frequency of "leaks." It is also unclear whether Congress, in establishing a formal panel by law, could compel a president to appoint members to serve on it or to submit to examinations by its members. The separation of powers doctrine might well preclude both.[40] If a president declined to appoint panel members or refused to submit to their examinations, the questions of who or what could compel him to do so would naturally arise. Impeaching a president because he refused to staff an Impairment Panel or have his prescribed physical examinations is hardly a sensible notion.

Also, in the event he did agree to submit to the panel's examinations, the president undoubtedly would find himself badly compromised by any adverse or ambiguous medical "reports" it issued. Given the inherent likelihood that the physicians serving on such a panel would occasionally, perhaps even often, be sharply divided over the interpretation of medical data, the problem is greatly compounded. Indeed, conflicting medical opinions might well make it considerably more difficult for the vice president and cabinet to act, even when they see the need to do so.

Examples of sharply divided medical opinions, and the confusion they produce, are not difficult to come by. After Boston Celtics basketball star Reggie Lewis collapsed during a game in the early 1990s, he was examined by many physicians. Subsequent to these examinations, one group of physicians argued that Lewis had a potentially dangerous heart condition and should no longer play basketball. Another group argued, however, that Lewis's condition was not life threatening and that he could continue to play. He did and he died. When Lewis's widow sued the latter group of physicians for malpractice in 1999, the jury was simply unable to weigh the conflicting medical opinions and the proceedings ended inconclusively in a mistrial.[41]

Another recent instance is the internationally famous court case in which a British nanny was tried and convicted in Massachusetts for causing fatal injuries to the child entrusted to her care. As we now know, medical opinion varied widely in this case. Some physicians believe that the dead child, on the basis of his injuries, had been shaken to death; some physicians argue that he had been slammed into a hard object; some physicians believe that he had been strangled; some physicians believe that he had been abused over a long period of time; some physicians believe that he had not been so abused.[42] The public—as well as court officials—continue to be confused and confounded, as well they might.

Disagreements among the physicians associated with these cases have been understandable but unfortunate. Disagreement among physicians serving on a standing Presidential Impairment Panel would also be understandable but, as will be shown later, would have potentially devastating repercussions for both the president and the nation.

Some proponents of a standing Impairment Panel try to explain away this difficulty by arguing that Supreme Court decisions are often by divided votes and that a divided judiciary has not harmed the country.[43] This argument is quite weak. It overlooks the fact that the Supreme Court is a formally constituted branch of government and that its decisions, whether unanimous or divided, are *binding*; a Presidential Impairment Panel would *not* be a branch of government and its findings, whether unanimous or divided, would only be *advisory*. It also overlooks the fact that closely divided Supreme Court decisions are often seen as weak decisions, likely to be reconsidered and possibly overturned at a future date.[44] A divided decision by any Presidential Impairment Panel, however, could not be reconsidered and overturned at a future date since the damage it rendered would be immediate and confined to a particular presidential administration.

Significant, too, is the fact that even a unanimous Impairment Panel might well be incorrect in its diagnosis and prognosis of the president's health. For this reason alone, its formal and periodic intrusion into the political life of the nation would be arbitrary and unacceptable. Just as presidents are not supermen, so too doctors are not gods. If the former are not blessed with immortality, the latter certainly are not imbued with infallibility. Any expectation that presidents would submit docilely to their judgments or that the public would accept those judgments unquestioningly is wholly unrealistic.

It should be noted that any president faced with a negative report by a standing Impairment Panel would almost certainly respond in kind. The White House would quickly assemble another group of medical experts, who would then issue a quite contrary report to the nation. There would then exist two reports on the president's health status, each with quite different conclusions. Confusion, partisan conflict, and paralysis would ensue, to the country's great detriment.

Furthermore, the proposal for establishment of a formal Presidential Impairment panel carries real dangers for the presidential office. Presidential power is very much the power to persuade; it is only rarely the power to command. A president must use all of his bargaining advantages in trying to convince others to do as he wishes them to do. In his landmark study, Richard Neustadt explains that in the act of presidential persuasion, one important factor is the president's professional reputation.[45] By this is meant that those whom the president must persuade have, at any particular time, a dominant opinion of him—whether he is in control of his Administration or not, whether he is knowledgeable or not, whether he is safe to follow or not, whether he is safe to ignore or not. Presidents, therefore, must keep this in mind and must do all they possibly can to enhance, rather than damage, their professional reputations so that their bargaining advantages and persuasive abilities will not be diminished.

Barbara Kellerman agrees, pointing out that "personal power is an essential component of effective presidential leadership."[46] Presidents must carefully guard their sources of personal power—which she describes as authoritative, instrumental, and libidinal—in order to lead the nation effectively. Authoritative powers are those derived by the president from the Constitution and laws of the United States. Instrumental powers are those used by the president to elicit compliance from others through his ability to reward and punish them. Libidinal power enables the president to convince others to follow him through his ability to engender in them an emotional response.[47] Presidents must do nothing or allow nothing to be done to jeopardize these sources of influence and must be politically skilled in guarding their prerogatives, in safeguarding their image as president, and in protecting the aura that surrounds the office they occupy.

A standing Presidential Impairment Panel would inescapably damage the president's "presidentiality."[48] In the process of formally and periodically assessing possible presidential impairment, it would itself impair or even destroy the president's ability to persuade, particularly by weakening his instrumental and libidinal powers. The damage done to the president would perhaps be unintended, but it would be grievous nonetheless.

Proponents of a Presidential Impairment Panel sometimes compare the president to an airline pilot since both are so important to the lives and well-being of their "constituents." They argue that just as the health of airline pilots is formally "screened" periodically, so should the health of presidents be.[49] But their analogy is extremely poor, because the nature of these two positions is so thoroughly dissimilar. If an airline pilot is relieved of his responsibilities, the act would be carried out quietly and behind the scenes. Travelers, to say nothing of the general public, would be unaware that anything unusual had occurred. But if a president should be relieved of his responsibilities, the act would shake the globe. The stock market would fall, international crises may be precipitated, terrorists may be emboldened, and every media outlet in the world would analyze and dissect the story for months. Also, airline pilots do not have to concern themselves with lessening their personal power or with damaging their public prestige. Presidents of the United States do.

A case study might illustrate the dangers that an Impairment panel would present to presidents and to the presidency. After President Eisenhower's heart attack in 1955, he was treated by a number of physicians. When the time came for Eisenhower to decide whether to seek a second term, these physicians took widely varying positions. Dr. Howard Snyder, the White House Physician, urged Eisenhower to run in 1956 and saw no medical reason why he should not. Boston cardiologist Paul Dudley White announced publicly that Eisenhower could certainly run for and serve out a second term but privately believed that the health risks for Eisenhower were formidable and weighed against candidacy. In fact, his confidential recommendation to the president was that he retire at the conclusion of his first term and become an "Ambassador for Peace." Army cardiologist Thomas Mattingly was even more pessimistic. He was convinced, although neither Snyder nor White agreed, that Eisenhower's heart had developed a dangerous aneurysm of the left ventricle which he anticipated would lead to future complications. Since such aneurysms often resulted in congestive heart failure and death, Mattingly thought that Eisenhower should not run for a second term but kept his opinion within "the family."[50] We now know, of course, that, despite these conflicting medical judgments, Eisenhower ran for and won a second term in 1956, served out that term, outlived his Democratic opponent, Adlai Stevenson, as well as Stevenson's vice-presidential running mate, Estes Kefauver, and survived until 1969, almost fourteen years after his heart attack and eight years after leaving the White House. Indeed, he exceeded the life expectancy for males of his birth cohort by several years, a rather impressive performance for someone with his adverse medical history.[51]

But what would have happened to Eisenhower and to the country if these three differing physicians had sat on a formal Presidential Impairment Panel and had gone public, either directly or indirectly, with their conflicting opinions? The country, to say nothing of the vice president and the cabinet, would have been thoroughly confused and unable to weigh the conflicting medical judgments. Perhaps Eisenhower would have been pressured by an avalanche of media coverage to step aside in the "national interest." Possibly he would have run again and gone down to defeat at the hands of an electorate unwilling to re-elect a "dying" man to the presidency or to put Vice President Nixon in a position where his elevation to the presidential office seemed guaranteed. Even if Eisenhower had run again and been re-elected, would not his conduct of office during his second term have been affected negatively by publication in 1956 of medical prognoses that cast a pall over his very survival? It is difficult to imagine how his relationship with the Washington community (Congress, the bureaucracy, the media, etc.) and with the international community would not have been badly undermined by publication of such medical judgments. His friends would have been afraid to follow him and his enemies would have been emboldened to oppose him, because both groups would now see him as standing at death's door. A president is unlikely to be very persuasive if his very continuance in office, and even his life itself, are seen as being in peril. Under such circumstances, he will necessarily be an impaired "leader," but the impairment will have been inflicted by others, no matter how lofty their intentions.

In the case of Dwight Eisenhower, the problem would have been compounded greatly by the fact that the negative medical prognoses in question were simply incorrect.[52] Indeed, if the Impairment Panel proposal had been operative here, history may well have been unfairly and inappropriately altered by physicians who, quite simply, were wrong in their medical judgments but who went public with them, either directly or through "leaks." In this instance, then, a standing Impairment Panel would have institutionalized human error and human fallibility, with potentially far-reaching effects on both the president and the country.

THE VIRTUES OF THE TWENTY-FIFTH AMENDMENT

As a way of safeguarding against the serious problems of a highly bureaucratized system for achieving medical input as described above, the Twenty-Fifth Amendment allows for an informal mechanism for assembling medical consultants, an alternative much preferred by the Amendment's authors and by the Congress that adopted it.[53] The precise nature of medical consultation seems better left to the Senior White House Physician and/or even to the vice president and members of the cabinet, depending on the particular circumstances prevailing at the time. Instead of establishing a standing Impairment Panel consisting of two neurologists, two internists, a surgeon, and a psychiatrist, as has been suggested,[54] flexibility in the process seems more desirable. Any attempt to preordain the nature of the medical advice required in the evaluation of the president's health or in the management of his care by adding language to the Constitution, by enacting a law, or even by adopting a concurrent resolution seems unnecessary and counterproductive. The nature of the president's illness should determine the type of medical practitioners brought into consultation by the Senior White House Physician. If, for example, the president is suffering from cancer, the Senior White House Physician would likely involve eminent oncologists in his care. If the president is suffering from depression, psychiatrists would likely be the consulting physicians, rather than surgeons or internists. In other words, an ad hoc group rather than one of a standing nature seems far more sensible.

An ad hoc group would be able to provide selective and confidential advice, through the Senior White House Physician, to the vice president and cabinet; a formal Impairment Panel, standing squarely in the public domain, would not. Its report would, almost by necessity, go to the press and the public, either directly or indirectly. At least one prominent journalist has already indicated that the press would do all it could to expose and analyze the deliberations of such a group.[55] Although it would be comforting to believe that the press and the public could receive this medical information and be able to process it competently and dispassionately, this is simply not the case. First, neither the press nor the public typically has the training required to process such information competently and dispassionately. Second, even those who do have the requisite training might well disagree on the interpretation of such information. Third, medical information would likely be interpreted throughout the country from a partisan perspective and used for partisan purposes. Fourth, recent history has shown that the press and the public react quite negatively to certain kinds of illness, particularly those that are psychological in nature, and that political figures who have suffered from—or even been rumored to have suffered from—such illnesses are likely to encounter political rejection.

Later in this volume, Jerrold M. Post illustrates this point well when he discusses the unhappy experience of Senator Thomas Eagleton in the 1972 presidential campaign. A more recent illustration of the same phenomenon came sixteen years later during the Bush–Dukakis campaign of 1988.

When rumors circulated that the Democratic presidential nominee, Governor Michael Dukakis of Massachusetts, had received treatment for an alleged psychological breakdown several years earlier, his opponents immediately used the issue against him. Asked about Dukakis, President Reagan quipped, "Look, I'm not going to pick on an invalid." Although Reagan later apologized for speaking carelessly, his remark dominated the news that day. For his part, Vice President Bush warned that the Democratic nominee would make the world a riskier place.[56] Almost immediately, Dukakis's standing in public opinion polls dropped by eight percentage points. Although the initial story was untrue and denied by Dukakis's doctor,[57] the damage was done. The press gave full coverage to the rumors, and the candidate's political opponents used them to good effect. Apparently, a segment of the public changed its voting intentions out of fear that this candidate *may* have received treatment for mental stress many years earlier.

Reflecting on this episode some eleven years later, Dukakis still described it with great feeling. He commented that:

> Candidates now have to ward off attacks not only on their political positions but on their medical status—real and contrived—as well. Allegations of mental instability are devastating in American electoral politics. Although the allegations were wholly unfounded in my case, they nevertheless did real damage to my campaign. But even apart from the 1988 election, this might well have broad, and serious, implications for the future. My experience might well persuade other political figures to avoid consulting mental health specialists even when they see a real need to do so because it will likely damage their careers.[58]

This concern is a very real one and represents dangers to both political leaders and the country. More narrowly, however, the experience of 1988 illustrates all too clearly that medical information can be abused, distorted, misunderstood, and politicized. Even when such information is accurate, the media tend to sensationalize it, and the public confronts the very difficult task of sorting fact from fiction. Therefore, it must be treated in every instance with great sensitivity.

Moreover, the public simply does not have the right to know all there is to know about the health history or health status of a presidential candidate or a sitting president, and great care must be shown in deciding what to release and what to withhold. Information that is unrelated to the present or future exercise of presidential power has no legitimate public purpose and may properly be kept in confidence. Whereas medical information about candidates is sensitive because it can affect their chances for election, medical information about presidents is particularly so because its release can damage their ability to lead. Strength or the image of strength is essential to leadership. Weakness or even the illusion of weakness injures it.[59]

Upon taking the oath of office, the president does not forfeit all his privacy rights as an American citizen. His medical records are protected by the principles of doctor–patient confidentiality, as are the medical records of others, but he must balance his rights to privacy against the welfare of the nation. Also, the American Medical Association's Council on Ethical and Judicial Affairs has indicated that a physician is freed from the rules of confidentiality in the presence of "overriding social considerations" and where there is the "need to protect the welfare of the individual or the public interest."[60] Under such circumstances, medical information gathered by the Senior White House Physician could be released to appropriate public officials (the vice president and members of the cabinet) in order to implement, if necessary, relevant provisions of the Twenty-Fifth Amendment.

Because the vice president and members of the cabinet view the president from the vantage point of close association, they are particularly well positioned to evaluate his health status and his ability to function as chief executive of the nation. If, however, Congress should decide to replace the cabinet as a participant in the process outlined in Section 4 of the Twenty-Fifth Amendment, the president could use his veto power to prevent it from doing so. Such a veto could be overturned only by a two-thirds vote in both houses. If the override attempt is unsuccessful, the cabinet would remain at the center of the displacement process, along with the vice president, who cannot be replaced by Congress. If, for whatever reason, the cabinet was unwilling to vote to separate the president from his powers, the president would continue to exercise those powers. If a majority of the cabinet, or even the entire cabinet, went on record as favoring the president's separation from his powers and duties, and if the vice president, for whatever reason, did not concur, the president would remain in power, since the Amendment makes the vice president's concurrence mandatory.

Some fear that the allegiance of the vice president and cabinet to the president would make invocation of the Twenty-Fifth Amendment extraordinarily difficult. But they perhaps miss one overriding point. The separation of a president of the United States from his powers and duties for any reason *should* be extraordinarily difficult and should not even be contemplated except under extraordinary circumstances. A stable and mature democracy demands no less.

Since the vice president is elected by the people and cabinet members are confirmed in their positions by the people's representatives in the United States Senate, a determination of presidential disability by the vice president and cabinet, with the advice of competent medical personnel, seems likely to win the greatest degree of public acceptance. The vice president, in his role as acting president, must be seen by the public as *legitimate* in order to provide leadership to the nation. Although his status as an acting president will present problems of their own for the vice president since he will be viewed as a temporary, even transient, chief executive, these problems pale in significance when compared with those that would result from the belief that some sort of cabal had taken place and that the vice president had been its beneficiary.

The problems of presidential impairment and presidential disability are not completely solved by the Twenty-Fifth Amendment, nor could they be by additional constitutional procedures or new laws. Quite simply, many problems linked to human pathology and human mortality are unsolvable. But, as one astute observer writes, the Twenty-Fifth Amendment "provides an approach to presidential succession which allows for an effective transfer of power in all cases of presidential inability."[61] Further, it makes clear that a disabled president remains president of the United States and that the vice president only *acts* as president; at the same time it places the exercise of presidential power by this acting president within an important constitutional framework.

Invocation of the Twenty-Fifth Amendment will depend on a wide range of variables. Such factors as the nature and degree of the president's impairment, the relationship existing between the president and the vice president, the pressure of domestic and international events, the president's and vice president's standing in public opinion polls, whether the president is in the first or second term, and whether his disability is likely to be short- or long-term will each be weighed. Given both the complexity of political life and the imponderables of ill health, invocation of the Amendment will necessarily be uneven.

The Amendment, however, remains an invaluable addition to the Constitution, seen even by many international legal scholars as providing one of the most impressive and best codified procedures in the world for constitutional succession.[62] Despite this fact, invocation of its provisions should never be taken lightly or become routinized. Routine invocation of Section 3 would not only trivialize the Amendment but also damage the president's "presidentiality" and thereby his ability to lead. More specifically, as previously discussed, presidential power itself would be diminished if those officials with whom the president must interact both at home and abroad acquired the view—in this instance from the president himself—that he was incapacitated or seriously compromised by illness. In addition to all the structural and institutional factors that already make presidential leadership so difficult in the United States,[63] any weakening of a presidency by frivolous invocation of Section 3—as, for example, when the president undergoes a medical procedure that does not affect his cognitive functions or his ability to communicate—would amount to a form of self-destruction by the president.

Presidents seem instinctively to recognize this fact. They have been extremely reluctant to invoke the disability provisions of the Twenty-Fifth Amendment, understanding all too well that giving up their *powers*, even for a short period, might well reduce their *power*. As an example, although Section 3 can be invoked for non-medical reasons, such as allowing a president to devote his full energies to fighting impeachment proceedings in the House and/or Senate, such invocation typically should be avoided by a politically astute leader. Voluntarily relinquishing the formidable powers of the presidential office at the precise moment when they are likely to be vital in protecting the president's political life and viability would represent political naïveté in its starkest form.

In fighting his recent impeachment battle, President Clinton never seriously considered invoking Section 3 and making Vice President Gore acting president. Instead, he retained and used the prestige of his office as well as its powers—delivering a State of the Union Address, proposing new laws to Congress, traveling abroad on diplomatic missions, ordering air strikes against Iraq—to successfully mobilize the support of the public and his party behind him. Significant political benefits clearly accrued to the president from the use of these powers and prerogatives. For example, his personal popularity increased some 13 percent after he delivered his televised State of the Union Address in January 1999,[64] and Democrats in Congress rallied enthusiastically behind him, praising his proposals and his vision.

As an example, Senator Charles Schumer (Democrat-New York) argued that "the speech was the best argument for ending the impeachment trial with dispatch because it showed all the important things we should and could be doing."[65] Even conservative television evangelist Pat Robertson, who earlier had been outspoken in pressing for Clinton's removal, admitted that the president had hit a "home run" in his State of the Union Address and that, from "a public relations standpoint, he has won. They might as well dismiss this impeachment hearing and get on with something else."[66] A few weeks later, the Senate voted to acquit Clinton on both articles of impeachment that had been brought against him by the House. Although a two-thirds majority is required for conviction in the Senate, not even a simple majority could be attained on either article.[67]

Stepping aside and allowing Vice President Gore to deliver the State of the Union Address as acting president would certainly have reduced pressure on President Clinton in January 1999 and given him more time to work on his defense. But it also would have deprived him of an unsurpassed opportunity to vanquish his opponents in the court of public opinion. In this instance, the voluntary forfeiture of presidential power, through invocation of Section 3, might well have sealed the president's fate, and he showed very good judgment—and a firm understanding of power—by refraining from doing so.

Section 4 of the Twenty-Fifth Amendment should become operative only under the most dire of circumstances, such as massive trauma, coma, severe dementia, major psychological disorders, kidnapping, and capture. Precisely because they are so closely associated with the president and are seen widely as his staunchest political allies, the vice president and cabinet seem particularly well suited to the process of ultimate decision-making here and, again, most likely to win public acceptance for the decisions they make. In cases of presidential ill health, the medical input these officials receive should come not from a formally constituted and standing Impairment Panel but rather from the Senior White House Physician and medical consultants assembled by this physician. A formal Impairment Panel would have an even more deleterious effect on the presidential office than that produced by excessive invocation of Section 3, because it would not only damage the power of the president but also diminish the prestige of the presidency.

It is important to note that within the past ten years two different groups of "experts" have studied and assessed the Twenty-Fifth Amendment to the Constitution. An edited summary of the findings of each group is included later in this volume. Briefly, however, in 1988, the Miller Center Commission on Presidential Disability concluded its lengthy deliberations by asserting that the Amendment "offers excellent standard operating procedures for times of temporary presidential disability" and "under most circumstances, is clear, simple and easily implemented."[68] Some nine years later, the Working Group on Presidential Disability concluded its own set of extended deliberations by pointing out that the Twenty-Fifth Amendment "has enhanced America's ability to respond to presidential inability" and urging that the Amendment *not* be changed since revision or augmentation by amendment "might create greater problems than it sought to correct."[69]

Neither group accepted the notion that the cabinet should be replaced in the process of determining presidential disability, and both groups rejected the proposal that a standing Impairment Panel of physicians should be established to screen the president's health periodically.[70] The Working Group, in fact, debated the Impairment Panel proposal for a lengthy period of time over two years before finally voting overwhelmingly (83–17 percent) against it.[71] This is particularly significant since a large majority of Working Group members were themselves physicians. In the instance of both the Miller Center Commission and the Working Group on Presidential Disability, the unique nature of the presidential office was seen as definitive.

CONCLUSIONS

Providing for occasions of presidential disability is prudent, especially given our history. That history should long since have taught us that presidents of the United States are all too mortal and, like other mortal beings, suffer serious maladies and personal problems.[72] It is vital to recognize, however, that safeguards against the dangers of a disabled president must not be allowed to damage the office of the presidency itself. In a system characterized by separation of powers and checks and balances, a sick presidency poses far greater risks to the republic than a sick president. The Twenty-Fifth Amendment provides a means for dealing with presidential disability that does not disable the institution of the presidency. By allowing for flexibility in the implementation of its disability provisions and informality in the marshaling of medical personnel to care for the president, it avoids the rigidity that can cripple the institution or shatter the delicate balance provided for by the framers. This is the genius of the Twenty-Fifth Amendment, and its contribution to the American constitutional order must not be underestimated.

NOTES

1. John Ferling and Lewis E. Braverman, "John Adams's Health Reconsidered," *William and Mary Quarterly*, 55 (Fall 1998), 83, 98, 104.

2. Irving Brandt, *James Madison: Commander in Chief, 1812–1836* (Indianapolis: Bobbs-Merrill, 1961), p. 210.

3. Rudolph Marx, *The Health of the Presidents* (New York: G. P. Putnam's Sons, 1960), p. 131.

4. Jerrold M. Post, M.D., and Robert S. Robins, *When Illness Strikes the Leader: The Dilemma of the Captive King* (New Haven, Conn.: Yale University Press, 1992), pp. 7–9.

5. Gene Smith, *When the Cheering Stopped* (New York: William Morrow, 1964), p. 91.

6. Kenneth R. Crispell and Carlos F. Gomez, *Hidden Illness in the White House* (Durham, N.C.: Duke University Press, 1988), p. 68.

7. Robert H. Ferrell, *The Strange Deaths of President Harding* (Columbia: University of Missouri Press, 1996), p. 15.

8. Robert E. Gilbert, *The Mortal Presidency: Illness and Anguish in the White House*, 2nd ed. (New York: Fordham University Press, 1998), pp. 32–42.

9. Ross McIntire, *White House Physician* (New York: G. P. Putnam, 1946), pp. 183–84.

10. Thomas Mattingly, A Compilation of the General Health Status of Dwight D. Eisenhower, Box 1, "General Health," Dwight D. Eisenhower Library, Abilene, Kans., pp. 99–100.

11. Janet Travell, *Office Hours, Day and Night* (New York: World, 1968), p. 330.

12. See, for example, Kenneth P. O'Donnell and David M. Powers, *Johnny, We Hardly Knew Ye* (Boston: Little, Brown, 1970), pp. 99, 103.

13. Gilbert, *Mortal Presidency*, p. 195.

14. James M. Young, M.D., interview with author, August 16, 1997.

15. Benjamin Aaron, M.D., interview with author, June 20, 1991.

16. Nancy Reagan, *My Turn* (New York: Random House, 1989), p. 10.

17. Joel K. Goldstein, "The New Constitutional Vice Presidency," *Wake Forest Law Review*, 30, No. 3 (Fall 1995), 517.

18. *Records of the Federal Convention of 1787*, ed. Max Farrand, vol. 2. (New Haven, Conn.: Yale University Press, 1911; rep. 1937, 1966), p. 495.

19. Gilbert, *Mortal Presidency*, pp. 85–112.

20. The previous Presidential Succession Law, that of 1886, bypassed congressional leaders and placed members of the cabinet, in order of departmental seniority, behind the vice president in the line of presidential succession.

21. Marie D. Natoli, *American Prince, American Pauper* (Westport, Conn.: Greenwood Press, 1985), p. 16.

22. Joel K. Goldstein, *The Modern American Vice Presidency: The Transformation of a Political Institution* (Princeton, N.J.: Princeton University Press, 1982), p. 229.

23. John D. Feerick, *The Twenty-Fifth Amendment: Its Complete History and Applications* (New York: Fordham University Press, 1976; repr. 1992), pp. 197, 200.

24. Ibid., p. 155.

25. Lawrence C. Mohr, M.D., interview with author, October 21, 1997.

26. E. Connie Mariano, M.D., interview with author, September 11, 1997.

27. Post and Robins, *When Illness Strikes the Leader*, p. 172.

28. See Paul B. Stephan III, "History, Background and Outstanding Problems of the Twenty-Fifth Amendment," *Papers on Presidential Disability and the Twenty-Fifth Amendment*, ed. Kenneth W. Thompson (Lanham, Md.: University Press of America, 1988), p. 67; see also Louis W. Koenig, *The Chief Executive* (New York: Harcourt, Brace, 1996), p. 85.

29. *Public Papers of the Presidents of the United States, Ronald Reagan, 1985* (Washington, D.C.: Government Printing Office, 1986), p. 919.

30. Ronald Reagan, *An American Life* (New York: Simon & Schuster, 1990), p. 500.

31. During President Garfield's lengthy final illness, Vice President Arthur was described as "sympathetic and self-effacing," typical behavior for vice presidents in such situations. See Irving G. Williams, *The Rise of the Vice Presidency* (Washington, D.C.: Public Affairs Press, 1956), p. 7.

32. Alexander Haig, *Caveat* (New York: Macmillan, 1984), p. 160.

33. Reagan, *An American Life*, p. 271.

34. Richard F. Fenno, *The President's Cabinet* (Cambridge, Mass.: Harvard University Press, 1959), p. 5.

35. Bert E. Park, "Presidential Disability: Past Experiences and Future Implications," *Politics and the Life Sciences*, 7, No. 1 (August 1988), 59.

36. Norman J. Ornstein and Shirley Elder, *Interest Groups, Lobbying, and Policymaking* (Washington, D.C.: Congressional Quarterly Press, 1978), p. 62.

37. See Working Group on Disability in U.S. Presidents, *Disability in U.S. Presidents: Report, Recommendations, and Commentaries* (Winston-Salem, N.C.: Bowman-Gray Scientific Press, 1997), p. 22.

38. Park, "Presidential Disability," 58.

39. Bert E. Park, "Resuscitating the 25th Amendment: A Second Opinion Regarding Presidential Disability," *Political Psychology*, 16, No. 4 (December 1995), 823.

40. Katy J. Harriger, "Who Should Decide: Constitutional and Political Issues Regarding Section 4 of the Twenty-Fifth Amendment," *Wake Forest Law Review*, 30, No. 3 (Fall 1995), 582.

41. John Ellement and Judy Rakowsky, "A Juror Says Panel Favored Mudge by 9–6; Drug Allegation Called Non-Issue," *Boston Globe*, June 26, 1999, p. A1.

42. Andy Dabilis, "Theory on Eappen Baby's Death Aired: Doctors Cite Evidence of Strangling, but Prosecutor Calls Idea 'Outrageous,' " ibid., March 8, 1999, p. B1.

43. See, for example, Herbert L. Abrams, "Can the Twenty-Fifth Amendment Deal with a Disabled President? Preventing Future White House Cover-Ups," *Presidential Studies Quarterly*, 29, No. 1 (March 1999), 124.

44. Henry J. Abraham, *The Judiciary*, 4th ed. (Boston: Allyn and Bacon, 1977), p. 44.

45. Richard E. Neustadt, *Presidential Power and the Modern Presidents* (New York: The Free Press, 1990), chap. 4.

46. Barbara Kellerman, *The Political Presidency* (New York: Oxford University Press, 1984), p. 15.

47. Ibid., pp. 20–21.

48. Robert E. Gilbert, Remarks, Working Group on Disability in U.S. Presidents, Atlanta, Georgia, January 27, 1995.

49. See Abrams, "Can the Twenty-Fifth Amendment Deal with a Disabled President?," 128.

50. Gilbert, *Mortal Presidency*, p. 97; see also Clarence G. Lasby, *Eisenhower's Heart Attack: How Ike Beat Heart Disease and Held On to the Presidency* (Lawrence: University Press of Kansas, 1997), p. 252.

51. For a fuller discussion of Dwight D. Eisenhower's medical history, see Gilbert, *Mortal Presidency*, pp. 74–141.

52. Eisenhower's 1969 autopsy photographs revealed the existence of a large, calcified ventricular aneurysm, just as Mattingly had diagnosed in 1955. Perhaps Mattingly was correct in his view that this aneurysm bore a relationship to the president's 1957 stroke, but it did not result in either sudden or premature death or significantly impair Eisenhower during his second term. See ibid., pp. 91, 109.

53. Birch Bayh, *One Heartbeat Away: Presidential Disability and Succession* (Indianapolis: Bobbs-Merrill, 1968), p. 86.

54. Herbert L. Abrams, "The Vulnerable President and the Twenty-Fifth Amendment, with Observations on Guidelines, A Health Commission and the Role of the President's Physician," *Wake Forest Law Review*, 30, No. 3 (Fall 1995), 465.

55. Tom Wicker, Remarks, Working Group on Disability in U.S. Presidents, Atlanta, Georgia, January 28, 1995.

56. *Newsweek*, November 21, 1988, p. 113.

57. Michael S. Dukakis, interview with author, August 31, 1998.

58. Michael S. Dukakis, interview with author, August 10, 1999.

59. Francis X. Clines, "Does Clinton Need to Turn to Ministers, or a Psychotherapist, Too?," *New York Times*, September 17, 1998, p. 14.

60. American Medical Association, Council on Ethical and Judicial Affairs, "Current Opinions," Chicago, 1989, Section 5.05; see also, AMA, Council on Ethical and Judicial Affairs, "Fundamental Elements of the Patient-Physician Relationship," June, 1990, p. 2.

61. John D. Feerick, "The Twenty-Fifth Amendment: An Explanation and Defense," *Wake Forest Law Review*, 30, No. 3 (Fall 1995), 503.

62. Post and Robins, *When Illness Strikes the Leader*, p. 171.

63. For an examination of the role of the presidency in a fragmented political environment, see Charles O. Jones, *The Presidency in a Separated System* (Washington, D.C.: The Brookings Institution, 1994).

64. "Clinton Ratings Near All-Time Peak," *Boston Globe*, January 21, 1999, p. A21.

65. *New York Times*, January 20, 1999, p. A21.

66. Ibid., January 21, 1999, p. A1.

67. On the first article of impeachment, perjury, the Senate voted 45 for, 55 against; on the second article of impeachment, obstruction of justice, the Senate voted 50–50.

68. White Burkett Miller Center of Public Affairs, *Report of the Miller Center Commission on Presidential Disability and the Twenty-Fifth Amendment* (Lanham, Md.: University Press of America, 1988), p. 23.

69. Working Group on Presidential Disability, *Disability in U.S. Presidents*, p. 11.

70. White Burkett Miller Center, *Report of the Miller Center Commission*, pp. 11–12, 17; Working Group on Presidential Disability, *Disability in U.S. Presidents*, p.17.

71. Working Group on Disability in U.S. Presidents, *Original Recorded Transactions Before Editing* Washington, D.C., December 2, 1996, pp. 281–82.

72. For a discussion of the high rate of premature death experienced even by non-assassinated presidents of the United States, see Gilbert, *Mortal Presidency*, pp. 2–18.

3

Reflections on the Twenty-Fifth Amendment As We Enter a New Century

Birch Bayh

The Twenty-Fifth Amendment provides an effective and predictable method for dealing with presidential disability. Although not perfect, the Amendment need not be changed. Congress, however, might consider enacting laws that would facilitate implementation of the Amendment in various ways. Our objective always must be to protect the national interest.

In the American system of government, the office of the presidency is the focal point of the public's attention. The recent impeachment trial of President Clinton has demonstrated once again that a vast amount of information regarding a president's public and private life is readily available for anyone able to open a newspaper or turn on a television set. However, despite our intimate knowledge of those who occupy the Oval Office, we tend to give relatively little thought to the dangers that continually threaten the lives and health of our presidents. Our view of them as physical supermen is reinforced by the carefully developed images put forward by professional public relations advisers. Scenes of Ronald Reagan on horseback or chopping wood reflect the desire of the public to see their president as an active, powerful figure. Understandably, these images are important tools for presidents eager to portray themselves as men capable of carrying the heavy burdens of leadership. Unfortunately, history reminds us that presidents are just as likely to be hospitalized as they are to be on horseback. Additionally, presidents must guard themselves against threats from demented individuals who, given the opportunity, are prepared to assassinate them.

Eight presidents of the United States have died in office, four by natural causes, four by assassination. Several past presidents, including Andrew Jackson, Theodore Roosevelt, Franklin Roosevelt, Harry Truman, Gerald Ford (twice), and Ronald Reagan, have narrowly escaped serious attacks by potential assassins. To date, President Clinton has been the target of two would-be assassins during his years in the White House. In 1994, twenty-nine rounds of ammunition were fired from a semi-automatic rifle by an assailant at a man resembling President Clinton as he emerged from the White House. In 1995, a potential assassin who had lain in wait along the president's favorite jogging route for a week armed with a .45-calibre automatic handgun was arrested. These events remind us once again of the dangers facing the president.

When, after the death of President William Henry Harrison in 1841, John Tyler boldly struck the word "acting" from his title and insisted that he was then president of the United States, he created a powerful precedent for those vice presidents who would succeed a *deceased* President. A *disabled but living* president posed far more serious difficulties. It was not until the ratification of the Twenty-Fifth Amendment that a clearly specified means was provided to cope with circumstances in which a sitting president is unable to perform the duties of his office. The Founding Fathers recognized that this was a possibility. However, at the Constitutional Convention in Philadelphia, reference made to the issue was scant as well as ambiguous. Article II, section 1, clause 6 reads:

> In Case of the Removal of the President from Office, or of his Death, Resignation, or Inability to discharge the Powers and Duties of the said Office, the same shall devolve on the Vice President, and the Congress may by Law provide for the Case of Removal, Death, Resignation or Inability, both of the President and Vice President, declaring what Officer shall then act as President, and such Officer shall act accordingly, until the Disability be removed, or a President shall be elected.

At the Convention, John Dickinson, a delegate from Delaware, asked the question that would echo through the years and not be answered until passage of the Twenty-Fifth Amendment in 1967: "What is the extent of the term 'disability' & who is to be the judge of it?"[1] As history demonstrates, prior to passage and ratification of the Twenty-Fifth Amendment, failure to resolve this basic question created serious consequences for the nation. The well-known case of Woodrow Wilson lying incapacitated for several months as the result of a massive stroke is only one of many instances in which a president has been effectively disabled. In the previous century, for example, President Zachary Taylor, stricken with an ailment diagnosed by one physician as cholera, sank slowly but perceptibly toward death over a period of five days. During this difficult time, he was essentially too ill to function as president. The country's business virtually came to a halt until Taylor died on July 9, 1850, and was succeeded by Vice President Millard Fillmore.[2]

As discussed earlier in this volume, President Eisenhower tried to deal with the potential effects of his own ill health by entering into a private agreement with Vice President Nixon. Drawn up under the direction of Attorney General Herbert Brownell, this agreement enumerated the duties the vice president was to perform in the event the president was unable to do so,[3] but it represented only a short-term and quite imperfect solution. As a result of his personal experiences, former President Eisenhower enthusiastically supported the Twenty-Fifth Amendment, the provisions of which are designed to cover just the types of disabilities he suffered.[4] Before we proceed any further, it is necessary to review the provisions of the Amendment that refer to presidential disability.

PROVISIONS OF THE TWENTY-FIFTH AMENDMENT

The Twenty-Fifth Amendment provides for the vice president to serve as acting president if the president becomes unable to perform the powers and duties of his office. It provides for this eventuality in three ways.

First, Section 3 provides for the president to voluntarily notify the Congress and assign the powers and duties of his office to the vice president, who will then serve as acting president during a period of disability. Upon recovery, the president may reclaim his powers and duties by notifying Congress. This section is intended to be utilized in cases of anticipated disability, such as surgery that would require general anesthesia. The voluntary nature of Section 3 was designed to lessen the temptation to treat a presidential disability as insignificant or hide it altogether, as has been the case historically.[5]

Second, Section 4, clause 1 provides for those occasions when the president is unable or unwilling to act voluntarily. The vice president and a majority of the cabinet may decide that it is in the national interest for the vice president to serve as acting president during the president's disability. President Eisenhower's heart attack, which rendered him unconscious, is an excellent example of a disability for which this provision would be applicable.[6]

Third, Section 4, clause 2 is designed for those instances in which the vice president and cabinet disagree with the president's assessment of his ability to serve. Such disagreement is to be resolved by Congress, and a two-thirds vote of both houses is required to deny the president the right to perform his powers and duties.

All these provisions, and the Twenty-Fifth Amendment in general, recognize that presidents are not physical supermen. They suffer from the same maladies and infirmities as the rest of us. They undergo various minor surgeries. More seriously, they are stricken by heart attacks, strokes, and, tragically, assassins' bullets. The Twenty-Fifth Amendment is intended to guarantee an orderly, consistent, and constitutionally mandated transfer of power in the very real event that a president is unable to perform the functions and duties of his office. Some question, however, whether the provisions of the Twenty-Fifth Amendment are adequate to deal with the situations for which they were intended.

RONALD REAGAN AND THE TWENTY-FIFTH AMENDMENT

On March 31, 1981, President Ronald Reagan literally came within millimeters of losing his life. The attempted assassination by John Hinckley, Jr., left the newly inaugurated president hospitalized, essentially unable to perform the duties of his office. Clearly, the Twenty-Fifth Amendment should have been invoked in this instance, yet it was not. The more immediate concerns with saving the president's life, along with a lack of familiarity with the Amendment on the part of Reagan's doctors and White House staff, explain why the provisions of the Twenty-Fifth Amendment were overlooked. White House Counsel Fred Fielding has explained that:

> [Prior to the assassination attempt] . . . one of the things that I had my staff working on was a book, basically an emergency book. What do you do about X, Y, Z, events concerning the President's health? I state in all candor that [the book] was not completed on March 30. [It was] early afternoon, and suddenly the president was shot and we all realized (a) it was an incident, (b) the President was shot, (c) it was very serious. To be very frank with you, that day, when I mentioned the Twenty-Fifth Amendment I could see eyes glazing over in some parts of the cabinet. They didn't even know about the Twenty-Fifth Amendment.
>
> The book [was later] finished . . . [and] whenever I could travel with the President . . . I would always carry a copy of the book.[7]

Unfortunately, this was not the only time that President Reagan faced the problem of considering invocation of the Twenty-Fifth Amendment. Before he underwent surgery for colon cancer in 1985, it was fully expected that he would temporarily transfer power to Vice President Bush under terms of Section 3 of the Amendment. Instead of doing so, he sent an ambiguous letter to Congress suggesting that the Amendment did not apply to the circumstances at hand, yet he was designating Bush as acting president.[8] Although this has led to disagreement about whether the Amendment was invoked on this occasion, it should be noted that, from a constitutional perspective, the only basis for the president's action was, in fact, Section 3.

In 1987, President Reagan was again ill. This time he underwent prostate surgery and recovered very slowly from the procedure, much more slowly than his aides had expected.[9] The President had to follow a sharply reduced schedule but, once again, the Twenty-Fifth Amendment was not invoked, either while he was under anesthesia or afterward.

Though these opportunities were missed to demonstrate to the world that the United States could function responsibly even though the president was disabled, the experience seems to have provided Presidents Bush and Clinton with an example: both presidents developed contingency plans and outlined the actions that were to be taken in the event a tragedy occurred, or either of them became disabled.[10]

CONTINGENCIES

The announcement several years ago that former President Reagan was suffering from Alzheimer's disease has added to the concern expressed by medical professionals, political scientists, journalists, and presidential scholars over the procedures to be followed when a president suffers from varying degrees of mental illness.[11] Those who drafted the Twenty-Fifth Amendment fully expected that, just as physical illness requires expert medical diagnosis, so, too, does mental illness. Indeed, every president is fortunate to have the best minds in the medical profession available to him. However, as discussion among those concerned with the Twenty-Fifth Amendment has illustrated, questions about how to and who should determine the president's physical and/or mental disability abound.

The drafters of the Twenty-Fifth Amendment were concerned about historical circumstances, like those surrounding Taylor and Wilson, where presidential disability was handled improperly, or deliberately kept from the public. At these and other times in the nation's history, presidential disability was readily apparent to available medical consultants and political advisers, but the system did not function in a manner that permitted the vice president to perform those duties that were being neglected. The steps that should be taken to ensure that this kind of deception or indecision is avoided are fundamental. There are some who believe the Amendment fails to do this adequately.

To strengthen the process, former President Jimmy Carter has suggested that the responsibility for determining presidential disability should rest with a formally constituted panel of distinguished physicians.[12] This idea of a blue ribbon panel is one that received much attention even prior to Carter's suggestion. It is one, interestingly, that former Presidents Ford and Bush oppose.

On the surface, a nonpolitical panel of independent and distinguished physicians sitting in judgment of the president's capacity to perform the duties of his office seems to have merit. Many of those who advocate the panel idea believe that its nonpolitical nature would enhance the credibility of the Twenty-Fifth Amendment in the minds of the American people.[13] Others are not so sanguine. Dr. Burton Lee, physician to President Bush (1989–92) offered an argument against this proposal in a 1994 letter to the *Journal of the American Medical Association*:

> I discussed this matter, while in the White House, with many strong advocates of a "committee of experts". I persuaded them that this always produced the lowest common denominator of medical decision making, that this is the main reason so many VIP's receive bad medical advice. This also disregards how every proficient and expert clinician conducts his clinical affairs.When we see a patient, and there are difficult and subtle decisions to be made, both in our specialty and out of it, we call in the best person or persons we know in the world to help us make these decisions. It might be 2 or 3 people, or it might be a dozen, but in the end the physician in charge makes the decision, after listening to the most persuasive voices, not the loudest or the most "important".
>
> There are other difficulties with a "committee of experts." Who will pick the committee? For what length of term? How will it operate? By majority decision? Can politics be kept out of it? How can it possibly be "non partisan"? "Leaks" to the press? Who will decide if indeed one of these experts may not be ill? Etc. Etc.
>
> No, the physician to the President must make those decisions, and must execute the responsibility to declare disability, while in concert with the President's family and associates.[14]

No one would argue that medical professionals have a unique capacity to diagnose the presence of physical and mental disease. But, in general, the proposal of a blue ribbon, standing panel of physicians suffers from three major flaws.

First, the proposal assumes that a panel, concluding in unanimity that a President is unable to fulfill his responsibilities, would bolster the credibility of the process. But the distinct possibility remains of differing diagnoses among physicians. This would be especially true in regard to mental illness, the diagnosis of which is often imprecise. Anything less than a unanimous decision, either way, would do little to ease possible concerns of the American public over the health of the president. Even a five-to-two vote that the president is not disabled would have a chilling effect on the country.

Second, especially in questions of mental illness, the proposal fails to appreciate the environment in which such a decision must be made. Determining if a president is mentally unfit to perform the duties of his office would require nearly continuous observation of his interaction with people in different situations. This not only is logistically impossible for a panel of physicians, but also discounts the ability of people, especially presidents, to play to the audience when they are being watched. The manifestations of mental illness are often transitory, coming and going depending on the environment in which a person is operating and the health of the person at a particular time. Certainly, presidents operate under enormous pressure and unique circumstances. Should a panel observe the president during a heated debate with congressional leaders, in the middle of a national security crisis, or during periods of solitude in the Oval Office? Moreover, depending on the stage of development, the effects of mental illness are more likely to be displayed in certain situations than in others. The inability of a panel to observe the president regularly and under all circumstances would severely limit panel members in their ability to make a comprehensive diagnosis of the president's ability to carry out the duties and responsibilities of his office.

Conversely, those people who are in a position to interact with and observe the president on a consistent basis, the White House Physician, the cabinet, the president's family and staff, the vice president, and others close to the president are much better situated to notice changes in behavior or character that could indicate an erosion of mental capacity. The White House Physician, in particular, is in an advantageous position to diagnose medical aspects of the president's fitness because of the close association over a significant period of time and also because of close association over a significant period of time with others who are close to the president.

Third, as President Eisenhower recognized, the determination of presidential disability is really a political question.[15] A blue ribbon panel of physicians would undoubtedly consist of some of the most brilliant and respected medical minds in their field. However, despite their recognized expertise, a panel would be ill equipped to understand the various political factors that would need to be considered in determining if a specific president or vice president is better able to fulfill the powers and duties of the office at any given time. For example, would a standing panel of physicians have been the best source for determining who was more qualified to serve, an impaired FDR or a well, but untested, Vice President Henry Wallace, an ill Dwight D. Eisenhower or Vice President Richard Nixon, a seriously wounded Ronald Reagan or Vice President George Bush? The Twenty-Fifth Amendment gives the ultimate responsibility for making this determination to the vice president and cabinet, precisely because they are best equipped to make a *professional* judgment of the *political* circumstances existing at the time and whether those circumstances mitigate against a transfer of presidential power to the vice president.

USING THE AMENDMENT PROPERLY

The Twenty-Fifth Amendment, like most other legislative products, is imperfect. The concerns that have been expressed over its perceived flaws are not without foundation. However, after careful assessment of them, I believe that the recommendations that have been offered to correct these flaws are likely to create greater problems than those that currently exist. The Twenty-Fifth Amendment, when used properly, provides an effective and predictable way to deal with presidential disability. However, the responsibility for ensuring that its provisions are invoked in a manner consistent with the intentions of the drafters ultimately lies at any given time with the individual president and with members of the president's administration. To enhance the implementation of the rules designed to deal with presidential disability, a few key steps should be taken.

First, as the Bush and Clinton administrations have done, each new administration should draft a detailed contingency plan to be followed in the event of a presidential disability. The president, vice president, their spouses, White House staff, White House Physician, and others close to the president should all be aware of the details of the plan. This should be done *before* the inauguration to ensure that the kind of confusion surrounding the assassination attempt on Ronald Reagan just two months after he was sworn into office is not repeated.

Second, the diagnosis of the White House Physician will undoubtedly weigh heavily in the minds of those charged with making the ultimate decisions about a president's ability to carry out the duties of his office, including the president himself. In order to make this diagnosis more comprehensive, steps should be taken to upgrade the stature of the White House Physician. In doing so, recognition should be given to the fact that the more sustained and day-to-day contact the physician has with the president, the better able he or she will be to judge the president's ability to carry out the duties of his office. Also, steps should be taken, fully recognizing the doctor–patient relationship, to ensure that the physician is able to inform the relevant people when he or she believes that the president is disabled. This is an important consideration that must be a part of each administration's contingency plans. If necessary, an Act of Congress could assert that the President's Physician is responsible for promptly informing the chief of staff, vice president, and other close associates of the president if he or she believes that the president is unable to carry out the powers and duties of the presidency. Importantly, the White House Physician's primary responsibility is to the national interest.

Third, a national dialogue about presidential disability should occur. The more people come to realize that presidents of the United States are just as likely to be stricken by debilitating illness as the rest of us, the better society as a whole will be able to deal with this situation when it does arise. Along with that, familiarizing the American public with the steps that are in place to deal with these unfortunate incidents will ease uncertainty at times when reason and calm are especially needed.

Finally, legislation should be considered that makes it illegal for any official to hide or distort information that would be necessary to invoke the Twenty-Fifth Amendment. The Wilson experience, where for several months his strong-willed wife, Edith, and his loyal aide, Joseph Tumulty decided who and what information got to and from the President,[16] and what information got to Congress and the press, must not be repeated.

It must be made clear to officials who engage in this sort of behavior that covering up presidential disability is simply not acceptable. In any attempt to educate the public about the realities of presidential disability, special emphasis should be given to the consequences of ignoring it. Wilson's massive stroke of 1919 is only the most tragic example of what can result when the president of the United States is unable to perform the duties of his office. In 1970, Edwin Weinstein, a prominent neurologist, published a provocative book contending that Woodrow Wilson had suffered a series of minor strokes, beginning in 1896 and reoccurring in 1900, 1904, 1906, and

1907.[17] These strokes, later accepted as fact by eminent Wilson scholar Arthur S. Link, are claimed to have seriously affected Wilson's mental capacity and judgment. Most notably, this series of strokes is said to have been responsible for brain damage that, combined with a severe case of influenza contracted during the Paris Peace Conference in 1919, contributed to Wilson's failures during the negotiations.[18]

These problems were greatly intensified by the massive stroke Wilson suffered as he fought for ratification of the Treaty of Versailles later that year. After he was stricken, the president did not deny to his associates that he was ill. He knew only too well that the functioning of the limbs on the left side of his body was affected, and he referred to himself as "lame." Yet, he did not accept the fact that his illness prevented him from properly executing his responsibilities, and he even considered running for a third term. On some matters, particularly those that did not endanger his strong sense of morality, his judgment was sound. On others, it was not.[19] Despite this tragic situation, the country just "muddled along."

This was an unfortunate instance of undiagnosed presidential disability. But, in this age of advanced technology, high-tech nuclear and conventional weaponry, and sophisticated computers, the consequences of ignoring new instances of presidential disabilities could be much more dangerous.

The Twenty-Fifth Amendment provides a blueprint of standard operating procedures to deal with presidential disability. As mentioned earlier, critics and supporters alike acknowledge that the Amendment is not entirely perfect. Yet, despite its flaws, several factors make it increasingly likely that its provisions will be followed by those for whom they are intended.

As Joel Goldstein discusses in chapter 9, the status of the vice presidency has grown over time. In the early 1900s, Woodrow Wilson's vice president described the office as similar to being in a cataleptic fit in which one "is conscious of all that goes on but has no part in it."[20] More recently, however, the office has taken on new responsibilities and become much more visible. This should make it easier for the vice president to assume the role of the acting president, and for the country to accept his or her assuming of that role.

Also, as the press has become more aggressive in investigating the possibility of presidential disability, and opinion leaders understand the importance of keeping the subject on the nation's agenda, the public is more aware of the possibility that a president may become disabled, and of the importance of ensuring continuity if he does suffer such a disability. In short, the public will know the truth. Not only does this make it difficult for the participants in the Twenty-Fifth Amendment process to ignore their responsibilities, but it also makes it politically unacceptable for them to do so. The national interest must always come first, and the Twenty-Fifth Amendment is designed to ensure that, in cases of presidential disability, it will. This fact must be understood with clarity by officials of both the executive and the legislative branches and by the people of the United States.

NOTES

1. Ruth C. Silva, *Presidential Succession* (New York: Greenwood Press, 1968), p. 85. Max Farrand, ed., *Records of the Federal Convention of 1787*, vol. 2 (New Haven, Conn.: Yale University Press, 1911; repr. 1937), p. 427.

2. K. Jack Bauer, *Zachary Taylor: Soldier, Planter, Statesman of the Southwest* (Baton Rouge: Louisiana State University Press, 1985), pp. 314–16.

3. "Agreement Between the President and Vice President on Procedures in the Event of Presidential Disability," *Public Papers of the Presidents, Dwight D. Eisenhower, 1958* (Washington, D.C.: Government Printing Office, 1959), pp. 196–97.

4. John Feerick, *The Twenty-Fifth Amendment: Its Complete History and Application* (New York: Fordham University Press, 1976; repr. 1992), pp. 62–63.

5. For a discussion of attempts to hide presidential disabilities, see John D. Feerick, *From Failing Hands: The Story of Presidential Succession* (New York: Fordham University Press, 1965), pp. 118–29. Kenneth R. Crispell and Carlos F. Gomez, *Hidden Illness in the White House* (Durham, N.C.: Duke University Press, 1988), pp. 75–159; Herbert L. Abrams, *The President Has Been Shot: Confusion, Disability, and the Twenty-Fifth Amendment in the Aftermath of the Attempted Assassination of Ronald Reagan* (New York: W. W. Norton, 1992), pp. 165–66. See also Robert E. Gilbert, *The Mortal Presidency: Illness and Anguish in the White House*, 2nd ed. (New York: Fordham University Press, 1998), chaps. 3–7.

6. Feerick, *Twenty-Fifth Amendment*, pp. 17–18.

7. White Burkett Miller Center of Public Affairs, *Report of the Miller*

Center Commission on Presidential Disability and the Twenty-Fifth Amendment (Charlottesville, Va.: Miller Center, 1988), p. 7.

8. President's Letters to the President Pro Tempore of the Senate and the Speaker of the House, *Weekly Comp. Pres. Doc*. 21 (July 13, 1985), 902; White Burkett Miller Center, *Report of the Miller Center Commission*, pp. 6–9.

9. Gilbert, *Mortal Presidency*, p. 240.

10. Judith Havermann and David Hoffman, "Presidential Disability Discussed," *Washington Post*, April 28, 1989, p. 1.

11. Bettina Boxall and Deborah Schoch, "Reagan Says He is in Early Stages of Alzheimer's," *Los Angeles Times*, November 6, 1994, p. 1.

12. Jimmy Carter, "Presidential Disability and the Twenty-Fifth Amendment: A President's Perspective," *Journal of the American Medical Association*, 272 (December 1994), 1698.

13. See, generally, Bert E. Park, *Ailing, Aging and Addicted: Studies of Compromised Leadership* (Lexington: University Press of Kentucky, 1993), pp. 195–228.

14. Letter from Burton J. Lee, III, M.D., to the Editor of the *Journal of the American Medical Association*, 272 (December 1994).

15. *Presidential Inability and Vacancies in the Office of Vice President: Hearings Before the Subcommittee on Constitutional Amendments of the Senate Committee on the Judiciary*, 88th Congress, 2d Session, 1964, p. 232 (testimony by Dwight D. Eisenhower).

16. Apparently, Woodrow Wilson's physician, Admiral Cary T. Grayson, and neurology consultant, Dr. Francis X. Dercum, wanted to make a full public disclosure of the president's medical condition. Feerick, *From Failing Hands*, pp. 171–73. Neither physician, however, was willing to oppose Mrs. Wilson's strong opinion to the contrary.

17. Edwin A. Weinstein, *Woodrow Wilson: A Medical and Psychological Biography* (Princeton, N.J.: Princeton University Press, 1981), pp. 141–80; 349–70

18. Ibid., p. 359.

19. Michael F. Marmor, "Wilson, Strokes and Zebras," *New England Journal of Medicine*, 307 (August 26, 1982), 528.

20. Feerick, *From Failing Hands*, p. 167.

4

Presidential Illness and the Twenty-Fifth Amendment: A Former White House Physician's Perspective

James M. Young, M.D.

The temporary but informal transfer of presidential power to the vice president that occurred in 1965 while I was serving as White House Physician paved the way to enactment of the Twenty-Fifth Amendment. This Amendment now brings such transfers within the purview of the Constitution. The role of the Senior White House Physician in the process of invoking the Amendment's disability procedures should be established and acknowledged at the beginning of every administration.

In this chapter, I will explain something of the responsibilities of White House Physicians and outline some factors that affect their professional lives as members of the White House Medical Unit, including those that have developed in recent years with regard to the disability provisions of the Twenty-Fifth Amendment. My service at the White House began in June 1963 and continued until September 1966 when I returned to the practice of medicine in the Navy's teaching hospitals. During my assignment as White House Physician, I served two sitting presidents, their families and staffs, and former President Harry S. Truman, when he represented the United States, along with Mrs. Lyndon Johnson, at the funeral of King Paul of Greece in 1964.

Throughout my tenure as White House Physician, my colleagues and I in the Medical Unit obviously had the health and care of the president as our primary responsibility. But almost as important was our contribution to the health and care of the president's immediate and extended family as well as those presidential assistants, secretaries, and cabinet members who were part of the executive branch of our government. We were also the primary caregivers for a large contingent of military personnel supporting the president. This group consisted of the White House Communications Agency, the White House garage personnel, the military personnel staffing Camp David, and, frequently, the members of the Secret Service on the White House detail.

We felt very strongly that we would make the president's job that much easier and relieve some of the tremendous personal burdens that could be shared by his staff if we were able to provide excellent health care to those persons surrounding the president and keep them well. So, if one considers the broad definition of being a White House Physician, it could more appropriately be termed Physician to the President, his family, and the executive branch of our government.

I was selected to come to the White House by then Captain George G. Burkley (United States Naval Medical Corps), who held the title of White House Physician and whose associate physician, Dr. Janet G. Travell, held the title of Physician to the President. My original Navy orders instructed me to report to the White House as Assistant White House Physician. Shortly after I arrived in June 1963, I was appointed White House Physician, and Captain Burkley was given the title of Physician to the President, a title identical to that of Dr. Travell.

My title of White House Physician enabled the Navy to advance my rank from Lieutenant Commander to Captain by virtue of a law that provides that "an officer of the Medical Corps of the Army, or a medical officer of the Air Force, who is below the grade of colonel and who is assigned to duty as physician to the White House has the rank, pay and allowances of colonel while so serving. An officer of the Medical Corps of the Navy who is below the grade of captain and who is assigned to that duty has the rank, pay and allowances of captain while so serving."[1] Such promotions are made in order to enhance a White House Physician's status in the military. Also, if they wished to do so, and with the advice and consent of the Senate, presidents could make promotions to even higher ranks. For example, President Johnson promoted Captain Burkley to the rank of Rear Admiral in the Navy and then to the rank of Vice Admiral.

Just as the military title assigned a White House Physician is important for reasons of status and prestige in the military, so, too, is the civilian title held by this official important for reasons of status and prestige in the White House. As I will later discuss, an additional civilian title, beyond that of White House Physician or Physician to the President or even Senior White House Physician, seems to make good sense, particularly since the Twenty-Fifth Amendment is now an integral part of the Constitution and the physician responsible for recommending its invocation would benefit from enhanced status. During my tour of duty in the White House Medical Unit, an additional title would also have gone a long way toward mitigating the confusion that resulted from the indeterminate titles held by medical personnel there.

Since several physicians inside the White House carried similar titles (White House Physician, Physician to the President), one can well imagine the confusion that might have occurred if the Twenty-Fifth Amendment had been in effect and a recommendation under Section 4 (which allows the vice president and a majority of the cabinet to relieve the president of his powers) were to be made to the vice president. Who would have been the physician to make it? Which physician's recommendation would have been viewed as authoritative by the vice president, the cabinet, the Congress, and the public? At the time, such questions had no clear answers.

MEDICAL CARE OF PRESIDENT KENNEDY

As one of the physicians to President Kennedy, I saw him only occasionally. At least once a month, the physicians in the White House Medical Unit joined with a group of consulting physicians and met with the president. During this meeting, we all would examine and question him about issues relating to his health. We had as members of our consultant group an endocrinologist from Cornell University and New York City, Dr. Eugene Cohen; an orthopedic physiatrist (specializing in rehabilitative medicine), Dr. Hans Krauss, also from New York City; and a gastroenterologist from the Lahey Clinic, Dr.

Russell Boles. We made suggestions to the president about his medications and his exercise program.

Dr. Krauss was very successful in providing a set of exercises that President Kennedy performed three times a day after swimming for about a half hour in the White House pool, which was heated to almost 90 degrees Fahrenheit. The president performed these prescribed exercises for his painful back problem under the supervision of Navy corpsmen assigned to the White House medical staff who had been trained by Dr. Krauss. These corpsmen were also trained in body massage, which they provided to the president after each exercise session. If the president were on a trip and had overnight stays, our medical personnel took with them a portable hydrocollator unit (which heats pads almost to boiling for application to injured areas of the body) to provide moist heat to the president's back as a substitute for swimming in the heated pool and then would follow this treatment with exercises and massage.

On a daily basis, Dr. Burkley and I would provide the president's dose of oral cortisone and florinef to fulfill the hormonal replacement requirements of his adrenal insufficiency. In small plastic cases labeled with appropriate instructions, the pills were supplied every day to Mrs. Evelyn Lincoln, the president's personal secretary, who gave them to him at the designated times.

In my opinion, President Kennedy was not significantly disabled. He clearly required oral hormone replacement to correct his hormonal deficiency and obviously benefited tremendously from the physical therapy and exercise programs prescribed by Dr. Krauss. His two major medical problems—a bad back and Addison's disease—caused him inconvenience and an inability to be totally independent of medical care, but in no way could he have been considered unable to perform the duties of the presidency.

The cortisone and florinef medications required close medical supervision. If too much cortisone is given to a patient, emotional instability can result. We were obviously aware of this and monitored the president's daily medications and emotional stability very closely. On occasion, he would take forty-five seconds of ultraviolet irradiation to his face to give him a rosy complexion, particularly when he had to appear before television cameras at his fabled news conferences. He also had some mild stomach problems, which were adequately controlled by an occasional pill as prescribed by Dr. Boles. A practice followed by many in the Washington, D.C., area at the time was the occasional use of an injection of Vitamin B-12 to provide a "lift" to the patient. The president occasionally was given a Vitamin B-12 injection.

Since there has been some speculation about President Kennedy's possible use of amphetamines, I must state here for the record that I never saw needle marks on any part of his body and the naval corpsmen assigned to his care, who regularly gave him body massages, never reported such marks to me.

When I was appointed to the White House, I was thirty-four years old, the same age as Jacqueline Kennedy. As I indicated earlier, the White House Physician is responsible not only for the president's health, but also for that of the president's family and others in the executive branch. The president's wife and children were provided health care primarily by Dr. Travell. Dr. Travell did not travel with the president or Mrs. Kennedy very often. Instead, Dr. Burkley or I would travel with them on extended trips. We usually melded into the group of Secret Service men surrounding the president or Mrs. Kennedy, carrying our medical bags, which appeared to be brief cases.

Occasionally, Mrs. Kennedy would go to Camp David by automobile, a day earlier than the president. I would often accompany her and the children, riding in the Secret Service backup car. Upon occasion, just before reaching Camp David and the Catoctin Mountain Park outside of Thurmont, Maryland, the children would be given some exercise and diversion. We would stop at a reptile farm where John, Jr., and Caroline would be entertained by the demonstrations of the staff and I would stand ready in case of some sort of medical problem. President Kennedy would usually arrive at Camp David the following day by helicopter, accompanied by Dr. Burkley. Upon the president's arrival, one of the two doctors would stay at Camp David with the Kennedys until they returned to the White House, and the other would have a short vacation.

I mention these trips to Camp David—and even to the reptile farm—to illustrate how close we physicians sometimes became to the president and members of his family. Occasionally, it almost seemed as though we *were* members of the president's family. For example, after President Kennedy's assassination, I actually lived at the White House for three days, being immediately available for calls from Jacqueline Kennedy and the Kennedy family. After the funeral, at her request, I accompanied Mrs. Kennedy to Hyannisport and spent a week there with her and her children, trying to console them and get them through that very sad and trying time.

MEDICAL CARE OF PRESIDENT JOHNSON

After becoming president, Lyndon Johnson asked all three physicians to stay on in the White House. He did not wish to appoint as White House Physician either of his two civilian doctors, Dr. James Cain of the Mayo Clinic, a close family friend for many years, or Dr. J. Willis Hurst, a cardiologist who had treated his 1955 heart attack. Instead, he preferred to keep on duty the existing team of White House Physicians with whom he felt comfortable, although Dr. Travell did leave the White House shortly after the 1964 election.

During the Johnson years, the White House Physicians met with and examined the president frequently, much more frequently than had been the case during the Kennedy Administration. As often as three times a week, we would monitor his blood pressure and take various readings of his vital signs. This was largely because of his cardiac history, particularly the serious heart attack he suffered while he was serving as the Majority Leader of the Senate.

Johnson demanded much attention from his doctors. In addition to the several physical examinations we gave him each week, the president also insisted that we insert his contact lenses whenever he used them and then remove them afterward. If he felt that we had inserted them in his eyes incorrectly, he would become quite irascible, making very evident his displeasure.

Despite the various ailments that Johnson suffered while president, the only significant disabling periods of health for him, during my time at the White House, were the occasions when he was confined to Bethesda Naval Hospital for severe bronchitis and laryngitis in January 1965 and for the removal of his gall bladder and a ureteral stone in October 1965.

During the latter hospitalization, President Johnson paved the way toward enactment of the Twenty-Fifth Amendment by signing over the powers of the presidency to Vice President Hubert Humphrey under terms of an agreement that existed between them. Shortly after recovering from the anesthesia of his gall bladder surgery, President Johnson resumed the presidency and all its awesome responsibilities. To my knowledge, we physicians, including the Johnsons' close friend, Dr. Cain, and the president's cardiologist, Dr. Hurst, had little input into the decision by the president to relinquish the powers of his office to Vice President Humphrey during his surgery, when he was under anesthesia. The president and vice president simply implemented procedures that they had established beforehand. The transfer of power to the vice president took place smoothly, and the resumption of the powers and responsibilities of office by President Johnson later that same day took place just as smoothly.

In discussing the president's medical condition, his press secretary frequently bent the truth. For example, in the case of President Johnson's surgery for the removal of his gall bladder, the press secretary had indicated that the president would have his surgery at 0830. In reality, we had him in the operating room at 0700 and out by 0830. Also, the surgery included the removal of the ureteral stone about which no prior announcement had been made, even though its removal by a Mayo Clinic urologist, Dr. Ormond Culp, certainly had been planned. President Johnson's gallbladder was removed by Dr. George Hallenbeck and Dr. Donald McIlrath, also of the Mayo Clinic. Of interest is the fact that a backup team of Navy surgeons and anesthesiologists were scrubbed and assisted the surgeon during the operation. Of even greater interest, perhaps, is that during this surgical procedure, the president's heartbeat increased significantly, a potentially dangerous condition known as supraventricular tachycardia. Dr. Hurst and I immediately detected the problem and prescribed an intravenous dose of atropine. After its administration to the president, his rapid heartbeat subsided quickly and converted to a normal rhythm.[2]

Without any firm knowledge, I can presume that this surgery, resulting in the turning over of the powers of the presidency to Vice President Humphrey, had provided a considerable impetus to the president for accelerating enactment of the Twenty-Fifth Amendment. The temporary transfer of presidential power to an acting president is, after all, one of the most significant features of the Amendment.

DISCUSSIONS ABOUT THE TWENTY-FIFTH AMENDMENT

In the thirty years since the Amendment's passage, considerable discussion has focused on ways to implement its procedures, particularly Section 4. In the mid-1990s, I became actively involved in these discussions as a member of the Working Group on Presidential Disability, a body whose formation was suggested by former President Carter as a step toward improving the way our nation deals with presidential disability.[3] Emerging from the meetings of the Working Group were eight recommendations, presented later in this volume. Since I had a particular interest and role in formulating the sixth of these, I think it appropriate that I discuss it here.

The sixth recommendation of the Working group provides that "The President should appoint a physician, civil or military, to be Senior Physician in the White House and to assume responsibility for his or her medical care, direct the Military Medical Unit and be the source of medical disclosure when considering imminent or existing impairment according to the provisions of the Twenty-Fifth Amendment."[4] Because of a need for more clarity and after considerable discussion by the members of the Group, I agreed to serve as chairman of a subcommittee of past and present White House Physicians to suggest more definitive procedures regarding the sixth recommendation. Besides me, the members of our subcommittee were Drs. John E. Hutton, Jr., White House Physician to President Reagan; Lawrence C. Mohr, White House Physician to Presidents Reagan and Bush; and E. Connie Mariano, White House Physician to President Clinton. I believe this was the first time in history that White House Physicians from the past and present functioned as a formal body. We met, discussed, and unanimously agreed on several points that are now included in the Report as an appendix to the sixth recommendation:

(1) "The President has and will continue to exercise his or her choice of physician to provide health care while he or she occupies the office of President of the United States."

Subcommittee members felt that it was necessary to emphasize that the president, like any other citizen of the United States, must have the freedom of choice as to which physician he or she wishes to minister health care to him and his family. In the practice of medicine, personalities remain a very significant part of the choice of one's own personal physician. A patient's confidence in and rapport with a physician has a significant effect on the response to treatment of the patient's illness by that physician. All members of the president's family need to have faith in their physician, as must the president.

(2) "It is recommended that the President appoint a Senior Physician to a position as his or her personal physician in the Executive Office of the President."

This recommendation emphasizes again that it is the president who should select the physician, rather than having that physician selected by some extraneous political body. It also suggests that the president's physician have significant medical training and experience as indicated by inclusion of the word "Senior" in his or her title.

(3) "This physician should be the Senior Physician in the White House with responsibility for facilitating the application of the Twenty-Fifth Amendment."

This recommendation was prompted by my personal experience when I arrived at the White House to be "Assistant White House Physician." It was no secret that Dr. Burkley and Dr. Travell disagreed on many issues, particularly those relating to President Kennedy's health care. Essentially they were at loggerheads. Dr. Travell had relinquished the responsibility of controlling President Kennedy's steroid replacement to Dr. Burkley shortly before I came to the White House. Both Drs. Travell and Burkley used the title of Physician to the President. As I explained earlier, if the Twenty-Fifth Amendment had been in effect then, and if some presidential disability had brought about consideration of invoking Section 4, I do not know which physician would have been empowered to report appropriate findings to the vice president. So our subcommittee of White House Physicians offered a recommendation designed to resolve such problems clearly and definitively.

(4) "The Senior Physician in the White House could be designated as Physician to the President, Physician to the White House, or Senior Physician of the White House Medical Unit."

This recommendation makes clear that there is one Senior Physician to the President who would, if necessary, be the physician to report to the vice president his or her opinion of the president's inability to discharge the powers and duties of his office. It is important that this responsibility be lodged unmistakably in the person of the

Senior White House Physician and that all parties understand this fact throughout the president's term in office.

(5) "It is recommended that the Senior White House Physician be accorded a title such as Assistant to the President or Deputy Assistant to the President or equivalent military rank."

This recommendation was made in an effort to address two different but interrelated concerns. First, as commander-in-chief, the president could order a subordinate military officer, who happened also to be White House Physician, to perform as the president wished. Although this concern is mitigated somewhat by a physician's dedication to the oath of Hippocrates and responsibility to the nation, as well as to the patient, it is further mitigated by giving the Senior White House Physician a significant civilian title that might permit somewhat greater independence from an obverse order issued by the president. Second, to bolster the position of the Senior White House Physician within the power structure of the White House, our subcommittee sought to provide him or her with an additional title commensurate with that held by other key members of the president's staff. Such a title should give added weight, among other high-level staff members, to any recommendation by the Senior White House Physician concerning invocation of the disability provisions of the Twenty-Fifth Amendment.

(6) "The office of Senior Physician in the White House should be an entity separate from the White House Military Office."

This recommendation was suggested in order to facilitate the ability of the Senior White House Physician to staff the White House Medical Unit appropriately, without possible interference by the Military Aide's office. The ability to provide excellent medical care by the White House medical staff is essential to the support of the president and his office. Military personnel of one military specialty, such as artillery, have varied opinions of other military specialties, such as military physicians, based on their personal military experiences. In addition, now that computerization has been introduced into the White House Medical Unit, interchanges with civilian, military, or foreign medical facilities is essential in planning for any emergency. Independence of the medical department provides more latitude and flexibility in planning for various presidential trips.

(7) "Because the Senior White House Physician may be a civilian

or military physician, it is recommended that she or he have military medical support."

This recommendation was made because of the multiple and varied military supporting facilities that provide assistance for the White House and the president. The use of military hospitals for presidential care ensures greater security for the president and his family. Various evacuation sites for the president, his family, and key members of the president's cabinet or members of Congress are staffed by the military. A request by the Senior Physician in the White House, if he or she be a military physician, to another military person has a degree of additional weight that a request by a civilian physician to the same military person might well not have. This is a very subtle but ever-present schism that is easily accommodated by having one or more military medical persons on the White House Medical Staff.[5]

The seven recommendations of our subcommittee embody significant procedures for presidents to consider and, it is hoped, adopt. One very important recommendation, outside the purview of our subcommittee, should nevertheless be a vital part of every president's pre-inaugural transition plan: a written agreement between the president and the Senior White House Physician about the way that issues of medical care should be managed. It is almost a presidential living will. I understand that President Bush had such an agreement with Dr. Burton Lee, his physician. Dr. Mariano has indicated to me that she and President Clinton and his family have such an agreement, modeled on the agreement between President Bush and his physician.[6] When an emergency arises, it is always too late to plan for it. All the exigencies of medical matters regarding the president should have been discussed and agreed upon with the president and his family prior to the president's inauguration.

An important additional point is this. During the meetings of the Working Group on Presidential Disability, there were frequent introductions of a proposal endorsed by a small minority of attendees that called for the appointment of a Standing Commission of Physicians for the purpose of evaluating the president's health status on an annual basis and assessing his capability of continuing to perform the duties of the presidency. The four White House Physicians on our subcommittee were unanimously opposed to this concept. Instead, our strong preference, based squarely on our combined experience in the White House, was to allow the Senior White House Physician to select whatever medical consultants he or she deemed appropriate under the particular circumstances of the moment, taking into account the precise nature of any medical problem that may arise and the medical specialties that seem most useful in dealing effectively with it.

CONCLUSIONS

In my view, after serving two different presidents as White House Physician, the Twenty-Fifth Amendment is adequate to solve the problem of presidential disability. In the one clear instance of presidential incapacitation that I encountered during my years in the White House (Lyndon Johnson's surgery for gall bladder removal in 1965), the voluntary transfer agreement existing between President Johnson and Vice President Humphrey became operative easily and without incident. I do not believe that a constitutionally established procedure for transferring presidential power to the vice president under similar circumstances would have worked any less perfectly or would work any less perfectly in the future. Indeed, since the disability provisions of the Twenty-Fifth Amendment now stand in codified form, future transfers of power should be even more effortless since both the public and executive branch officials will be acquainted with the parameters under which such transfers take place. Additionally, if, as has been suggested here, the position of the Senior White House Physician is bolstered so that the important role that physician has in recommending invocation of the Twenty-Fifth Amendment is recognized and acknowledged at the outset of every administration by the president, the president's family, the vice president, and members of the cabinet, the application of the Amendment's disability provisions for reasons of ill health should be accomplished as smoothly as the Amendment's authors intended.

NOTES

1. See *United States Code*, Ch. 1041, 70A Stat. 34.
2. For a detailed discussion of John F. Kennedy's and Lyndon B. Johnson's health, see Robert E. Gilbert, *The Mortal Presidency: Illness and An-*

guish in the White House, 2nd ed. (New York: Fordham University Press, 1998), chaps. 6 and 7.

3. Personal communication from James F. Toole, M.D., co-chair of the Working Group.

4. See Working Group on Disability in U.S. Presidents, *Disability in U.S. Presidents: Report, Recommendations, and Commentaries* (Winston-Salem, N.C.: Bowman-Gray Scientific Press, 1997), p. 16.

5. Ibid., Appendix II, p. 22.

6. Personal communication from E. Connie Mariano, M.D.

5

In Sickness and in Health: Medical Care for the President of the United States

E. Connie Mariano, M.D.

The White House Medical Unit has grown over time in both size and range of activities. Its primary responsibility is to protect and preserve the health and well-being of the president. During the last two administrations, the director of the unit—the Senior White House Physician—has been assigned the additional responsibility of recommending invocation of the disability provisions of the Twenty-Fifth Amendment under clearly delineated circumstances.

George Washington, the first president of the United States, set many precedents for the chief executives who succeeded him. One such precedent was to have a personal, presidential physician who conscientiously ministered to his health needs.

Washington's medical history has been described as "alarming."[1] At various points in his life, he suffered from malaria, smallpox, tuberculosis, pleurisy, influenza, and dysentery. After becoming president in 1789, he developed a serious infection, probably of staphylococcal origin, and was gravely ill for several weeks.[2] When it was suggested to the new president that he have a physician available to him on a regular basis, Washington thought immediately of Dr. James Craik, whom he had met many years earlier while he was serving in the army as a lieutenant colonel and Dr. Craik was serving as regimental surgeon. During one of Washington's illnesses at that

---

The views expressed in this chapter are those of the author and do not necessarily reflect the views of the Department of Defense, the United States Navy, or the White House Military Office.

time, Dr. Craik told him prophetically, "the fate of your friends and country are, in a manner, dependent on your recovery."[3]

Years later, whenever the president needed medical care, Dr. Craik was summoned to perform house calls on the "First Patient" at the nation's capital, New York City, and at the president's home in Mount Vernon, Virginia. Dr. Craik remained Washington's physician until the very end when he ministered at the bedside of the dying former president. In fact, it was to Dr. Craik that Washington uttered some of his final words: "Doctor, I die hard, but I am not afraid to go. My breath cannot last long."[4] A few hours later, President Washington was dead, most likely of acute bacterial epiglottitis, which involves a covering of the opening to the windpipe, preventing food and drink from entering the larynx.[5] The loyal and dedicated Dr. Craik stood grief-stricken at his bedside.

THE EVOLUTION OF THE WHITE HOUSE MEDICAL UNIT

Since the era of Dr. Craik, medical care for the president has expanded and evolved greatly. In the 1920s, the medical team formally charged with the care of the president was given the name White House Medical Unit (WHMU). In 1927, Congress recognized the title "White House Physician" as that of the doctor responsible for the medical care of the president. This physician would serve as the director of the WHMU. Also in the late 1920s, President Hoover insisted that the White House Physician, Navy doctor Joel Boone, be given an office on the ground floor of the White House. This office remains to this day as the Doctor's Office and serves as the medical office for the president's physician.

The function and role of the WHMU have been shaped by presidential morbidity and mortality. The assassination of President Kennedy in 1963 prompted the WHMU to increase pre-hospital emergency medical training for its staff. WHMU members also began regularly training with the United States Secret Service to coordinate medical response with presidential protection.

In 1981, the attempt on the life of President Reagan focused attention on medical contingency planning. Tactical questions arose such as: Where will the WHMU medical providers be located at the time of an attack? What medical equipment will be available at the scene?

Where should an injured president be taken? What type of medical facility is needed? How far is the hospital? How should the president be transported?

The assassination attempt on President Reagan led the WHMU to work closely with the American College of Surgeons to develop the Capital Program. Under this plan, the College prepares an annual report to the WHMU cataloguing the medical facilities in the United States and presenting such data as the number of physicians available, the number of operating rooms, the hospital's most recent accreditation date, and so forth. The WHMU uses this report to decide which hospital to designate in a particular city to handle a presidential emergency.

Each individual sitting president has also influenced the function and composition of the Medical Unit. When President Clinton was inaugurated for his first term in 1993, he presented the challenge of providing medical coverage to a relatively young leader who regularly jogged, worked long hours, and traveled frequently.

Medical Unit Changes

In February 1994, I was named Physician to President Clinton and Director of the White House Medical Unit. I began my tenure with the good fortune of having already served as a White House Physician for seven months under President Bush, and I had witnessed a year of transitional leadership in the Medical Unit. By then, I had seen the Unit from all levels of operation and had studied the challenges faced by my predecessors in providing care to the president, vice president, and their families. The lessons of the past, and the imperative to make the Unit responsive to the needs of a new president, motivated me to institute five major changes. These changes are designed to allow the Medical Unit to provide sustained professional care and attention to the president both at home and abroad. They also are intended to help the Senior White House Physician to respond to conditions that might lead to invocation of the disability provisions of the Twenty-Fifth Amendment. The five changes are as follows:

(1) *Provide twenty-four–hour on-site coverage.* Wherever the location of the president, there is always a medical provider a "few heartbeats away." During the working day, a WHMU physician and

assistant (WHMU nurse or medic) "shadow" the president, being always within a minute of being able to reach his side. When the president retires for the evening in the family quarters of the White House, a WHMU nurse or medic stands overnight watch in the Presidential Emergency Operations Center, seconds away from the president should a medical emergency arise.

When the president travels outside the eighteen acres of the White House compound, he is accompanied by a minimum of two WHMU members, a physician and a nurse or medic. When the president travels to another city or country, there is always at least one WHMU physician and nurse aboard Air Force One who travel with him to every city he visits.

In March 1997, when President Clinton took a bad fall in Florida and tore his quadriceps tendon, his condition was immediately evaluated by Dr. William Lang, the White House physician on duty. Dr. Lang initially treated the injured leg by immobilizing it and applying an ice pack. When I received word at my Florida hotel shortly afterward that the president had been injured and was being taken to the hospital, the duty nurse and I departed immediately and arrived at the hospital twenty minutes before the ambulance transporting the president arrived. Thus, at a time of medical emergency, members of the WHMU were immediately available to provide care to the injured president.[6]

(2) *Focus on acute care "in the trenches."* Previously, White House Physicians have been subspecialists. My predecessors included a neurosurgeon, urologist, cardiologist, nose and throat specialist, cancer expert, and so on. I have shifted the focus from in-house subspecialty care to acute primary care with expertise in emergency medicine and resuscitation in the field. The best neurosurgeon in the world cannot help if the patient dies in the field because the team does not know how to resuscitate a victim in that environment.

Because of our emphasis on primary, acute, and emergency care, the WHMU selects and trains professionals to practice medicine in austere and difficult environments. The five physicians at the White House, all board-certified in their respective fields, include one general internist, three family medicine physicians, and one emergency medicine specialist.

In addition, our five physician assistants are experts in acute and primary care; one is certified in emergency medicine. All five White

House nurses are certified in trauma and emergency care as well as inpatient intensive care. All three medics/hospital corpsmen are selected from Force Recon, Delta Force, and Seal Team environments where they provide medical care to military forces in hazardous settings.

Members of the WHMU are certified in Advanced Cardiac Life Support and Advanced Trauma Life Support. Many members of the Unit are instructors in these courses. While the WHMU medical care providers are experts in outpatient medicine and resuscitation in the field, consultants at our designated trauma centers, of which there is at least one in each major city, are experts in their respective specialties of surgical and medical care.

(3) *Build the model for medical contingency planning.* Wherever the president travels outside the Washington, D.C., area, we assign a member of the WHMU to "advance" the destination. The Unit member designates and visits the hospital(s) we would use should the president become ill or be injured. In addition, the WHMU representative works closely with the Secret Service and White House Military Office to prepare plans for response and evacuation should an emergency arise. For foreign countries, the WHMU assigns members to "advance" presidential, vice-presidential, and selected first lady overseas trips.

Domestic and foreign advance missions account for a major part of the WHMU's work. Foreign advance missions are the most challenging, especially in Third World countries. WHMU members conduct health risk assessments of the cities to be visited (including such factors as altitude, temperatures, air quality, incidence of malaria, and so forth), develop liaison with State Department and host-nation health representatives, conduct walk-through visits of each site planned for the visit, and render care to traveling White House staff members.

To support the Clinton administration's heavy travel schedule, the WHMU advances an average of twenty-five foreign countries a year to support presidential, vice-presidential, and first lady overseas trips. During the past seven years, the WHMU has sent members to advance cities in every continent except Antarctica.

(4) *Develop and formalize the field of protective medical support.* Protective medical support refers to providing medical care to a patient under security protection ("the protectee"). To ensure an efficient response that also preserves security, the WHMU extensively

trains with the Secret Service. Wherever the president travels, the WHMU travels with him not only to provide medical care but also to respond to attempts on his life. The WHMU members are trained to shift into the protective medical support mode, which strategically positions our team members to respond rapidly to an attack on the protectee. If there is an attempt on the life of the protectee, the Secret Service protects and rescues, while the Medical Unit evaluates and resuscitates.

(5) *Establish an Executive Medicine Curriculum with required reading for WHMU personnel.* In addition to readings on the history of the White House prepared by the White House Historical Society, members of the Medical Unit must read and be familiar with a number of key books, each of which relates to their professional responsibilities.[7] The WHMU also hosts lectures by speakers with expertise in related fields. Our Executive Medicine Curriculum broadens the perspectives of WHMU medical personnel, familiarizes them with lessons from the past, and sensitizes them to possible problems of the present and future.

The changes instituted in the White House Medical Unit are intended primarily to improve the overall quality of health care given the president. Medical contingency planning, preparations for emergency medicine, medical training with the Secret Service, a continuous medical presence around the president, and an "academic" curriculum designed to link the past with the present also aim to facilitate applications of the Twenty-Fifth Amendment if such applications become necessary. Notably, the White House Medical Unit is key to ensuring quality medical care and facilitating determination of medical disability.

THE PRESIDENT'S ANNUAL EXAMINATION

The delivery of medical care at the White House comes in many forms. Besides the support and care just discussed, the WHMU also arranges annual examinations for all its primary patients. The president's annual physical examination is traditionally organized by the president's physician. Because medicine should never be practiced in a vacuum, the president's physician selects consultants and specialists from outside the White House to participate in this annual examination. The evaluations for President Bush and President Clinton were conducted in the Presidential Medical Evaluation and Treatment Unit suite at Bethesda Naval Hospital. During the Clinton Administration, I selected consultants from both military and civilian medical centers to compose the panel of specialists who evaluate the president. These have included a gastroenterologist, cardiologist, urologist, allergist, dermatologist, podiatrist, ophthalmologist, otolaryngologist, and an orthopedic specialist. At the conclusion of the examination, I prepared a summary of findings as well as the press release. The president reviews and approves the press release before it is disseminated. The release of medical information is normally at the discretion of the patient rather than the physician, whether or not the patient is president of the United States.

In September 1999, a panel of physicians which included twelve board-certified consultants from both the military and civilian sectors gave the president his most recent physical examination. Following the examination, I arranged for this panel to meet the press and answer specific questions about its findings. The press secretary served as moderator for this open question-and-answer session. At the outset, I made a statement summarizing the results of the physical exam, and then the floor was opened to questions that were answered by members of the panel. Reporters asked questions concerning many aspects of the president's physical condition, including his reflux disease (when acid flows up into the esophagus), the medications he takes for it, his weight, his allergies, his diet and exercise program, his actinic keratoses (due to chronic sun exposure), and the hoarseness of his voice. Each question was answered by the relevant specialist, and, at the conclusion of the press conference, all parties seemed well pleased with the results.

OTHER MEDICAL UNIT SERVICES

The Medical Unit occasionally has been asked to provide care to visiting dignitaries and heads of state. In 1998, President Clinton offered my assistance to King Hussein of Jordan, and I traveled to the Mayo Clinic to meet with the medical team treating the king. The patient population treated by the Medical Unit ranges from heads of state, to kitchen staff, to visitors to the White House compound. On an average, 1.5 million people visit the White House each year. During the December holiday season, more than 160,000 visitors view the "President's House." On a single winter night during Candlelight Holiday Tours, more than eleven thousand visitors come through the gates. The WHMU provides tour coverage year round to respond to emergencies on the compound. Such emergencies have ranged from cardiac arrest in an elderly tourist to a fainting spell in a teenager during the summer months.

MEDICAL UNIT COMPOSITION

Because of the mission demands on the Unit, the size of the WHMU is now the largest in history. Twenty-one active-duty military personnel from the Army, Navy, and Air Force are currently assigned there.

The professional groups within the Unit and their primary roles are as follows:

White House Physicians: five (four during the Bush Administration; includes the president's physician who is the Senior White House Physician). The physicians' responsibilities are to:

- provide duty coverage for the president, vice president (both domestic and overseas), and first lady (overseas trips only)
- evaluate and treat patients at the WHMU Clinic located in the Old Executive Office Building adjacent to the White House
- perform advance missions of foreign sites for presidential and vice-presidential trips
- maintain credentials at the National Naval Medical Center in Bethesda
- teach introduction to clinical medicine as assistant professors at the Uniformed Services University School of Medicine

White House Physician Assistants: five (three during the Bush years; all are certified physician assistants trained in primary and acute care; one physician assistant has specialty training in emergency medicine). The physician assistants' responsibilities are to:

- accompany the vice president during domestic travel
- advance domestic and foreign sites for presidential missions
- advance foreign sites for vice-presidential and first lady missions
- evaluate and treat patients in the WHMU Clinic

White House Nurses: five (six during the Bush Administration); all are registered nurses trained in critical care, with additional training in trauma and emergency medicine). The nurses' responsibilities are to:

- provide nursing coverage on all presidential flights aboard Air Force One and all vice-presidential foreign flights aboard Air Force Two
- provide inpatient nursing care at the National Naval Medical Center
- assist in treating patients in the WHMU Clinic
- provide patient instruction and medical education
- perform both domestic and foreign advances of presidential missions, advances of vice-presidential and first lady foreign missions
- stand overnight watch in the President's Emergency Operations Center.

White House Medics/Hospital Corpsmen: three (the same number as during the Bush Administration). EMT and paramedic responsibilities are to:

- advance domestic and foreign presidential trips and vice-presidential and first lady overseas trips
- evaluate and treat patients in the WHMU Clinic
- provide tour coverage and respond to emergencies on the White House compound
- stand overnight watch in the President's Emergency Operations Center

White House Administrative Support: three (one in the Bush Administration). Non-medical support personnel include:

- certified Health Care Administrator, who is responsible for WHMU budget, planning, and logistics
- Clinic Office Manager
- Executive Assistant to the President's Physician.

WHMU PERSONNEL SELECTION PROCESS

A rigorous process results in the selection of all Unit members. The three military branches nominate the candidates, who are then screened by the Department of Defense. Candidates are then interviewed by the WHMU and White House Military Office Security.

Upon selection, the candidate must obtain a top-secret clearance before joining the Unit.

Members of the Unit usually serve two-year tours. Occasionally, members are invited to serve a third year in roles of leadership and additional responsibility. As the President's Physician and Director of the Medical Unit, I have been assigned until 2001 to allow for continuity of care until the next administration takes office.

TWENTY-FIFTH AMENDMENT PLANNING

Shortly after being named the President's Physician, I discussed the Clinton Administration's Twenty-Fifth Amendment Plan with the chief of staff, the president's legal counsel, and members of the Presidential Contingency Program, an organization run by the military in the White House that has as its main function the preservation of the office of president. The Presidential Contingency Program selects the individual cabinet member each year who is to be absent from the president's State of the Union Address in order to preserve the line of succession to the presidency should a catastrophe occur. A military aide is assigned to be with the designated cabinet member during the State of the Union Address.

Plans concerning utilization of the Twenty-Fifth Amendment were already in place when President Clinton assumed office, and as his physician, I had the opportunity to review them and make suggestions. Under the terms of these plans, I play a significant role, as the President's Physician, in determining medical disability and in advising the administration about the president's health. To gain a variety of additional perspectives, I served as a member of the Working Group on Presidential Disability, established in 1994 by the Bowman Gray School of Medicine and the Carter Center, and participated in its several two-day meetings between January 1995 and December 1996. I was also a member of the White House Physicians' subcommittee set up by the Working Group to develop recommendations concerning the position of the Senior White House Physician, particularly regarding the disability provisions of the Twenty-Fifth Amendment. Both the Working Group and the White House Physicians' subcommittee composed a list of recommendations for facilitating applications of the Twenty-Fifth Amendment (included in chapters 4 and 11) to which I subscribe.[8]

The White House staff and WHMU members are fully cognizant of the Twenty-Fifth Amendment. Throughout my tour of duty at the White House, every WHMU exercise and emergency drill ends with the question: Should the Twenty-Fifth Amendment be invoked?

Only once to date during the Clinton Administration has the Twenty-Fifth Amendment issue even potentially arisen. During President Clinton's quadriceps tendon repair at Bethesda Naval Hospital in March 1997, he received a spinal anesthetic. This anesthesia did not affect his consciousness or his cognitive abilities. If the president had undergone general anesthesia for this surgery, however, I was fully prepared to recommend invoking Section 3 of the Twenty-Fifth Amendment, which would have allowed the powers and duties of the presidency to pass into the hands of Vice President Gore. In fact, I had informed Bruce Lindsey, a key presidential adviser, that, if the president required general anesthesia, Section 3 should be invoked. As general anesthesia was unnecessary, I did not recommend its invocation.

CONCLUSION

Medical care for the president of the United States has come a long way since the days of President Washington and Dr. Craik. The incidence of presidential illness and the violence directed against presidents throughout American history, as well as the growth of terrorism in recent years, has stimulated the WHMU to evolve into a dynamic and responsive team of professionals dedicated to maintaining the health of the nation's leader. The modern WHMU provides not only medical care but also protective medical support in a dangerous era. The Unit stands trained and prepared in times of both presidential sickness and presidential health.

The unit's director, the Senior White House Physician, is particularly well placed to oversee the care provided the president by both the WHMU and consulting physicians. For this reason, I see no need for the appointment of any formal, standing board of physicians, as has been suggested, for the purpose of evaluating the president's health each year. The involvement of outside physician-consultants in assessing the president's health is already a well-established practice in the White House. As previously noted, in my years as Senior White House Physician, I have regularly involved a sizable number of military and civilian medical consultants in the president's care. These consultations have provided the president with expertise in different medical subspecialties. The existence of an independent panel of consultants to evaluate the president's health would dilute the authority of the Senior White House Physician in the important role in deciding whether to recommend invocation of Section 3 of the Twenty-Fifth Amendment to the president or Section 4 to the vice president and members of the cabinet. The establishment of an independent panel would run directly counter to the recommendation of both the Working Group on Presidential Disability and that of the Miller Center Commission on Presidential Disability (included in chapter 12 of this volume).[9]

My experience over the past seven years convinces me that the Twenty-Fifth Amendment provides a workable constitutional framework for dealing with issues of presidential disability. Throughout my tour as Senior White House Physician, which I believe is the longest in recent history, I have studied the Amendment's provisions and am prepared to face the prospect of recommending their invocation under appropriate medical circumstances. This responsibility, after all, is outlined in the administration's long-standing contingency plan and I would have no hesitation in fulfilling that duty.

I do recommend, however, that future administrations follow the lead of Presidents Clinton and Bush in developing plans for possible applications of the Twenty-Fifth Amendment prior to or very shortly after the inaugural ceremonies. These plans, at least in part, should clearly define the role for the Senior White House Physician in assessing presidential disability and in recommending invocation of Section 3 or Section 4 as appropriate. This role should be understood as fully as possible by the president, the president's family, the vice president, the cabinet and the White House staff, so that recommendations concerning invocation of the Amendment for reasons of ill health can be made under agreed-upon guidelines and as efficiently and dispassionately as possible.

NOTES

1. John Luter, "James Craik: The First 'White House' Physician," *Today's Health*, February 1964, p. 49.

2. Ibid., p. 68

3. James Thomas Flexner, *Washington: The Indispensable Man* (Boston: Little, Brown, 1974), p. 32.

4. Willard Sterne Randall, *George Washington: A Life* (New York: Henry Holt, 1997), p. 502.

5. David M. Morens, M.D., "Death of a President," *The New England Journal of Medicine*, December 1999, p. 1847.

6. For a fuller discussion of the Clinton injury and subsequent surgery, see Robert E. Gilbert, *The Mortal Presidency: Illness and Anguish in the White House*, 2nd ed. (New York: Fordham University Press, 1998), pp. xi–xiii.

7. The reading list includes the following: Jerrold M. Post, M.D., and Robert S. Robins, *When Illness Strikes the Leader: The Dilemma of the Captive King* (Yale University Press, 1993); Gilbert, *Mortal Presidency*; Kenneth R. Crispell and Carlos Gomez, *Hidden Illness in the White House* (Durham, N.C.: Duke University Press, 1988); Bert E. Park, *The Impact of Illness on World Leaders* (Philadelphia: University of Pennsylvania Press, 1986); Herbert L. Abrams, *The President Has Been Shot: Confusion, Disability, and the Twenty-Fifth Amendment in the Aftermath of the Attempted Assassination of Ronald Reagan* (New York: W. W. Norton, 1992); Joel K. Goldstein, *The Modern Vice Presidency: The Transformation of a Political Institution* (Princeton, N.J.: Princeton University Press, 1984).

8. See Working Group on Presidential Disability, *Disability in U.S. Presidents: Report, Recommendations, and Commentaries by the Working Group* (Winston-Salem, N.C.: Bowman-Gray Scientific Press, 1996).

9. See, in particular, "Report by Former and Current Military Physicians Assigned to the White House Regarding Recommendation VI," ibid., p. 22; see, also, White Burkett Miller Center of Public Affairs, *Report of the Miller Center Commission on Presidential Disability and the Twenty-Fifth Amendment* (Charlottesville, Va.: Miller Center, 1988).

6

Medical Consideration in the Determination of Presidential Disability

Lawrence C. Mohr, M.D.

It is a responsibility of the White House Physician to assess the functional impairment of the president as a consequence of any illness or injury. The physician's assessment of impairment is a medical judgment, which is based on a medical examination and the results of medical tests. Disability occurs if an impairment is of sufficient nature and magnitude to prevent the president from performing his constitutional duties. The determination of disability is a political decision, which can be made only by the president himself or by designated government officials in accordance with the provisions of the Twenty-Fifth Amendment. The Bush Administration, in developing a contingency plan under which the disability provisions of the Amendment would be implemented, made the single most important contribution to the development of the Twenty-Fifth Amendment since ratification more than thirty years ago.

For the past two decades there has been increasing public interest in the health and health care of the president of the United States.[1] Indeed, during this period the health of both presidents and presidential candidates[2] has emerged as a major factor in consideration of fitness for office. The primary reason for this interest, I believe, is the fact that many of our recent presidents have had serious health problems while in office. Even a former president who was largely healthy during his one term in the White House has called urgent attention to this matter.[3]

Consider the health statistics of the eleven presidents who have served since the beginning of World War II. At least nine of these presidents (almost 90 percent) had significant illnesses or injuries while in office. Two of them died in office: Franklin Delano Roosevelt from cerebral hemorrhage and John F. Kennedy by assassination. Five other presidents in this group (almost 50 percent) had illnesses or injuries that were serious enough to require hospitalization while in office. Three of these had major surgery that required general anesthesia and postoperative pain control. During this same period, there were also six unsuccessful assassination attempts on five different presidents. Although five of these attempts failed completely, the attempted assassination of Ronald Reagan resulted in a life-threatening chest wound that required emergency surgery.

What can be learned from these statistics, beyond the fact that the United States of America has had a large number of sick or injured presidents in recent times? First of all, they make evident the fact that sick presidents can be good presidents. Franklin Delano Roosevelt, for example, lost the use of his legs from polio at age thirty-nine and had several serious, chronic illnesses while in office. These included malignant hypertension, cerebrovascular disease, chronic obstructive lung disease, and congestive heart failure.[4] Yet, history shows him to be one of our greatest presidents: he was elected to four terms and led the nation through two of its greatest crises, the Great Depression and World War II.

Similarly, Dwight D. Eisenhower had a myocardial infarction, major surgery for ileitis, and a stroke during his two terms in office. Although acutely aware of his precarious health status, Eisenhower steadfastly and adroitly led the nation through a difficult period of the Cold War and is generally regarded as one of our better presidents.[5] These cases illustrate the fact that a sick or injured president who receives proper and timely medical care may be able to function quite well in office, even in times of crisis.

On the other hand, there have been episodes of illness during which several of our recent presidents could not possibly have performed their constitutional duties, at least for some period of time. Examples would include the periods of time during and immediately after President Eisenhower's myocardial infarction in 1955 and surgery for ileitis in 1956, President Johnson's gall bladder surgery in 1965, and President Reagan's emergency surgery for his gunshot wound to the chest in 1981, as well as his subsequent surgery for colon cancer in 1985.[6] In each of these situations the functional capacity of the president to perform his constitutional duties had to be significantly impaired, if only for a short period, as a result of the medical condition itself or as a consequence of the sedative and hypnotic effects of general anesthesia and pain medication.

In any consideration of presidential disability, it is the functional capacity of the president to perform his constitutional duties, not the underlying illness or injury itself, that is of paramount importance. There are several aspects of functional capacity that are particularly important with respect to the president of the United States: cognitive function, alertness, judgment, appropriate behavior, and the ability to communicate. Cognitive function is the ability of the president to think clearly. Alertness is the ability of the president to be fully aware of his environs and to be fully engaged with the responsibilities of his office. Judgment is the ability of the president to choose between options and to make rational decisions. Appropriate behavior is the ability of the president to interact in a decorous, scrupulous, and rational manner with those around him. The ability to communicate is the capacity of a president to clearly express his will and his decisions. Any illness or injury that impairs the functional capacity of the president of the United States in one or more of these critical areas has the potential to adversely effect his performance of a president's constitutional duties and can have significant political, economic, and national security consequences for the country.

THE TWENTY-FIFTH AMENDMENT

If an illness or injury impairs the functional capacity of the president to an extent that he cannot effectively perform his constitutional duties, consideration must be given to transferring the powers of the presidency to the vice president.[7] The Twenty-Fifth Amendment contains two sections that pertain to presidential disability and the transfer of presidential powers. Section 3 provides a mechanism for the voluntary transfer of presidential powers from the president to the vice president. Section 4 provides mechanisms for the involuntary transfer of presidential powers to the vice president in circumstances in which the president is unable or unwilling to acknowledge disability. In both cases, the vice president becomes acting president for the period during which the president is disabled. Also, in both cases, the president may reclaim the powers of the presidency by declaring, in letters to the President pro tempore of the Senate and the Speaker of the House of Representatives, that no disability exists.

The reclamation of powers following an involuntary transfer of powers to the vice president can become somewhat complicated if the vice president and a majority of the principal officers of the executive departments, or other such body as Congress may by law provide, disagree with the president's declaration that no inability exists. In such a situation the president's fitness for office must be determined by Congress. Congress is required to assemble within forty-eight hours after written notification is provided to the President pro tempore of the Senate and the Speaker of the House of Representatives that the vice president and a majority of the principal officers of the executive departments, or other such body as Congress may by law provide, conclude that the president is unable to discharge the powers and duties of his office. This notification must be received within four days of the president's declaration that no disability exists. Congress must then determine within twenty-one days whether the president is able to discharge the powers and duties of his office. A two-thirds vote in both houses is required to prevent a president from reclaiming the powers of his office, in which case the vice president continues to serve as acting president.

It is important to appreciate that a declaration that the president of the United States is disabled from an illness or injury, the transfer of presidential powers from a disabled president to the vice president, and the reclamation of presidential powers by a previously disabled president are *political* decisions. They are *not* medical decisions.[8] They are decisions that can be made only by the president himself in the case of a voluntary declaration of disability under the provisions of Section 3, or by the elected and appointed government officials specified in Section 4 in the event of an involuntary determination of disability and transfer of powers. In this regard, the authors of the Twenty-Fifth Amendment were very careful to ensure that any transfer of powers from a disabled president to the vice president, and the reclamation of those powers by a previously disabled president, would remain entirely within the boundaries of the political process.

Although all decisions related to presidential disability and the reclamation of presidential powers are purely political, it is reasonable to expect that medical information related to the nature and severity of any underlying illness or injury, as well as an assessment of the degree of functional impairment caused by the illness or injury, would be carefully considered in any contemplation of presidential disability, either voluntary or involuntary. The White House Physician has several important roles in this regard.

ROLE OF THE WHITE HOUSE PHYSICIAN

First and foremost, as the president's doctor, the White House Physician must ensure that the president receives the best possible medical care for any illness or injury he may have. In this respect, he or she must be fully prepared to deal effectively with a panoply of medical problems, ranging from minor illnesses to serious, life-threatening conditions requiring admission to a critical care facility. Whether the medical problem is major or minor, the medical care provided to the president must be of the very highest quality.

All medical care given to the president should be provided in accordance with the usual procedures, standards, and ethics of medical practice. No exceptions should be made for purposes of political expediency. This includes the maintenance of confidentiality within the doctor–patient relationship. It is also important that the White House Physician pay very careful attention to the use and effects of any mind-altering or sedative-hypnotic drugs given to the president during the course of medical treatment.

Secondly, the White House Physician must make a medical assessment of the extent to which any illness, injury, or medical treatment impairs the functional capacity of the president to perform the constitutional duties of his office. Particular attention should be given to those areas that are critical to the performance of the president's constitutional duties. As previously described, these are: cognitive function, alertness, judgment, behavior, and the ability to communicate. It is reasonable to expect that both the medical care of a sick or injured president and the assessment of functional impairment would involve the use of medical consultants who are experts in the medical conditions for which the president is being treated. This is consistent with the usual course of good medical practice and should not be construed as an unusual or special accommodation for the medical care of the president of the United States.

If at all possible, the White House Physician must discuss both the medical care and the impairment assessment directly with the sick or injured president. If a voluntary transfer of presidential powers to the vice president is a consideration, the president himself must make the political decision as to whether the degree of impairment is sufficient to invoke Section 3 of the Twenty-Fifth Amendment. It is reasonable to expect that any such decision would be made in close consultation with the first lady, other members of the president's family, the vice president, the White House chief of staff, and the president's inner circle of senior political advisors because the influence of those close to the President is likely to be substantial.[9] The White House Physician must be prepared to brief these individuals on the state of the president's health and functional impairment if directed to do so by the president.

If circumstances are such that an involuntary transfer of presidential powers must be considered under the provisions of Section 4 of the Twenty-Fifth Amendment, the White House Physician should transmit an assessment of functional impairment to the vice president and principal officers of the executive branch, or other such body as Congress may by law provide, who have the constitutional authority to make the political decisions regarding presidential disability and whether a transfer of presidential powers should occur. A similar assessment of functional impairment should, in my opinion, be transmitted to these same government officials in any consideration of reclamation of powers by a previously disabled president under the provisions of Section 4.

It is important, once again, to emphasize two key points. Impairment is a medical judgment of the extent to which an illness or injury effects the functional capacity of the president. The physician's assessment of impairment is based on the findings of a medical examination and the results of medical tests. It should be the duty of the White House Physician to assess the degree of impairment and to provide this assessment to the president, and other individuals as directed by the president or required by law, during the course of any illness or injury that provokes consideration of a transfer of presidential powers to the vice president. Disability, on the other hand, is a political decision that an impairment is of sufficient nature and magnitude to prevent the president of the United States from effectively discharging his constitutional duties. Disability can be determined only by the president himself or by those government officials who are explicitly given the authority to make this determination in Section 4 of the Twenty-Fifth Amendment.

It is also important to emphasize that all medical decisions and recommendations concerning the president should be made by the White House Physician in consultation with outside specialists. These are the physicians who will have examined and treated the president on a firsthand basis. These are the medical practitioners who will know him best. Therefore, it is this group who will have thorough and detailed knowledge of the medical reasons for any determination of disability. Although it has been suggested that a standing panel of physicians, a so-called Presidential Disability Panel, could effectively play such a role, I disagree.[10] Such a group would be very unlikely to have firsthand knowledge of the president's medical condition and would not be involved in providing medical care to him. Therefore, it would likely serve to complicate and confuse the very sensitive, complex, and important issue of determining presidential disability and make the process more protracted. By their very nature, panels tend to be rather ponderous and slow in reaching conclusions and in framing recommendations, particularly when the subject matter of their deliberations is complicated and there are significant differences in opinion among their members. In determining whether the Twenty-Fifth Amendment should be invoked, needless delay should be avoided, especially, of course, when a transfer of presidential power is necessary. Therefore, the medical input essential to any such determination should come from those physicians most familiar with the president and the president's medical status and those best able to make an expeditious and well-informed judgment about the president's overall health.

CONTINGENCY PLANNING FOR PRESIDENTIAL DISABILITY

There is considerable room for judgment concerning both impairment and disability in any medical situation involving the president of the United States. From previous discussions with former Senator Birch Bayh and John D. Ferrick, key legislative architects of the

Twenty-Fifth Amendment, I am confident in stating that the authors of the Twenty-Fifth Amendment wanted to ensure that there is appropriate opportunity for both judgment and flexibility in implementing the provisions of the Amendment in any given situation.[11] Given the countless possible situations in which implementation of the Twenty-Fifth Amendment should be considered, and the seriousness of any transfer of powers from the president to the vice president, their prescient wisdom in this regard is praiseworthy.

There is also substantial room for confusion in implementing the provisions of the Twenty-Fifth Amendment. This is particularly true in emergency situations, such as cases of sudden but insidious illness and cases of traumatic injury to the president. Therefore, careful forethought must be given to the Amendment's possible use.

George Bush, who served as Ronald Reagan's vice president for eight years, had particularly keen insight into the importance of implementing the Twenty-Fifth Amendment quickly and efficiently in appropriate situations. As a result, as president, he directed that a contingency plan be developed for the implementation of the Twenty-Fifth Amendment in every conceivable situation that warranted its use. Development of this plan began during the transition period after his election to the presidency in November 1988 and was finalized and approved by him as president in April 1989.

The contingency plan developed during the Bush Administration had three enormous benefits: (a) it removed any questions or ambiguities about circumstances in which the Twenty-Fifth Amendment should be implemented; (b) it provided an advance directive by the president for certain specific actions to be taken by designated individuals if a medical condition or injury impaired his functional capacity to the extent that he could no longer perform the constitutional responsibilities of his office; and (c) it provided informed consent of the president for pertinent medical information to be given to the vice president and principal officers of the executive departments, or other such body as Congress may by law provide, in the event that the president developed an illness or injury of sufficient nature and magnitude to consider an involuntary transfer of presidential powers under the provisions of Section 4. This would preclude any conflict of interest regarding the confidentiality of pertinent medical information that would be transmitted to these government officials and taken into account during a determination of presidential disability.

The historical importance of the contingency plan developed during the Bush Administration should not be underestimated. For the first time since the ratification of the Twenty-Fifth Amendment in 1967, detailed guidelines were written for its implementation in specific situations. As explained in chapter 11, the 1996 *Report of the Working Group on Presidential Disability* calls for the development of a similar contingency plan by every future president during the post-election transition period and its finalization by the time of inauguration. In providing a model for future presidents to follow, George Bush has made the single most important contribution to the use of the Twenty-Fifth Amendment since the ratification of the Amendment itself. The precedent-setting contingency plan developed during his administration will serve the nation well should the disability of a president need to be considered at some point in the future. In fact, the Clinton Administration followed the Bush precedent in adopting a contingency plan of its own in 1993, perhaps a sign that the practice is already becoming regularized.

CONFIDENTIALITY OF MEDICAL INFORMATION

In any consideration of presidential disability, the maintenance of confidentiality within the doctor–patient relationship is a major concern for the White House Physician. Such confidentiality is one of the basic principles of medical practice and must be taken very seriously by every physician. As such, it is my belief that the sanctity of the doctor–patient relationship should not be violated by any physician caring for the president of the United States unless there is a compelling legal or ethical reason to do so in the public interest. An illness or injury of the president that provokes consideration of an involuntary transfer of presidential powers to the vice president *would*, in my opinion, constitute a compelling reason to release medical information to the vice president, principal officers of the executive departments, or other such body as Congress may by law provide. However, any medical information released by the White House Physician should be transmitted in a secure manner through properly established channels and due process of law solely for the purpose of implementing the provisions of the Twenty-Fifth Amendment.

The contingency plans developed during the Bush and Clinton Administrations clearly delineate both the channels and the process for transmitting medical information to designated government officials in any situation that would provoke consideration of a voluntary transfer of presidential powers under Section 3 or an involuntary transfer of powers under Section 4 of the Twenty-Fifth Amendment. As previously mentioned, these plans provide the White House Physician with advance directives and informed consent of the president for the release and transmittal of medical information to designated government officials, through the channels and procedures specified in the plan. Thus, in such a situation, the White House Physician would release and transmit medical information in strict accordance with specific procedures previously approved by the president. This removes any legal and ethical ambiguities regarding the confidentiality of medical information that the White House Physician provides to designated government officials for their consideration of presidential disability and the transfer of presidential powers to the vice president under the provisions of Section 4. In my opinion this is one of the most important benefits that a contingency plan provides.

It has become customary in recent years for presidents to issue written statements to the press when illnesses or injuries interfere with the performance of their duties or their official schedules. It needs to be stressed that the release of medical information through such statements must always be the decision of the president. It is not, and must not be, the decision of the White House Physician to release such information. All such statements, in my opinion, should be directed by the president, written by the White House Physician, edited by the White House press secretary, and approved by the president prior to release. They should contain timely, accurate, and complete information regarding the president's diagnosis, treatment, condition, and prognosis. False or misleading information about the president's health should never be provided to the press or the general public.

I also believe that the details of specific discussions and events that take place within the context of the doctor–patient relationship should remain forever private and not be divulged to the public. A press release that adheres to these principles will satisfy the public's right to be informed about the health status of a sick or injured president and, at the same time, maintain the sanctity of the relationship between the president and his physician.

CONCLUSIONS

The role of the contemporary White House Physician is a multifaceted one. He or she not only must provide excellent medical care to the president but also, on occasion, be involved in the extraordinarily sensitive matter of assessing presidential impairment under the Twenty-Fifth Amendment. As stated in the *Reports* of both the Miller Center and the Working Group on Presidential Disability, White House Physicians must be of such high caliber that they are accorded the greatest degree of respect and recognition within the medical profession (see chapters 11 and 12). They and their work should be well known within the medical establishment and they should be viewed as eminent in their field of expertise. Their background should provide them with the capability to analyze the medical literature with scientific precision and to consult and work well with the very best medical specialists from across the country.

It is also important for White House Physicians to develop and maintain a sound working relationship with the president's political staff. Although they must never yield to political pressure to "cut corners" in caring for the president, White House Physicians will interact frequently with the president's political advisers, minister medically to some of them, and work with them on issues related to the health and medical care of the president. At all times, however, it is essential for White House Physicians to maintain their professional objectivity and avoid becoming involved in political controversy. Their medical mission must always be central.

My view is that the position of White House Physician should not be subject to confirmation by the United States Senate since the president should have the right to choose his or her own physician without formal interference from the outside—in this instance, from another branch of government. Since the relationship between the White House Physician and the president will be a rather intimate one, it must be based on complete trust and confidence and should not be politicized.[12]

One of the most important qualifications of the White House Physician is that he or she must be fully at ease with the enormous—and unique—responsibilities that come with the position he or she occupies. These responsibilities have clearly grown since the Twenty-Fifth Amendment was added to the Constitution in 1967. In the final analysis, White House Physicians must recognize that their responsibility is to the president and to the country. Further, they must accept an additional important fact. The record reveals not only that many of our presidents have been ill during their terms in office but also that White House Physicians who have provided inadequate medical care or who have compromised their integrity have received the reproach of history.

NOTES

1. See, in general, Kenneth R. Crispell and Carlos F. Gomez, *Hidden Illness in the White House* (Durham, N.C.: Duke University Press, 1988); Robert E. Gilbert, *The Mortal Presidency: Illness and Anguish in the White House*, 2nd ed. (New York, Fordham University Press, 1998); Bert E. Park, *The Impact of Illness on World Leaders* (Philadelphia: University of Pennsylvania Press, 1986); Jerrold M. Post, M.D., and Robert S. Robins, *When Illness Strikes the Leader: The Dilemma of the Captive King* (New Haven, Conn.: Yale University Press, 1993).

2. For an examination of the 1992 presidential candidacy of Paul Tsongas, see Robert E. Gilbert, "Presidential Disability in Law and Politics: Lessons from 1992," *Miller Center Journal*, 5 (Spring 1998) pp. 3–21.

3. Jimmy Carter, "Presidential Disability and the Twenty-Fifth Amendment: A President's Perspective," *Journal of the American Medical Association*, 272 (1994), 1698.

4. Robert E. Gilbert, "Disability, Illness, and the Presidency: The Case of Franklin D. Roosevelt," *Politics and the Life Sciences*, 7 (1988), pp. 33–49.

5. See, especially, Fred I. Greenstein, *The Hidden-Hand Presidency: Eisenhower as Leader* (Baltimore: The Johns Hopkins University Press, 1994).

6. Gilbert, *Mortal Presidency*, chaps. 4, 6, 7.

7. See Arthur S. Link and James F. Toole, "Presidential Disability and the Twenty-Fifth Amendment," *Journal of the American Medical Association*, 272 (1994), 1694–97.

8. Lawrence C. Mohr, "The White House Physician: Role, Responsibilities, and Issues," *Political Psychology*, 16 (1995), 787.

9. Robert S. Robins and Henry Rothschild, "Ethical Dilemmas of the President's Physician," *Politics and the Life Sciences*, 7 (1988), 7.

10. Bert E. Park, "Resuscitating the Twenty-Fifth Anmendment: A Second Opinion Regarding Presidential Disability," *Political Psychology*, 16 (1995), 823.

11. See Birch Bayh, *One Heartbeat Away: Presidential Disability and Succession* (Indianapolis: Bobbs Merrill, 1968); John D. Feerick, *The Twenty-Fifth Amendment: Its Complete History and Applications* (New York: Fordham University Press, 1976; repr. 1992).

12. For an interesting discussion of the White House Physician's role, see Lawrence K. Altman, "Unique Problems for a Physician Who Makes (White) House Calls," *New York Times*, February 21, 1989, p.19.

7

Broken Minds, Broken Hearts, and the Twenty-Fifth Amendment: Psychiatric Disorders and Presidential Disability

Jerrold M. Post, M.D.

Because the public wants a president who is strong, wise, decisive, and stable, disorders that impair the president's cognition and emotional reactions are particularly stressful to the political system. Psychiatric illness, both functional and organic, unfortunately is still stigmatized. This puts a premium on concealing such illness, a situation that is dangerous for the president and the nation. How a leader reacts to illness, both physical and emotional, is a function of both leader personality and political considerations. To appear strong, leaders will often return to office prematurely after surgery or a heart attack, interfering with their recovery and impairing their leadership. Substance abuse also affects decision-making and judgment and is easily concealed. A routinization of the use of the Twenty-Fifth Amendment is suggested, with enumeration of conditions that should prompt consideration of the Amendment's temporary invocation.

In considering the problem of disability in the White House, there is a paradox. The more severe the disability, the less the problem in terms of the potential for political distortion of medical diagnosis and treatment.[1] The acute disability——stroke, myocardial infarction, acute gastrointestinal bleed—that is dramatic in onset and medically incapacitating cannot readily be concealed. It will almost certainly come to public notice, and medical treatment will be administered in the bright glare of public attention.

To be sure, assessing the recovery from illness may be subject to political cross currents. Even in this open democracy, with a vigorous opposition and aggressive media, the degree of residual incapacity can be masked, witness Woodrow Wilson after his stroke and Ronald Reagan during the recovery from trauma surgery after the assassination attempt by John Hinckley.

But it is the insidious illness, the subtle disability, not readily obvious, that in many ways is the most problematic for the political system. When the onset is gradual and the symptoms are fluctuant, the leader is unlikely to present an obvious or consistent public image of medical impairment, even though the disability is evident to the inner circle. In such a circumstance, if the leader and his inner circle ignore how much the illness is compromising his decision-making and effectiveness and carefully orchestrate his public appearances, the presence or degree of the disability can be significantly obscured. Such a situation can present to a conscientious leadership circle a choice between being loyal to what may be a temporarily ill leader and deceiving the public.

But there is another hazard as well. The insidious illness, gradual in onset, varying in degree, may not be readily apparent to the inner circle, including the president's physician. They may collectively "cast a blind eye" toward the disability, for the cost of recognizing it would be too high. Especially when the leader is ascribed God-like stature, there may be a collective denial, as exemplified by Mustafa Ataturk's terminal illness. Ataturk was the founder of the modern state of Turkey. Although he demonstrated the full panoply of signs of terminal liver disease from life-long alcohol abuse, no one in his entourage, including his physicians, recognized that he was ill. It was a case of collective denial of the leader's mortality.

The Need to Conceal Illness to
Preserve the Leader's Image

Serious illness—both physical and mental—is an equal opportunity employer. It does not discriminate between the poor and the wealthy, between the man in the street and the VIP, between the private citizen and the public official. But when illness strikes the president, unlike the man in the street, it poses a special problem, because the president must be seen as strong and wise and in control. This image of strength and stability is critical to public confidence. Accordingly, there is a premium on concealing illness, as exemplified by the cover-up of the recurrence of lymphoma by former Massachusetts Senator Paul Tsongas and his physicians during the Democratic presidential primaries of 1992. Moreover, the need to preserve the image of health may lead VIPs to avoid comprehensive diagnostic evaluation and treatment altogether or to undergo inadequate treatment secretly, as exemplified by Governor William Casey of Pennsylvania, who underwent a heart-lung transplant in 1993. His cardiologist acknowledged that Casey's regular cardiac evaluation was omitted during the fall of 1990, for fear the results would leak and adversely affect Casey's campaign.

THE SPECIAL POLITICAL PROBLEMS OF ILLNESS AFFECTING THE PRESIDENT'S MENTAL AND EMOTIONAL REACTIONS

Because of the collective need for the leader to be seen as wise, decisive, and in control, illnesses that affect the leader's mental processes and/or emotional reactions are especially threatening to his political followers. Accordingly, the perceived need to conceal is particularly strong for mental illness, such as the suicidal depression that tragically claimed the life of President Clinton's long-time friend and deputy White House counsel, Vincent Foster, in 1993. Despite the major advances in medical science concerning the etiology and treatment of depression, the victims of this serious mental illness continue to be stigmatized and are perceived by the public as weak and unstable.

The revelation of a VIP's psychiatric illness and treatment must be avoided at all costs, a lesson painfully learned during the 1972 presidential campaign. The Democratic Party's presidential nominee, Senator George McGovern of South Dakota, chose Senator Thomas Eagleton of Missouri to be his vice-presidential running mate. Ten days after the Democratic convention, aware that the Knight newspaper chain was about to break the story, Eagleton acknowledged that in his twenties he had been voluntarily hospitalized for depression and had undergone a series of electroshock treatments. The revelation produced a firestorm. Democratic prospects plummeted in the polls, and party leaders felt they had no choice but to remove Eagleton from the ticket, replacing him with Sargent Shriver. McGovern, perceived to be injudicious and ineffective as a leader, in part because he had initially chosen Eagleton to be his running mate, lost the election to Richard Nixon by a wide margin. Although the Eagleton episode occurred more than a quarter of a century ago, the passage of years has not done much to diminish the taint of mental illness. In an early 1990s survey, in fact, 65 percent of respondents still saw "a lot of stigma" attached to it. Only 6 percent did not. More recent surveys disclosed little change.[2]

Shocking the Washington political community, John Wilson, the president of the City Council of the District of Columbia, committed suicide by hanging himself in the spring of 1993. Wilson had long suffered from severe depression concealed from all but his immediate family and closest friends. Aspiring to be mayor, he refused definitive inpatient treatment for his serious depression, and apparently was reluctant to take antidepressant medication because it interfered with his clarity of thinking. Wilson probably believed, with good reason, that to reveal that he was receiving psychiatric treatment would be politically fatal.

Like Wilson's, Vincent Foster's depression occurred in the intense, merciless political context of Washington, where, in the bitter last sentence of Foster's farewell note, "ruining people is considered sport." He reportedly had suffered a fifteen-pound weight loss, was having trouble sleeping, felt guilty and worthless, and was having problems concentrating—all classic symptoms of depression. His family physician in Little Rock had recently sent him a prescription for an antidepressant, but Foster had not sought psychiatric treatment in Washington. This is indeed unfortunate, because depression is a very treatable disease. Whether his special status as a White House insider inhibited him from seeking definitive treatment we cannot say with certainty, but the atmospherics of the case certainly suggest this strongly.

James Forrestal, secretary of defense in the late 1940s, became seriously depressed and paranoid after widespread media attacks on his integrity and loyalty. The gravity of his illness unrecognized, he was considered to be suffering from "exhaustion." A workaholic, Forrestal remained in office but was isolated from decision-making by President Truman, and the isolation only magnified his paranoia. When he ultimately was admitted to the Bethesda Naval Hospital, rather than being treated on the first floor psychiatric ward, Forrestal was hospitalized in the VIP suite in the tower—from which he committed suicide by plunging to his death. Had he been treated like an ordinary seaman, this talented public servant might well have recovered from his suicidal depression.

Like James Forrestal, Vincent Foster was stung by the media criticism and was unable to cope with the foreign culture of Washington. Reluctant to reveal the degree of his suffering and seek appropriate treatment, Vincent Foster, like James Forrestal, may have died of high status. The melancholic chorus from Sophocles's *Ajax* that Forrestal was copying before he leaped to his death may well have reflected Foster's last thoughts:

> Thy son is in a foreign clime
> Worn by the waste of time
> Comfortless, nameless, hopeless save
> In the dark prospect of the yawning grave
>
> Oh, when the pride of Graecia's noble race
> Wanders, as now, in darkness and disgrace,
> Better to die and sleep
> The never waking sleep than linger on
> And dare to live when the soul's life is gone.

Severe debilitating depression has been an occupant of the White House. As Robert E. Gilbert has persuasively demonstrated, President Coolidge's reputation for being a "do nothing" president in his second term was almost certainly the consequence of a severe depression precipitated by the death of his adolescent son.[3] Between Coolidge's two terms, his favorite son, Calvin, Jr., developed a blister after playing tennis on the White House grounds without wearing socks. The blister became infected, young Coolidge developed septicemia, and three days later died. Coolidge fell into a profound grief from which he never recovered, a case, in the judgment of Knight Aldrich, of pathological grief.[4] He withdrew, became hypersomnolent, spending eleven hours sleeping each day of his second term; he was both irritable and disinterested. Gilbert's description is vivid:

The President withdrew almost completely from interaction with Congress and showed little inclination even to participate in the activities of the departments of his own government. His workdays began to shrink in length and his naps grew considerably longer and more frequent. His shrewdness turned to disinterest; his involvement turned to indifference, and his well-developed leadership skills were abandoned.[5]

Both Dwight Eisenhower and Lyndon Johnson suffered from heart attacks from which they recovered. Calvin Coolidge, on the other hand, never recovered from the broken heart occasioned by his son's death.

One of the difficulties with mental illness in the White House is discriminating between transient emotional reactions or situation-appropriate reactions and mental illness. Richard Goodwin has written tellingly of Lyndon Baines Johnson's paranoia:

> . . . it was expectable that the "Kennedy crowd", as Johnson called them, should be the prelude to that swarming crowd of "enemies" and "conspirators" that began to affect Johnson's mind. Not only had he felt humiliated—and with some cause—during Kennedy's presidency, but the enduring shadow of Camelot—glamorous, popular, intellectual, enshrined in steadily growing myth—seemed to him to obscure the achievements of his own presidency, preventing others from seeing how much more he was accomplishing than had his predecessor. The omnipresent ghost of the past was, for Johnson, reincarnated in the person of Robert Kennedy and his followers. However, understandable hostility would soon be displayed by the more ominous conviction that Robert Kennedy was not just an enemy, but the leader of all his enemies, the guiding spirit of some immense conspiracy designed to discredit and ultimately, to overthrow the Johnson presidency.[6]

Were the President's rantings concerning conspiracies just his way of letting off steam or did he temporarily slip over the edge under the unremitting pressure from protesting youths chanting, "Hey, hey, LBJ, how many kids did you kill today?" And was it really paranoia, for, in fact, the increasingly disaffected youthful generation was "out to get him"?

During the last days of Watergate, the pressure on President Richard M. Nixon was immense. According to memoir reports, he was both drinking heavily and displaying paranoid and depressive symptoms, leading to fear that he might react in an aggressive paranoid manner, with grave international consequences. Nixon himself confided to his diary that he had "a sinking feeling" in his stomach and was suffering through sleepless nights. When, in mid-July, Vice President Ford met with him, Ford's reaction to the meeting was that Nixon was not "as strong mentally or physically as he had been before. I had a growing sense of his frustration, his resentment and his lack of a calm, deliberate approach to the problems of governing." A few weeks later, Secretary of State Henry Kissinger accompanied the West German Foreign Minister to a meeting with Nixon in California. Kissinger was shocked at the deterioration in Nixon's appearance and demeanor. He was very pale and, although the president seemed composed, Kissinger found that "it clearly took every ounce of his energy to conduct a serious conversation. He sat on the sofa in his office looking over the Pacific, his gaze and thought focused on some distant prospect."[7]

GETTING HIGH IN THE WHITE HOUSE

Substance abuse in political office is a particularly troublesome problem. The evidence is compelling that John F. Kennedy abused amphetamines.[8] Dr. Max Jacobson, known to the glitterati as Dr. Feel Good, administered energizing injections of a tonic containing amphetamine to his prominent clients. Dr. Jacobson was to lose his license, which was revoked by the state of New York, for flagrant abuse in the prescribing of controlled substances. Jacobson was flown to Berlin at the expense of the Kennedy family to accompany JFK during the critical visit when Kennedy made his dramatic "Ich bin ein Berliner" speech. The president may well have been high on speed during that speech.

In this case, Jacobson was not an official physician to the president. But what if the president were pressuring his official physician to administer pain killers, sleeping pills, stimulants? Could the physician resist? Lord Moran could not resist the pleas of Winston Churchill for his "reds, blacks, whites and Dr. Morans;" nor could he decline the pleas of Anthony Eden, who was addicted to amphetamine, when, during the Suez crisis, he pleaded, "Charles, I must have my Benzedrine." Consider the impact in crises of decision-making under the influence of amphetamine. But consider, also, the pressure and ongoing dilemma of the physician to the president or prime minister during a major crisis, when the fate of the nation is on the leader's shoulders and the leader is demanding sleeping pills and stimulants to keep him going.

The most frequently abused substance is the lubricant that makes the gears of Washington turn: alcohol. The world of politics is a particularly salutary environment for the concealment and facilitation of alcoholism. It is usually the case that it is only when there is an embarrassing public episode that the alcoholism finally comes to light. A colorful example is provided by the powerful chairman of the House Ways and Means Committee, Wilbur Mills, found frolicking while drunk in the tidal basin early one morning in 1974 with the stripper Fanny Fox. Two-time presidential contender and 1956 Democratic Party vice-presidential nominee Estes Kefauver greeted each day with a tumbler of straight Scotch. What are the boundary lines between social drinking, problem drinking, and alcoholism, especially in Washington? And how does the White House Physician monitor and limit the president's alcohol consumption? And should this be his or her role?

Organic Deterioration

Acute organic illnesses affecting the central nervous system are much more alarming to the public than those in which mental functioning is unaffected. Eisenhower's 1955 myocardial infarct produced little alarm, but the stroke he suffered in 1957 produced great consternation, for initially his speech and thinking were affected. Major columnists suggested that the president should delegate his responsibilities to Vice President Nixon. Several commentators urged that the president should resign, and the *New York Post* editorialized that it preferred having Nixon as president over having no president at all. A prominent senator, Wayne Morse of Oregon, suggested that the time had come for Eisenhower to step aside. Even White House staffers were gloomy and tense.[9] The impact of this particular illness, then, was particularly pronounced because the president's reasoning abilities seemed to be in question.

In addition to the problems of acute illnesses such as Eisenhower's in 1955 and 1957, a particularly vexing diagnostic problem concerns the gradual and progressive organic brain syndrome reflecting early Alzheimer's disease or multi-infarct dementia. There is a certain deterioration of mental functioning associated with the aging process. When Senator Howard Baker assumed the role of White House chief of staff after the Irangate debacle, replacing Donald Regan, he asked an experienced aide, James Cannon, to assess White House decision-making. In the process of interviewing senior White House officials, Cannon developed a picture of Ronald Reagan as inattentive, distracted, and apparently not interested in the job. "All he wanted to do was watch movies and television at the residence."[10] Cannon recommended that Baker consider the application of Section 4 of the Twenty-Fifth Amendment, having concluded that President Reagan was "at the brink of being physically and mentally incapable of carrying out his responsibilities." Baker interviewed President Reagan with Cannon present and concluded that Reagan *was* up to the job. Note the absence of medical participation in the evaluation. Because personal style persists in organic deterioration, lay observers regularly underestimate the degree of impairment consequent to the decline in cognitive function. Sophisticated neuropsychological testing is required to establish the degree of impairment from organic brain disease.

Moreover, the course of cerebral degeneration is characterized by wide fluctuation. Such fluctuations may occur within several hours, with the patient reasonably alert in the morning, semi-stuporous in the afternoon. An intercurrent infection may tip the afflicted individual over the edge. Estimating the capacity for sustained executive performance over time benefits from systematic observation over time.

IMPACT OF POLITICAL CONTEXT AND LEADER PERSONALITY ON
MEDICAL DECISION-MAKING AND TREATMENT

The degree to which political considerations bear upon decisions concerning executive capacity is strikingly illustrated by the manner in which President Reagan resumed the reins of power after surgery for colon cancer in 1985. It should be noted that, comments to the contrary notwithstanding, the Twenty-Fifth Amendment was not officially invoked at this time despite the exchange of letters with Vice President Bush. Indeed, comments by White House staff at the time

weakened the intent of this part of the Amendment to ensure the
nation that an able leader was in charge. President Reagan was disoriented after awakening from surgery, a nearly three-hour procedure. Herbert L. Abrams's meticulous research has documented the
casual, ad hoc manner in which the decision was made that the president was competent to resume official authority.[11] White House
Counsel Fred Fielding, Chief of Staff Donald Regan, and White
House Press Secretary Larry Speakes devised their own test. A two-
sentence letter had been drafted for the president to sign in order to
regain his office. The letter read: "Following up on my letter to you
of this date, please be advised that I am able to resume the discharge
of the Constitutional powers and duties of the President of the
United States. I have informed the Vice President of my determination and my resumption of those powers and duties."

Fielding, Regan, and Speakes decided that if the president could
read the two-sentence letter, he was sufficiently lucid to reclaim the
office. Fielding asked the attending surgeon if that would be evidence that the president was lucid. The surgeon responded, "Yup."
No other physicians, including the White House physician, were involved in this decision, no screening mental status exam was given,
and no consideration was given to using even the simplest test of
cognitive functioning. Nor was the president asked whether he felt
able to resume the presidency.

A year later when Irangate broke, President Reagan claimed he
could not remember the decision to ship arms to Iran—a decision
made while he was recovering from surgery. During the Irangate
hearings, Attorney General Edwin Meese stated that President
Reagan approved the shipment while "recovering from surgery and
that his memory could have been impaired as a result of post-opera-
tive medication." It was politically expedient to declare the president
competent to regain the office immediately after the surgery, and it
was politically expedient a year later to suggest the president's inability in order to exculpate him from responsibility for the Iran–Contra
affair.

Because a high-level political leader, with the support and assistance of members of his staff, wishes to demonstrate strength and
being in control, he may not take medicine that might impair his
sensorium during recovery from surgery or a myocardial infarct. This
was the case with Lyndon Johnson in the wake of his 1955 coronary.

Moreover, he met with aides in his hospital room, participating in important decisions. This is not recommended treatment. Not taking recommended medications or not adhering to a particular regime can be medically harmful.

Both these circumstances—the rapid resumption of executive authority by Reagan immediately upon awakening from cancer surgery, and LBJ's driven behavior as Majority Leader of the United States Senate right after his coronary—call attention to the interaction between political situation, patient personality, and medical needs.

CONSIDERATIONS FOR ROUTINIZING IMPLEMENTATION OF
THE TWENTY-FIFTH AMENDMENT

Absent a routine temporary invocation of the Twenty-Fifth Amendment in such situations, political circumstances will tend to override medical circumstances, to the patient's, and the nation's, detriment. Herbert Abrams has recommended a number of circumstances that should automatically trigger invocation of the Twenty-Fifth Amendment.[12] They include:

- any planned surgical procedure that requires general anesthesia
- any emergency surgical procedure that requires general anesthesia
- the use of psychoactive drugs in any significant amount (such medications as narcotics, tranquilizers, amphetamines, barbiturates, and anesthetics may profoundly alter consciousness, judgment, perception, and behavior)
- the perception by the president or his physician that an illness, injury, or emotional condition is interfering with his judgment or ability to govern
- any serious illness
- death or serious illness in the president's immediate family
- the diagnosis of Alzheimer's disease or any other progressive, mentally disabling condition
- significant alterations of the president's cognitive faculties or ability to communicate.

I believe there is much wisdom to these recommendations, but for some of these conditions, one might wish to step back from automatically triggering the Twenty-Fifth Amendment to automatically triggering active consideration of its temporary invocation. The routinization of temporary implementation of the Twenty-Fifth Amendment would make this a much less consequential act and diminish concern over the public loss of confidence. As an example, consider the death of President Clinton's mother, Virginia Kelley. We know from President Clinton how complicated the relationship and how powerfully influential. Yet his public responsibilities permitted him to stop only briefly at the funeral before resuming his travel to an important overseas summit meeting. Acute grief is disabling, and blocking the opportunity to grieve can be crippling. Would the American public have thought President Clinton weak if for several days he absented himself from public view to mourn the loss of his mother? I think not. Had a major crisis erupted in the immediate aftermath of his mother's death, could the president have brought all of his psychological faculties to bear on dealing with the crisis? Assuredly not. The president, no less than any other man, deserves the chance to grieve. But the absence of routinization of temporary implementation of the Twenty-Fifth Amendment for acute grief, surgery, and the other conditions enumerated by Dr. Abrams makes each decision a political decision, and, in such circumstances, politics regularly win out over the medical welfare of the ailing president, and both the president and the public suffer as a consequence.

In closing, let me draw attention to a psychological reaction of critical importance in considering presidential disability. As observed at the beginning of this chapter, the acute disability is not the most pressing problem. It is the unrecognized, insidious, subtle, and fluctuant disability that is the greatest concern. A slowly progressive malignancy, such as that which ultimately claimed the lives of Georges Pompidou of France and the Shah of Iran—a slowly deteriorating cardiomyopathy which led to the requirement for a heart-lung transplant for Governor William Casey of Pennsylvania—such hidden, progressive, non-dramatic illnesses can have profound psychological consequences for the ailing leader. Facing death powerfully concentrates the attention and can significantly distort decision-making. It can lead to a superimposition of the personal timetable on the nation's timetable, with deleterious consequences for both the leader and the nation.

The nation wants a president in full control of his mental faculties and emotional reactions—wise, knowledgeable, judicious, temperate, decisive. Disorders, both organic and functional, that impair the president's decision-making and judgment are the most stressful for the political system. These disabilities are the most difficult to evaluate and to manage, and the easiest to mask—a dangerous combination for the nation.

NOTES

1. This article draws significantly on "Disorders Affecting Cognition and Behavior and the Twenty-Fifth Amendment: Implications for Presidential Disability," a paper presented to the Working Group on Presidential Disability, The Carter Center, Atlanta, Georgia, January, 1995 and upon Jerrold M. Post, M.D., and Robert S. Robins, *When Illness Strikes the Leader: The Dilemma of the Captive King* (New Haven, Conn.: Yale University Press, 1993).

2. Andrew B. Borinstein, "Public Attitudes Toward Persons with Mental Illness," *Health Affairs*, 11 (Fall 1992), 191; U.S. Public Health Service, *Mental Health: A Report of the Surgeon General* (Rockville, Md.: Substance Abuse and Mental Health Services Administration, 1999), chap. 1.

3. Robert E. Gilbert, "Psychological Pain and the Presidency: The Case of Calvin Coolidge," *Political Psychology*, 9 (March 1988), 86.

4. Knight Aldrich, "Personal Grieving and Political Defeat," in *Papers on Presidential Disability and the Twenty-Fifth Amendment*, vol. 3, ed. Kenneth Thompson (Lanham, Md.: University Press of America, 1996), pp. 82–96.

5. Gilbert, "Psychological Pain and the Presidency," 94.

6. Richard Goodwin, *Remembering America* (Boston: Little, Brown, 1988), p. 396.

7. Stephen E. Ambrose, *Nixon*, vol. 3 (New York: Simon & Schuster, 1991), pp. 381, 387, 399.

8. See James Giglio, *The Presidency of John F. Kennedy* (Lawrence: University Press of Kansas, 1991), pp. 263–64; see also Thomas C. Reeves, *A Question of Character: A Life of John F. Kennedy* (New York: The Free Press, 1991), pp. 295–97.

9. Robert E. Gilbert, *The Mortal Presidency: Illness and Anguish in the White House*, 2nd ed. (New York: Fordham University Press, 1998), p. 109.

10. Jane Mayer and Doyle McManus, *Landslide* (Boston: Houghton-Mifflin, 1988), p. ix.

11. See, in general, Herbert L. Abrams, *The President Has Been Shot: Confusion, Disability, and the Twenty-Fifth Amendment in the Aftermath of the Attempted Assassination of Ronald Reagan* (New York: W. W. Norton, 1992).

12. Ibid., pp. 222–25.

8

The President's Spouse, the President's Health, and the Twenty-Fifth Amendment

Robert S. Robins

The politics of implementing the Twenty-Fifth Amendment will largely be the politics of "removal" of the president. An essential aspect of that process will be the role of the inner circle in evaluating and communicating their opinion of the state of the president's health. When Illness Strikes the Leader *demonstrated that members of a leader's inner circle tend to seek to put a leader in office and to keep him there regardless of the consequences to his health or the consequences of his health on the performance of his office. This chapter examines that tendency in relation to the role of the wives of five presidents: Wilson, Harding, Roosevelt, Eisenhower, and Johnson. The conclusion is that the spouse does not act substantially differently from other members of the inner circle such as the president's doctors or political confidants.*

Who knows first and who knows best about the president's health? Who is most likely to be believed by outsiders? The president himself? The president's physician? The president's closest associates? The president's spouse? In the event of a contested presidential removal, under terms of the Twenty-Fifth Amendment, all the members of the inner circle will have a powerful voice in what should be done. A plea by the president's spouse, even if it should differ from that of other members of the inner circle, is very likely to be decisive.

Politics, especially presidential politics, is a middle-aged and old person's game.[1] Of the seventeen presidents in the twentieth cen-

Special thanks to David B. Dyment, M.D., Vancouver, British Columbia, for his advice and comments. Of course, all errors of fact and interpretation are the author's.

tury, about half were at least briefly so medically impaired as to prevent them from carrying on their duties. Sometimes the disorder was
slow and fluctuant, like Franklin Roosevelt's arteriosclerosis-associ-
ated illnesses; sometimes it was sudden but declining in severity,
like Eisenhower's heart attack; sometimes it was intermittent, like
Kennedy's apparent amphetamine abuse;[2] sometimes it was traumati-
cally catastrophic, like Reagan's gunshot wound. The health of presidents, however, is likely to be worse than we know. Only after a
president's death—often only after decades after a president's
death—do we learn of the existence and severity of many presidential
medical conditions.[3] Even for presidents who have been dead for
decades, information regarding the gravity of their health conditions
continues to appear, as the recent work by Robert E. Gilbert[4] on
Lyndon Johnson and Clarence G. Lasby[5] on Eisenhower demonstrate. As of the writing of this chapter, five of the century's presidents are still alive. Thus, we begin this analysis with the assumption
that the medical facts about the presidents we survey are not only
incomplete, but also biased toward the side of good health.

Although many important leaders continue to rule well into what
the general population would consider the retirement years, most,
including American presidents, do not. American presidents are
short-lived in comparison with other white males, with members of
Congress, and with members of the Supreme Court. Perhaps it is a
different sort of person who seeks the presidency; perhaps the presidency takes a particularly severe toll on its incumbents. Though it is
always difficult and sometimes impossible to evaluate how important
it is in any case, stress is a contributing cause of cardiovascular disease and reduces immunity to many illnesses.[6]

Although the health care of VIPs is not completely different from
the health care of others, it is also not the same. This is even more so
with the president of the United States. In some ways his care is apt
to be much better than that of the general well-to-do population, but
often it has been worse. Anastasia Kucharski has pointed out that
health care for VIPs often proceeds by indirect, unusual, and confused referral channels; that too many or too few health care professionals are involved; that responsibility for health care is frequently
uncertain and diffuse; that clinical attention is very often misdirected;
and that there is an exceptionally high incidence of disagreement
about diagnosis and care.[7] These factors can lead to bad, even disas-

trous, health care. [8] Ironically, being a VIP, even being president, does not ensure superior health care.

It is not simply that the health care is problematic, but also that the information and advice presidents have received about their health has often been biased in an optimistic direction. Aside from the general advice that anyone should be told about his or her health, presidents should also be advised as to (1) the degree to which a medical condition and its treatment may affect their ability to carry out the unique responsibilities of the office; and (2) the likely course of such a condition and its likely effect on the president's competence. Except in extreme cases, such health-related matters should not be decided on medical grounds alone. Not only is the medical condition in question here, but also how that condition affects and is likely to affect the president's ability to function. The overwhelming majority of presidential physicians have been skilled and ethical, but some have not.[9] Some have put personal considerations before professional ones, and some have been lacking in medical skill. At times the president's condition has been kept a closely held secret, excluding all or all but a few other physicians. A doctor working with other doctors keeps a little, perhaps, of his humility. When he is wrong, he will be corrected, and his colleagues will not hold him in awe. But when he is the only medical expert among laymen, then even the most marginal graduate of the most obscure medical school may have an overwhelming influence.[10] The president's physician is the only member of the inner circle chosen by the president outside his area of competence.

In determining the current and future effect of their health on their duties, presidents, like the rest of us, have turned to those closest to them for advice. The spouse is likely to be the person most readily consulted. Parenthetically, members of the inner circle, unlike the rest of us, are under a moral obligation to offer such advice, even if not solicited.[11]

Those closest to the president constitute the inner circle. That somewhat varying and not always precisely defined group has in the past been composed of the president's health providers, especially his principal physician; his closest friends; favored relatives, including his wife; and long-time and well-trusted political associates. In *When Illness Strikes the Leader*, Jerrold M. Post and Robert S. Robins demonstrated that the tendency of members of the inner circle has been to subordinate the president's health to his winning and remaining in the presidency. This tendency is not surprising and not even necessarily wrong. Presidents, like many ambitious people, tend to subordinate their health to their ambition and to what they see as their duty, and those close to presidents see their role as one of support, not criticism. Although this chapter will look at the role of the president's wife in health-related decisions, it is essential to remember that the principal responsibility for evaluating the effect of his health on his office is the president's.

Have the thirty-eight women who have been married to sitting presidents acted any differently from other members of the inner circle regarding their husbands' health care? That is not an easy question to answer. Even more so than with the president's physicians and his closest friends, the relation between husband and wife is largely hidden from view and may be more likely to change over time. And even more than in other relationships, there are subtleties hardly sensed by the husband and wife, and much less so by an historian or political psychologist. We should also remember that not all presidents and their wives are emotionally intimate or partners in politics. In some cases, the spouse may have little or no influence, knowledge, or perhaps even interest in her husband's political life—or even in his private life. In others, the presidency itself may bring a couple together. As first daughter Margaret Truman noted:

> Living and working together in the same house, a president and his wife often see more of each other than they have in any previous era of their marriage. The first lady is frequently more intimately involved in her husband's political reactions and decisions than ever before. Betty Ford was one of several first ladies who told me this in unvarnished terms. Lady Bird Johnson made it even clearer. "You and your husband suddenly look at each other and say: " 'It's you and me.' Other people—our children, friends—will try to help. But in the end it's the two of us who are going to succeed—or fail."[12]

As with all other persons or groups connected with the Oval Office, however, the actions and role of first ladies have been frequently described and discussed in biographies, autobiographies, and other primary sources. This extensive material has been illuminated, especially in the past decade or so, by a rich and growing literature on first ladies and a robust comparative literature on the political context of ill leadership.

Any piece of advice can be understood only in terms of the context in which it is given. Therefore, the nature of the marriage—the relationship between president and first lady—will be described here as will the political context in which the advice was given. The evidence tends strongly to point in one direction: presidents' wives, like other members of the inner circle, have, with few exceptions, followed, supported, and encouraged their husbands' desire to become president and to stay in office, regardless of the apparent health consequences. Some wives believed (often on medical advice and perhaps with good reason) that the exercise of power and the prestige of the office were good for their husbands' health, viewing the office of the president as health therapy. Edith Wilson said that leaving the presidency would damage her stroke-stricken husband's health more than staying in office. She saw the presidency as treatment for her medically disabled husband without regard to the effect on the government. Others have told their husbands that staying in office despite bad health is good for the country and bad for his political enemies. Better him in power sick than his opponent in power well. Such was the case with Lady Bird Johnson, who nevertheless stated that every first lady feels it has been her primary duty "to make a comfortable area, an island of peace, if you will, a setting in which her husband can do his best work."[13]

Motivations are difficult, sometimes impossible, to assess. I believe that the spouses were honest, sincere, and well-intentioned in their advice to their husbands. In most cases, they were arguably accurate as well. As with anyone else, motives were mixed and acted one upon another. In every case, save perhaps one, the first ladies were supporting their husbands in what their husbands wanted to do. Regarding the point of this chapter, however, the advice followed the same general pattern as that of other members of the inner circle: seek or stay in office.[14]

Let us look at five of the seventeen presidents in the twentieth century and their wives.

Edith Bolling Wilson and Woodrow Wilson

President Woodrow Wilson was widowed in 1914 when his first wife, Ellen Louise Axson, died of chronic nephritis.[15] He experienced such a severe depression that he was unable to function for days at a time. Soon, however, he was introduced by his physician, Cary Grayson, to a widowed Washington businesswoman and socialite, Mrs. Norman (Edith Bolling) Galt. After an intense and romantic courtship, they married in December of 1915. Although Wilson appears something of a dry stick, he was a passionate man, very dependent on his wives.

As Judith L. Weaver demonstrates, the second Mrs. Wilson was a strong-willed and possessive person, who was quick to make her attitude and opinion known and followed.[16] Chauncey D. Leake, who later wrote on the Wilson presidency, characterized her as "imperious, determined, proud, and extraordinary."[17] Leake offers a firsthand vignette of the semi-public Mrs. Wilson. In 1917 at Fort Myer in Virginia, a minister was making what seemed to Mrs. Wilson an overly long invocation before the president's speech. Leake was a young man, serving in a military honor guard:

> I was standing on the ground not ten feet from [President Wilson] and a little to the rear, so that I could see clearly what was going on. I was conscious of an impatient tapping. Cautiously glancing up, I noted that Mrs. Wilson was looking at the minister disapprovingly, and it was she who was tapping her foot. The President showed no impatience. Mrs. Wilson's annoyance seemed to continue as the invocation went along, and I could hear her audible sigh of relief when the prayer finally closed. I have no memory of what the President said, except my feeling remains that it was clear, calm, and inspiring. Nonetheless, my impression persists much stronger to the effect that Mrs. Wilson was a domineering and probably an intolerant person.[18]

Leake is perhaps too severe—Mrs. Wilson was probably not the only one desiring a briefer invocation—but his description of the first lady is consistent with that of others.

In a different way, Wilson also was keen to make his opinions and attitudes known, but since he was a former college professor, these took a more intellectualized form. Wilson's doctoral dissertation, published as *Congressional Government*, remains one of political science's notable works. It advocates a shift in American government toward a parliamentary form, a policy that Wilson continued to consider while president. On November 5, 1916, two days before the election, Wilson wrote to his secretary of state, Robert Lansing, that if his opponent, Charles Evans Hughes, were elected, he would ask

Lansing to resign, appoint the victorious Hughes secretary of state, ask his vice president to resign, and resign himself. Thus, Hughes would immediately become president, much as a similar transition would occur in a parliamentary system.[19] Health was not an issue here, but the letter does suggest that Wilson had the courage to resign if he believed that the best interests of the country required it.

In late September 1919, while campaigning for the League of Nations treaty, the sixty–three-year-old Wilson suffered a stroke. At his direction, the organic nature of his disability was publicly denied by his wife and doctor. The story put out was that the president was suffering only from fatigue. In fact, Wilson was unable to read or otherwise carry out the functions of his office. This inability was not surprising in that from his return to Washington on October 2 the effects of the stroke rapidly extended themselves to his entire left side. His physicians were fully aware of the problem, diagnosing his condition as a massive cerebral thrombosis. He also required urinary catheterization and experienced respiratory problems when lying flat. Mrs. Wilson, who had an excessive fear of hospitals,[20] refused the type of hospitalization that the condition required.

Edith and Joseph Tumulty, Wilson's principal aide, sealed the president off from all but the presidential physician, Cary Grayson, who initially agreed to participate in the deception. In January of the following year, however, when the severe nature of the disability was evident, Grayson did recommend to the president that he resign, "but Mrs. W. objected."[21] After this attempt, Grayson resumed his role as a loyal member of the cover-up. Tumulty, after Wilson's stroke, said he would never cooperate in removing Wilson from office because the president had been so good to him.[22] Repeated requests by elected and senior government officials to see the president were refused. Meetings, Mrs. Wilson said, would upset the president. Secretary of State Robert Lansing, attempted to secure an audience, sought to convene a cabinet meeting, and then requested a certification of disability, but was dismissed from office for the attempts. The vice president, Thomas R. Marshall, refused to act as president for (among other reasons), his doing so would be an indirect certification of the president's disability.[23]

Mrs. Wilson was candid: "I am not thinking of the country now, I am thinking of my husband."[24] The president's doctor later approvingly concurred: "During the four and a half years of his illness she thought of practically nothing else."[25]

From the onset of Wilson's illness in September 1919 to Harding's accession to office in March 1921, the presidency hibernated. There were no proclamations, no pardons, no bills signed into law (though twenty-eight became law without Wilson's signature); no presidential supervision of the executive branch; and no legislative initiatives. Messages were given to Mrs. Wilson to give to the president, but there is no evidence that he received them. There is also no indication that Mrs. Wilson attempted to manipulate policy. The presidency was on hold; the government drifted. Nor were Grayson, Tumulty, and Mrs. Wilson alone in the cover-up. Decades later, the editor of the *Washington Post* stated that though he was aware of the president's disability, he chose not to publish that fact, apparently on the basis that such a discussion of the president's health was an invasion of privacy.

Immediately after his stroke, Wilson had ordered that his condition be kept secret. After his improvement, which still left him severely impaired, both psychologically and physically, the president appeared to be unaware of his condition. It may be that, as Edwin Weinstein argued, Wilson suffered from the condition of anosognosia, the unawareness of disability not infrequently experienced by stroke victims.[26] Anosognosia is affected by the pattern of brain damage, but it is also influenced by whether the victim's denial is reinforced by others.[27] Although Grayson did suggest that Wilson resign, we do not know how vigorously he made the argument; we do know that, after this attempt, he gave support to the denial. Another physician, Francis X. Dercum, a Philadelphia neurologist consulted by Mrs. Wilson, recommended against resignation on the belief that leaving office would damage the president's health. Dercum was influenced in this advice by his belief that Louis Pasteur had recovered from a similar disease. This may have been the case with Pasteur. Stroke victims sometimes do recover sufficiently to permit them to take up complex and important responsibilities. This was not the case with Wilson, however, despite the fact that he may have been a particularly determined patient. As Alexander and Juliette George show, Wilson had a strong belief that he was carrying out a divine mission as president.[28] Wilson's denial was so great that he hinted that he would be willing to run again in 1920, and he was surprised when he was not nominated.

Mrs. Wilson concealed the extent of the president's illness, and she frustrated efforts to make him resign. Did Mrs. Wilson put her husband's feelings and well-being as she saw it above national interests? She may have been right that remaining in the presidency was good for the president's spirits and the activity associated with the presidency aided his general well-being. "Stress" is not a self-defining term.[29] An environment that one person would find impairing, another would experience as stimulating. Like many ambitious people in public life, Wilson had thrived on conflict. That characteristic may, however, have changed after his stroke. We cannot tell at this distance. Clearly, his ability to function as leader declined, and there is no indication that he ever regained his former vigor.

FLORENCE KLING HARDING AND WARREN GAMALIEL HARDING

Warren Harding was the public picture of health but a private portrait of illness.[30] As early as his twenty-second year, Harding suffered the first of what would eventually be five episodes of psychiatric illness. Even when apparently healthy and cheerful, he was subject to severe depression, suffering from insomnia from at least his twenties. Returning from a successful presidential trip to Alaska, and with reassurances that a minor collision in Vancouver harbor between the presidential yacht and the destroyer *Zeilen* had not put him in danger, Harding simply lay on his bed, his face in his hands. "I hope the boat sinks," he moaned.[31] Not long afterward, plagued by hypertension consequent on a life of poor health habits, and bereft of good medical or spousal care, he died suddenly at the age of fifty-seven of cardiovascular disease. His wife's reputation was such, and Harding's evident misery so obvious, that false rumors circulated that his spouse had poisoned him as an act of mercy.[32] Florence Harding's not unsympathetic biographer refers to her role and that of Harding's doctors in the president's death as negligent homicide.[33]

Warren Harding was the young, handsome, and popular newspaper editor of the Marion, Ohio, *Star*. Hardly a muckraker, Harding had as one of his policies to make sure that at least once a year every one of Marion's citizens would see his name positively mentioned in the paper. Harding disliked printing any unpleasant news, at one time expressing the wish that the paper simply not print the police reports. The future president's father remarked that it was a good thing that Warren was a man because otherwise, given his inability to say no, he would always be pregnant.

How did this easy-going, self-indulgent, but psychologically fragile man come to be senator and then president?

Florence Kling came from a family socially above the middle-class Hardings. Her reputation was damaged, however, by her wildness as a young woman, going with what was called the rough set. Over her family's strong objections she married one Henry A. De Wolfe and bore him a son, Marshall, six months after the wedding. In less than two years, De Wolfe deserted her. Florence returned in humiliation to small town Marion, Ohio (population 4,000), and took up the profession of piano teacher. It was not long, however, until she met the owner/editor of the *Star*. She pursued him aggressively:

> At a large summer picnic [Florence] spotted [Warren] across a field lying in the hay with another woman, and trotted over to interrupt their love whispers, chatting enthusiastically about the weather until Warren's friend got the hint and left. On another occasion she waited for him at the train station, where he was returning from a visit to his girlfriend Nettie Hacker. Spying her from the window, he attempted to slip out on the other side of the train. "You needn't try to run away, Warren Harding," she yelled out. "I see your big feet." She drove him away in her buggy.[34]

In 1891, Florence and Warren married. At thirty-one, she was six years older than he, had gone through a difficult marriage, and had been self-supporting for several years. She was clearly the more mature and, as will be shown, the more ambitious and determined, even ruthless. She had already virtually lost interest in her son, who had by now been all but legally adopted by her father. Her father disapproved of this marriage as well, refusing to speak to his daughter for seven years. In this regard, Florence was following a well-worn path of future first ladies, marrying "beneath them" over the objections of their parents.

Florence was determined to prove her father wrong, as she noted years later while first lady,[35] and to make up for the time she had lost in the De Wolfe fiasco. She had as a child expressed the wish to be first lady—a sentiment reflected in her statement at the reception following her marriage to Harding that she would make him president.[36]

It would be wrong, however, to consider Harding only the prey in this pursuit. There was an element of calculation in his choice of Florence as a wife. Although he did not have the driving single-minded ambition of Florence, he was ambitious, and saw in her a person who would aid him in both business and politics. Also, Florence's father, Amos Kling, was a wealthy man with strong connections to the Ohio Republican Party. Marion was dominated by Democrats, and so Harding found it difficult to find a base there. Despite Amos's strong opposition to the marriage, Harding might have believed that he would eventually come around and be an aid, though he never did. On the contrary, even years after the marriage, when Harding was running for the state senate, Amos Kling publicly repeated the persistent rumor that Harding was of partial black ancestry, and that that should prevent his being elected to any office. However, it is clear that Amos's daughter saw something very special in Harding. As a *Star* writer put it, "Destiny alone never reached out for Warren. . . . Destiny in his case had an ally in a woman—his wife"[37]

As is so often the case when one person marries another hoping to change a major part of that individual's personality or character, the marriage was not an easy one. Florence quickly and decisively took charge of the business end of the *Star* and rapidly increased its revenues. This financial improvement was not associated with an improvement in the young Harding's emotional well-being. The future president began experiencing attacks of extreme anxiety and nocturnal dyspepsia so strong that the newlyweds moved in with Harding's father, a homeopathic physician. Harding began to take trips alone, to conventions, to the Chicago World's Fair of 1893, and to Washington. Perhaps the trips were self-therapy for his frequent depression. On January 7, 1894—eighteen months after his marriage—he checked into a Seventh-Day Adventist institution for treatment, including "laughing therapy." He did not return full-time to the *Star* for another year.

During his convalescence, not only did Florence manage the *Star* superbly, she also devoted herself to Warren's care. As Mrs. Harding's principal biographer, Carl Anthony, notes:

They were genuinely a team, and whatever else might later be said for his deficiencies as a husband, his respect for her opinion and independence was part of his commitment to this unusual and capable woman. The downside of this was that she often pushed him to meet her high expectations of himself, exacerbating his nervousness only then to coddle him. To some degree, she was the tonic for the nervousness she could prompt.[38]

About this time Harding changed his wife's nickname from The Boss to The Duchess. He respected and generally followed her political advice. As one senator's wife commented, "it was Florence whom [Harding's] friends and henchmen back home came to consult."[39] Florence's ambition was greater than Warren's. In 1916 he was being touted as a dark horse candidate for the Republican presidential nomination. He wrote to a political friend that ". . . I am unsuited to the higher position if it were possible for me to attain it, and you know that I am truthful when I say that I do not desire it," noting that the "responsibilities" and the "anxieties" would be too much for him.[40] Of course, Harding would not be the first person to acquire the virus of presidential fever once exposed to it, but this statement is consistent with his attitude and behavior throughout his life. Later, in 1919, Mrs. Harding also expressed a reluctance for her husband's candidacy, citing the mental and physical demands of the office as well as the risk of losing his senate seat but, as will be shown, she was readily persuadable.

Florence struggled with Warren's drinking and especially his continual and promiscuous adultery, at one point threatening divorce, though she eventually came to tolerate the behavior. Harding often visited prostitutes (at one point apparently contracting gonorrhea), but "his dalliances were not confined to the ladies of the evening. There were the young and single, mature and widowed, even the respectably married. While thousands of husbands had such episodes, for Warren it at times almost seemed to become a pathological obsession."[41] His drinking too was excessive.

Florence did not have the reputation as an easy person. Generally agreed to be the better politician, she directed much of Warren's political career, having "a ruthless ambition to become First Lady" and constantly making "Warren work toward that end."[42] Although it would be too much to say that Mrs. Harding forced her husband into state and national politics, she did persuade him. Harding had the normal ambition of a publicly oriented man; Florence was consumed with the desire for political prominence. A reporter at the time noted that even Harding acknowledged that "his automobile was the only thing Florence did not want to run."[43] Evalyn Walsh McLean, wife of a prominent Washington newspaper owner, knew Florence better than any other person, with the possible sole exception of Warren. Later, McLean described Florence as being "like those robot men . . . going on and having a terrific force . . . a driving power, a disregard for any except what was right in her path. She had a hard streak in her, and a ruthless streak."[44] She also had a reputation for vindictiveness. Alice Roosevelt Longworth stated that Florence kept a book of names of people with whom she wanted to get even.[45] She even boasted that Warren "seemed a little afraid of her."[46]

Aside from his multiple psychiatric illnesses and several hospitalizations, Harding had serious cardiovascular problems. In a letter to his mistress Carrie Phillips on August 17, 1918, he stated that he had become seriously out of breath and dizzy during a speech. The condition was of at least three years' standing. Harding was overweight, smoked cigars and cigarettes, drank to excess, and kept late hours. He had blood in his urine as well as elevated blood pressure.[47] His personal doctor, the homeopathic physician Brigadier General Charles E. Sawyer, largely ignored the symptoms. In 1919 he advised his patient to seek the presidency. "Why hesitate?" he wrote in a letter to Harding.[48] Eventually, despite the advice of society astrologer Marcia Champney, who predicted that Harding would win the presidency but die in office, Mrs. Harding changed her earlier opposition to his candidacy and came to support her husband's seeking the nomination. She was as active in this race as in the others, drawing on her newspaper experience to make Harding's run for office the first in which the press was systematically courted and manipulated. The presidential election of 1920 was also the first in which women had the vote, and Florence responded to that fact by making it the first in which there was a selling of the prospective president's wife equal to that of the selling of the nominee.

Harding, of course, defeated James Cox in 1920. Warren's and Florence's different attitudes to the winning of the presidency were evident in their first words on being alone in the White House, as recounted by Mrs. Harding in a letter to a friend: "'Well, Warren Harding, I have got you the Presidency. What are you going to do with it?' He turned to her solemnly. 'May God help me, for I need it.' "[49]

Clearly, as the president's sister said, "Florence enjoyed being mistress of the White House better than he did being the President of the United States."[50] Warren's unhappiness was hidden from the public, but not from his close allies such as Charlie Forbes, who recounted a walk on the White House grounds after the president and Florence had had a stormy argument. There Harding "told me how unhappy he was and how empty his life had been. 'You know something of it,' he said. He wept."[51] Although Harding gave his wife cause for fear of public scandal, her efforts to control even the smallest aspects of his behavior increased in the White House to extraordinary lengths, leading to heightened friction between them. Evalyn McLean describes a golfing party involving the president that Florence insisted on joining despite her lack of interest in golf. Warren remarked that he was so relaxed that he was reluctant to return to the White House, but then:

> Into Mrs. Harding's bossy eyes there came a glitter. She spoke to him in a whisper; he replied in a gruff undertone, and she talked back. Then he began to criticize her dress, her shoes, her hat; it was a kind of fencing game with sharp words for swords. I tried to change the subject several times, to draw the sting of what I saw was smarting in two people's eyes. They continued to rasp at each other at dinner. I walked ahead with the President. "Evalyn," he said abruptly, "I'll get even with her if it's the last act of my life. Damn her soul."[52]

It would be wrong to say that anyone drove Harding to be president. He sought the office and was responsible for his own actions and for the failure of his presidency. But there were those—a group of hypocritical and self-seeking "friends" (some of whom ended up in jail for corruption after his death) and his wife—who more than encouraged this weak and self-indulgent person. Never believing himself to be intellectually up to the job of president,[53] and being correct in that self-evaluation, as well as being psychologically ill-suited to the post, Harding fell victim to those who were more clever, more ruthless, and more ambitious. Harding died from heart failure, a type of illness that can be accounted for by his age, weight, and smoking, but also a disorder aggravated by psychological distress. If his mental well-being had anything to do with his physical well-being, Harding's wife served as a negative influence.

The case of Mrs. Harding certainly supports the thesis of this chapter: that spouses act as other members of the inner circle do when what is best for the president's health conflicts with what is best for his or their political influence. Is this, however, a case of diminished responsibility? Florence was a prisoner of her time. Today she would be a political figure in her own right, with her boozy, womanizing husband relegated to the background. And how much was Warren pushed? He wanted the presidency, and although he was not the sort of person to say no, does he not bear the responsibility for assuming an office unsuited to his abilities? On the other hand, Florence was clearly the stronger character and the smarter person. Did not those superior qualities put her under a greater obligation to her husband and to the country?

Eleanor Roosevelt and Franklin Delano Roosevelt

Eleanor Roosevelt was the most prominent of all first ladies both during her husband's tenure and afterward.[54] By the time of her husband's presidency, however, she and he had drifted apart. Both received affection elsewhere, and Eleanor rarely stayed in the White House, spending most of her time either in Manhattan or in a small house on the Roosevelt New York estate, Hyde Park.[55]

It is not clear just how much influence she had upon the president. Their son, James, was his father's secretary, and he said that Eleanor was part of the kitchen cabinet.[56] On the other hand, FDR's favorite child and White House hostess, Anna, described Eleanor's and Franklin's lives as separate.[57] Eleanor had access to Franklin, but not always influence. James Roosevelt noted that his father, like all presidents, received a great deal of unsolicited advice, much of which he dismissed, but that:

> It was harder for father to disregard mother's advice. She usually had plenty of it to offer, and it generally came by wire or mail, since she usually was off somewhere. . . .

> During the Spanish Civil War mother wired father in Warm Springs. "Just received wire signed Einstein, Dorothy Thompson, etc., about important leaders trapped in Madrid. Are you or State Department doing anything?" With his sense of humor, father wired back: "State Department doing everything possible in Spain. Had successful dedi-

cation of Medical and Education buildings. Lovely weather. Much love to all of you."

James Roosevelt goes on to summarize a letter from his mother questioning FDR's characterization of Charles Lindbergh as an appeaser and his refusal to promote another lend-lease critic to general. "Father didn't even answer that one," the president's son and personal secretary commented.[58]

Some scholars have characterized Eleanor as FDR's "eyes and ears" and as his conscience.[59] This is a partial truth. Roosevelt was himself intelligent and politically acute and was surrounded by many excellent political advisers. Also, like many husbands (and many presidents), FDR heard but did not always listen. He was, however, sometimes shamed/nagged into doing what Eleanor wanted:

> Even Eleanor's most ardent admirers in the Roosevelt inner circle admitted that she pushed her husband too hard at the end of the day, when he was tired and needed to relax. "She would come in after he'd been wrestling with major problems all day long and insisted that he find a job for some unemployed actor in New York," Anna's daughter, Eleanor Seagraves, recalled. "And if he refused to do something she asked, she would come back again and again until it reached the point where he had to tell his aides to keep her away."[60]

In another context, Anna recounted:

> I remember one day when we were having cocktails. . . . A fair number of people were in the room, an informal group. . . . I was mixing cocktails. Mother always came in at the end so she would only have to have one cocktail—that was her concession. She would wolf it—she never took it slowly. She came in and sat down across the desk from Father. And she had a sheaf of papers this high and she said, "Now, Franklin, I want to talk to you about this." I have permanently blocked out of my mind what it was she wanted to bring up. I just remember, like lightning, that I thought, "Oh, God, he's going to blow." And sure enough, he blew his top. He took every single speck of that whole pile of papers, threw them across the desk at me and said, "Sis, you handle these tomorrow morning."[61]

Eleanor was embarrassed and apologized, but her temperament was such that she could not help herself. One of Roosevelt's personal physicians, Dr. Howard G. Bruenn, noted that Anna was a good influence on Franklin's well-being, "but Eleanor was a different kind of person, more driven, more insistent. She couldn't accept that he was really sick or that he needed to cut down on his activities, if they related to her concerns."[62]

The relationship between Eleanor and Franklin was not a simple one. As Doris Kearns Goodwin notes:

> Over the years, the very qualities that had first attracted Franklin and Eleanor to one another had become sources of conflict in their marriage. After initially valuing Franklin for his confidence, charm and sociability, qualities that stood in contrast to her own insecurity and shyness, Eleanor had come to see these traits as shallow and duplicitous. After being drawn to Eleanor's sincerity, honesty, and high principles, Franklin had redefined these same attributes as stiffness and inflexibility.[63]

They were close in their early years, and Eleanor was sympathetic and supportive of Franklin when he fell victim to polio in August 1921, including overseeing and organizing much of his physical therapy. But even then their personalities did not mesh. In the summer of 1924, about a year into FDR's convalescence, Eleanor, he, and several friends went on a laid-back cruise on the seventy-one–foot houseboat *Laroocco*. After two weeks, Eleanor found the sailing boring and the wind-moaning nights a little frightening. She left him in the care of her attractive friend Missy LeHand while she went to New York to attend meetings and give speeches to keep Franklin's political name alive. Against the wishes of Franklin's mother, Missy became Franklin's "wife" for months at a time. Eventually a romantic affair developed between them.

As Karen O'Connor, Bernadette Nye, and Laura Van Assendelft have noted, in many ways Eleanor functioned as a loyal vice president (as assistant director of civil defense she was the first first lady to chair an official government commission) in a period before the vice president's role had been broadened.[64] As we have seen, the president sometimes felt her a nuisance, but she did have his ear when she wanted to make her opinions known.

It has been overwhelmingly documented that Roosevelt's health in his final year not only was very bad, it was evidently and obviously very bad. Lieutenant Commander Howard G. Bruenn was one of the two military physicians attending President Roosevelt (the principal physician, Vice Admiral Ross McIntire, is generally considered to have been less involved and of lesser competence and candor than Bruenn) during the president's final thirteen months, from March 1944 to the president's death on April 12, 1945. In his official report, "Clinical Notes on the Illness and Death of President Franklin D. Roosevelt,"[65] Bruenn noted that Roosevelt had for at least two years preceding his death persistent and largely uncontrollable hypertension. In April 1944, readings reached the medical emergency level of 226/118 mm Hg. In the election month of November 1944, the reading was 260/150. Digitalis, continuous bed rest, weight loss, and sedation to achieve good night-time rest were prescribed, but only the digitalis was tolerated by the president. His medical care, given the knowledge and resources available at that time, was appropriate. His medical conditions were hypertension and associated arteriosclerosis (a disease of the arteries leading to insufficient oxygen to the brain and other organs). Among the consequences of these conditions in this sixty–two-year-old man was a variable ability to function intellectually. That is, he would have periods of competence, when he would be as intelligent and vital as he was in 1933, and then periods of severe lethargy, when he would be incapable of doing anything but staring dumbly into space. Lord Moran, Churchill's personal physician was at the Yalta Conference in early February 1945 where Churchill, Roosevelt, and Stalin met to decide many of Europe's postwar arrangements. He wrote in his diary:

> The President looked old and thin and drawn; he had a cape shawl over his shoulders and appeared shrunken; he sat looking straight ahead with his mouth open, as if he were not taking things in. Everyone was shaken by his appearance and gabbled about it afterwards.

> Everyone seemed to agree that the President had gone to bits physically. . . . It was not only his physical deterioration that had caught their attention. He intervened very little in discussions, sitting with his mouth open. . . . I doubt, from what I have seen, whether he is fit for his job here.

> He [Roosevelt] has all the symptoms of hardening of the arteries [arteriosclerosis] of the brain in an advance stage, and I give him only a few months to live.[66]

With few exceptions, his children, his political associates, foreign dignitaries, and many others were aware that after 1943 FDR was a very sick man, often unable to stay awake or to concentrate on important matters. Only the public and Roosevelt himself were kept in the dark. James told his father at the January 1945 inauguration, "Old man, you look like hell." But FDR dismissed his appearance as only normal fatigue. When James went to Dr. McIntire with the same concern, the doctor replied that "a few days will fix him up."[67]

There is also reason to believe that Roosevelt had been diagnosed in 1944 with advanced cancer associated with a malignant melanoma and had been advised by Dr. Frank H. Lahey of Boston not to run again.[68] Because no autopsy took place, or at least no results were revealed, and because Roosevelt's medical records could not be found after his death, we cannot be sure of the accuracy of this report.

Dr. McIntire kept up a public and, the evidence indicates, a private stance that the president was capable of leading the country. What about Eleanor, the president's wife?

The issue of Roosevelt's health had arisen most pointedly in the private discussions in the White House in 1944 as to whether he should run for a fourth term. Robert E. Gilbert notes that:

> Despite the President's obvious and dangerous physical decline, he agreed to accept his party's nomination in 1944 for a fourth term. Although several of his associates intended to tell Roosevelt that he was too ill to seek another term, at the last moment they failed to do so. One New York leader urged the First Lady to try to dissuade her husband from running again; but her attitude was that it would have been extremely difficult to have a transition in power at that difficult point in history, and that if the President would follow his doctor's orders, "he could stand going on with his work."[69]

Given the advice of FDR's principal physician and the fact that Eleanor was not in close contact with her husband, this was not an unreasonable statement. The statement was also colored by Eleanor's own personality. It is not surprising that she expected Franklin to follow directions and do what she believed was his duty. Eleanor privately was somewhat different from Eleanor publicly, as her son James notes in his memoir, *My Parents*:

> Elliott [another son of Eleanor's and Franklin's] has written of "the father we loved, the mother we respected." My first inclination was to differ with this. We grew to love and respect both of them. But on reflection I see there is some truth to what Elliott says. Father was able to give love more freely than mother and showed more warmth.

Father could relax and, prior to polio, romp. Mother was always stiff, never relaxed enough to romp. She was a formal person who wore starched dresses to her neck. She found it easier to give than to get, to do for than to have done for her. Mother loved all mankind, but she did not know how to let her children love her.[70]

James then recounts how Eleanor described how her youngest son, Elliott, still a child, fell into a fire while he was wearing medical body braces:

Writing father in Washington, she began by speaking of "the splendid cruise" she'd had to St. Andrews's and went on with other chitchat before even getting around to the accident. "When I got home I found that poor baby Elliott had fallen into the ashes of a fire the children had on the beach." We had been burning litter and the beach now looked quite nice, she noted. As for Elliott, well, 'The ashes got under the strops of his braces and burned . . . but he only cried a little. . . . Nurse says they are only skin burns. . . ."[71]

James Roosevelt bitterly, and probably accurately, stated that the fourth term race was his father's death warrant. In this evaluation he was at least partially joined by his sister Anna, who was FDR's almost constant companion in the final White House years. Early in 1944 she had approached McIntire with severe concern about her father's health and been reassured, though she continued to note his appearance and continued to worry. Thus, Eleanor had medical, if not visual, support for her wish for Franklin to run in 1944. The point may have been moot. She publicly denied ever having been asked about his running by Franklin himself.[72]

Roosevelt lasted only a few months into his fourth term, a period that included the disastrous Yalta Conference, which he attended often in a daze. Had Roosevelt declined to run, the Democrats would likely have nominated William O. Douglas, Harry Truman, or James Byrnes—all strong choices. The Republicans nominated Thomas Dewey, another good choice. America probably needed the Roosevelt of 1932, but not the Roosevelt of 1944. At best, Mrs. Roosevelt's influence on his decision, if she had been given the opportunity of exercising it, would have been—to judge by her comments to the New York leader—mistaken as to what was in her husband's and the country's best interest, and at worst self-serving. In any event, she followed the pattern of all but a few in the inner circle.

Mamie Doud Eisenhower and Dwight David Eisenhower

Eisenhower's health is the best documented of any President's.[73] This is due in part to Eisenhower's policy of relative openness, the careful keeping of records, the making of many records available by his care-givers, and in part to the careful work of scholars, especially Robert Ferrell[74] and Clarence G. Lasby.[75] Eisenhower suffered through much of his life from severe intestinal disorders and in the final dec-ades of his life from heart disease and stroke. These problems may have been associated with his strong Type A personality, evidenced by never napping, taking vacations only under orders, and displaying a strong temper throughout his life. He was also a four-pack-of-Camels-a-day smoker into middle age. Though medical opinion is not in full agreement as to the relation of stress to Eisenhower's three major illness—-the heart attack in 1955, the ileitis in 1956, and the stroke in 1957—some argue that they were "all typical of the 'immod-erate' worker."[76]

His wife, Mamie, was also frequently ill, principally through what was described as a weak heart. Being an army wife was difficult for her. She was one of four daughters of moderately wealthy parents who kept a staff of four and entertained frequently. The girls were catered to. The eighteen-year-old Mary Geneva Doud (always called Mamie) met in 1914 and the following year wed the twenty-five-year-old second lieutenant Dwight David Eisenhower (always called Ike). His monthly salary was $141.67, and he was gently told by his pro-spective in-laws that he and Mamie would be financially on their own.[77] Stephen Ambrose writes that, after their marriage, Ike and Mamie:

> settled into Ike's three room [Bachelors' Office Quarters]. He concen-trated on his work; she concentrated on him. Ike had a firm expectation about his wife's role, which was to center her life around his. That suited Mamie. She was six years his junior; she had been trained for such a role in her Denver finishing school; she had watched her mother devote herself to pleasing her father. . . .
>
> Best of all she never complained, although she had much she might have complained about. In the first thirty-five years of their marriage, they moved thirty-five times [seven times in one year]. Not until 1953 did they have a home [at Gettysburg, Pennsylvania] that they could call their own. Until World War II, with one exception, in 1918, he

was never the [Commanding Officer], so she always had to defer to someone else's wife. His progress in the Army, after World War I, was excruciatingly slow. She had to manage the money to the penny, and watched as he turned down numerous offers for civilian employment at substantially higher salaries. But she never nagged him to leave the Army, never told him that the time had come to make something of himself.[78]

Because she could afford to and because she found the life of a peacetime army officer's wife sometimes difficult, Mamie returned frequently to her parents' home in Denver.[79] Her health was always frail, and in middle age she developed a disease affecting her carotid sinus, which damaged her sense of balance, making her stumble and fall and sometimes bump into objects. This behavior, combined with her habit of lying in bed well into the day, led to the false rumors that she was alcoholic.[80]

The Eisenhowers' relationship was sometimes tense. For example, it appears that on Eisenhower's return to the United States in 1945 to become chief of staff, Mamie was not willing to join him at the luxurious Fort Myers, Virginia, residence that went with the position. Records suggest that she was drugged with phenobarbital by Eisenhower's personal physician, Dr. Howard M. Snyder, to accomplish the move.[81] On the other hand, Mamie appeared to care greatly for her husband, especially about his health.

Perhaps she cared too much. The record is of a wife who fussed/obsessed/nagged/was controlling/was dedicated to the care of her husband. It is worth quoting Clarence Lasby, Eisenhower's health biographer, at some length here:

> "Dr. Mamie," as Snyder referred to her in private, was confident enough to make a medical determination in virtually every circumstance. . . .

> Whatever the case, Mamie wanted to act when she detected a problem, and generally she would go to her doctor to enlist his support. She asked him to direct the president to call his bridge game when she thought he was tense. She asked him to return to the White House to check Ike when he had a headache. She asked him to give him more or fewer pills depending upon her reading of the situation. And she "raised hell" with Snyder if he did something she considered ill advised. . . .

The president responded in many ways to his wife's attentiveness. Sometimes he did as she asked; sometimes he ignored her; sometimes he stayed up for only a little while, hoping to pacify her; sometimes he was contrary as when he would go to bed after she asked him to stay up or eat when she wanted him to wait; and sometimes he would leave for another room, as on an afternoon when he was sitting drinking his beer and she turned down his lip and said, "See, Howard [Dr. Snyder], how purple it is." On many more occasions, however, he became irritated and angry about her "dictating" to him. On a winter day in 1958 he was grouching about a cold, condemning all doctors in no uncertain terms, and told Mamie at lunch that he wanted to go to Thomasville [Secretary of the Treasury George Humphrey's plantation where Eisenhower liked to hunt]. "She immediately took exception to it and tried to persuade him to delay departure until Thursday," Snyder noted. "He agreed; however, he flew off in a rage and went into his dressing room, where he remained all afternoon. He would have no part of Mamie. She was quite alarmed for fear his anger would induce a recurrence of cerebral trouble [which he had experienced in November 1957], but there was nothing she could do to correct the initial reaction. . . . The irony was that despite her good intentions, Mamie became the most frequent and lasting source of her husband's anger.[82]

Though Mamie was quick to criticize the president and his doctors, she was reluctant to take on any direct responsibility for his health care. For example, in May 1956, Eisenhower was diagnosed as having a severe constriction of the intestine associated with ileitis. After he began to experience strong discomfort, the doctors not only sought Eisenhower's agreement to perform surgery but also asked Mamie to sign permission papers. For reasons we do not know, she declined, and so his son, John, did so.[83] Although she did not express strong opinions one way or another about Nixon, Mamie asked Dr. Snyder to request the president to stop campaigning for Nixon because "he might pop a cork."[84] There was reason for concern. Snyder claims that Eisenhower suffered from ventricular fibrillation during his campaign for Nixon.[85]

In some ways it is odd that she so often enlisted Snyder's help, for Eisenhower—a good patient once convinced of what his health required—was hardly respectful of Snyder. Once the president was playing golf, with Snyder as part of the party. Eisenhower was in one of his Type A angry moods, and his game was not going well:

by the seventeenth green he was doing abominably. He made a bad explosion shot out of the trap and Snyder yelled, "Fine shot!" He became livid with rage and shouted back, "Fine shot, hell, you son of a bitch," and threw his wedge at the doctor. The staff of the club fortunately wrapped itself around Snyder's shins and the heavy iron wedge missed him; otherwise he would have had a fractured leg. The president apologized perfunctorily and said, "Oh, pardon me."[86]

What, then, was Mamie's reaction when Eisenhower contemplated running for a second term, something he had said he would never do? Did she have or try to exert any influence? The Eisenhowers followed a strict division of labor. He was responsible for the public part of their life; she, for the home and family. Each was firm in maintaining the division. Once, for example, when the White House chief housekeeper, J. B. West, presented Mamie with a luncheon menu that the president had approved, Mamie sharply told him, "I run everything in my house. In the future all menus are to be approved by me and no one else."[87]

Eisenhower, like Mamie, did not like his plans interfered with, but he was also careful in consulting those he trusted before making major decisions. In January 1955, he arranged a secret dinner party of a group of intimates to discuss the possibility of his seeking a second term. The guest list consisted of Secretary of State John Foster Dulles, Media Spokesman James Hagerty, Chief of Staff Sherman Adams, Senator Henry Cabot Lodge, Republican Party Leader Leonard Hall, long-time friend and presidential aide Wilton Persons, political intimate Arthur Summerfield, Treasury Secretary George Humphrey, Attorney General Herbert Brownell, political adviser Thomas Stephens, and his brother, Milton Eisenhower. This was "the gang," as they were known to one another, the people Eisenhower most trusted politically. All were aware of the severity of Eisenhower's heart attack of September 24, 1955. We know, though the "gang" may not have known, that Eisenhower felt medically able to run and desired to do so. We also know that getting an approval from Dr. Paul Dudley White would take some manipulation on Eisenhower's part. We also know that Eisenhower would suffer a stroke not long after his inauguration.

With the exception of brother Milton, all were the president's subordinates. With the exception of Milton (and later Eisenhower's son, John), all said the country needed him, though they acknowledged that there were both political and health risks associated with his earlier heart attack. Later, Eisenhower's good friend George Allen also recommended against running.

Mamie was not at the meeting, but, like her son and George Allen, she was consulted. Scholars agree that she wanted him to run. Robert Ferrell writes that Mamie explicitly recommended running because inactivity would be bad for his heart.[88] If so, she must have been thinking of frustration, because Eisenhower was one of the most exercise-conscious of individuals, maintaining his West Point cadet weight up to and beyond his sixties. Clarence Lasby writes that Mamie believed that leaving the presidency would not only damage Eisenhower's health, but would even be fatal.[89]

Eisenhower did run, of course, was elected, but suffered a stroke, a disease that with some individuals is associated with stress, in November 1957. It is hard to argue that the presidency was good or bad therapy for Eisenhower, aside from the question as to whether the presidency should ever be used as personal therapy.

LADY BIRD JOHNSON AND LYNDON BAINES JOHNSON

For one of the least controversial first ladies, opinions about Lady Bird Johnson differ considerably.[90] Jackie Kennedy despised her as much as Jack despised Lyndon. Mrs. Kennedy was once heard to comment contemptuously that Lady Bird "would crawl down Pennsylvania Avenue on broken glass for Lyndon."[91] On the other hand, a survey of historians by the Sienna Research Institute in 1983 ranked Lady Bird third best among all first ladies, just behind Eleanor Roosevelt and Abigail Adams.[92] The two evaluations had something in common: both were true. Lady Bird Johnson was a shy and insecure twenty-two-year-old woman who, after two months of largely telephone courtship, married on November 17, 1934, probably the least shy and least insecure of all American presidents. Although she subordinated her life to her husband's career throughout that marriage, she always showed due concern for the good of the country and stood up for individuals who she thought were being ill treated.

Lady Bird's political education began immediately after their brief honeymoon. Lyndon gave her a list of the counties and their political leaders and other politically relevant facts in the constituency of the

congressman for whom he was then working and told her to memo-
rize them. Brought up in a well-to-do family where she was well
cared for, she had to adjust herself to a congressional aide's salary,
keep house, and learn to cook for an almost constant stream of sur-
prise guests. She also volunteered, as Lyndon expected, to borrow
against her inheritance for whatever Lyndon's (and by extension, her)
career needed. Nor was Lyndon an accommodating or agreeable husband. With her, as with so many of his intimates, he was a bully.

   As Betty Boyd Caroli recounts, at the very beginning of their
honeymoon while visiting friends, Lyndon noted that Lady Bird had
a run in one of her stockings and that she should go and change. She
hesitated, he again told her to leave immediately, which she did.
Lyndon had a long list of clothes she should and should not wear,
and was willing to talk about her publicly in ways that almost any
woman would find embarrassing.[93] Like many presidents, Lyndon
Johnson was a philanderer, but Lady Bird stands alone as being publicly sympathetic, bordering on approving, of this behavior:

> Barbara Walters inquired of Lady Bird [in February 1974, about a year
> after Lyndon died] about [Lyndon's] reputation as a "flirt and ladies'
> man." The ex-First Lady replied, "Lyndon was a people lover and that
> certainly did not exclude half the people of the world—women." When
> Walters persisted, asking "How did you handle it?," Lady Bird replied
> in a way that must have diminished considerably her stock with femi-
> nist listeners: "I hope that I was reasonable. And if all those ladies had
> some good points that I didn't have, I hope I had the good sense to try
> to learn a bit from it."[94]

But if Lady Bird was soft and subservient to Lyndon, she was not
otherwise a weak or inconsequential person. She managed his congressional office briefly during the early days of World War II and
was deeply involved in the management and building of what was to
become the Johnson's multi-million–dollar Texas Broadcasting Cor-
poration. She had no political or policy axes to grind, only to support
her husband. Lady Bird did have personal opinions, however, which
she expressed forcefully. For example, when a long-time political
aide of the president, who was also a friend of the family, Walter
Jenkins, was arrested in Washington for homosexual behavior, Lyndon remained quiet, seeing how the wind would blow. Lady Bird
immediately and without Lyndon's approval went to the *Washington
Post* with a personal statement of loyalty to Jenkins.

Health considerations figured strongly in LBJ's decisions about whether to run in 1964 and 1968. He had suffered a serious heart attack in 1955 and had long believed that he would die prematurely—he did die suddenly from a heart attack in 1973 at the age of sixty-four—as had so many men in his family. Johnson was influenced in these considerations by his wife, Lady Bird, who was his close political adviser. She stands alone among first ladies for advising her husband twice on whether his health should prevent him from running. In 1964 she advised him to run; in 1968, not to run.

Johnson stated in his memoirs that he was uncertain in 1964 whether his health would last through a term in office. He believed that the "strain of my work in the Senate had helped to bring on my severe heart attack when I was only forty-six. Now I was nine years older."[95] On May 14, 1964, a private medical conference was called including Drs. George Burkley, Larry Lamb, Janet Travell, and the Johnson's closest medical friend, Dr. James Cain of the Mayo Clinic.[96] Lady Bird said she wanted to be there to assist in their deliberations. She had previously written out a nine-page analysis for Lyndon of the pros and cons of his running. She had also written out a draft statement (which she hoped he would not use) in which the president would decline to run; contained in that statement were spaces for the inclusion of medical reasons. Lady Bird noted in the analysis that Lyndon "may die earlier if he continues in the role of the presidency and works as hard as he has been." She then went on to give other reasons for running—good of the country, regard of their friends and supporters—but then speculated on LBJ's possible post-presidential depression and frustration, returning to the question of death in office:

> Last, he might live longer if he didn't run for the Presidency. Who can tell? And if he did, would it be worth it?
> My final conclusion was that I thought he ought to run, facing clearly all the criticisms and hostilities that would come our way, pacing himself as well as his personality will permit, with Sundays off and occasional vacations, and then three years and nine months from now, February or March 1968, if the Lord lets him live that long, announce that he won't be a candidate for reelection. By that time, I think the juices of life will be sufficiently stilled in him.[97]

In an informal meeting that evening with Drs. Cain and Willis Hurst, the two physicians speculated to Lady Bird, before the physi-

cal examination, that the psychological aspects of Johnson's leaving
the presidency—inaction, frustration—would be harder on the fifty-
six-year-old president than the stresses of the presidency. We do not
have a record of the results of the physical examination. In a subsequent memorandum to her husband, Lady Bird suggested that not
only would retirement be bad for his psychological health but also
"Your friends would be frozen in embarrassed silence and your enemies jeering."[98] He should run, she said.

In his memoirs, Johnson comments that though he very much respected Lady Bird's opinion on this as on other matters, he was not
convinced.[99] From May 14 to 3 P.M. on August 25, 1964, Johnson
wrote that he looked at both sides of the question of running, consulting widely, deciding to run only after the Democratic convention had
convened in Atlantic City. It is not clear from the record how much
health considerations, as opposed to political ones, figured in his
delay.

Lady Bird's advice was accurate in terms of LBJ's physical health
during his first term. In that period Johnson suffered only from a
sessile polyp in his throat, which was removed, and required gall
bladder surgery. Neither procedure damaged Johnson's ability to
carry out the duties of the presidency. The racial and anti-Vietnam
war unrest that plagued the country in the late 1960s had, however, a
devastating effect on his emotional and mental well-being. Johnson's
brother, Sam, stated that Johnson looked very ill and suffered from
sleeplessness. By 1968, aides described the president as "old," "bat-
tered," "drained," "pallid," and "aged."[100] Johnson in his memoirs
stated that "Of all the 1886 nights I was President, there were not
many when I got to sleep before 1 or 2 A.M. and there were few
mornings when I didn't wake up by 6 or 6:30."[101] It is difficult to
believe that the 1964–68 presidency was good therapy for Johnson.

By 1967 Johnson was convinced that he could not live through
another term.[102] Lady Bird agreed, but she wanted medical support.
In a discussion on October 20, 1967, with Dr. Cain, who was a house-
guest in the White House, Lady Bird recorded in her diary that "I
told [James Cain] my feelings—that I did not want to go through the
grueling six months of another campaign, and that even more, if we
should win I did not want to face another four years as devouring as
these last four have been. . . . And for the first time in my life I
believe that Lyndon, too, could be happy [in retirement]."

She then turned to fear of a stroke, and continued:

But what I do not know is whether I could endure having Lyndon face the sort of trial that President Wilson did—that is, to be in office, to be incapacitated, or reduced to half his mental and physical abilities while still being President. . . . I asked Jim [Cain] frankly, as a medical man, what advice he could give me. He said "Obviously he has aged. The last four years have taken a lot out of him . . . but I cannot say, as I think the doctors should have said to FDR when he ran for his fourth term, that he won't live out this next term, that he won't be able to serve as he should. No man can say what will happen." . . . And so the dilemma continues.[103]

The fear of stroke was also prominent in Lyndon's considerations. He later wrote:

I did not fear death so much as I feared disability. Whenever I walked through the Red Room and saw the portrait of Woodrow Wilson hanging there, I thought of him stretched out upstairs in the White House, powerless to move, with the machinery of the American government in disarray around him. And I remember Grandmother Johnson, who had had a stroke and stayed in a wheelchair throughout my childhood, unable even to move her hands or to speak so that she could be understood.[104]

Two and a half months later, in January 1968, Lyndon and Lady Bird met with their old friends and allies John and Nellie Connally. Once governor of Texas and formerly as deeply involved in public life as Lyndon, Connally had retired from politics. He and Nellie were clearly happy. In response to Lyndon's request for advice, Connally said that, after retiring, at first "You are sad. You almost feel like you are dead. And then when that time passes, there is a great wave of relief."[105]

Lady Bird kept to her earlier belief that Johnson should not run again, and Johnson took Lady Bird's advice once again, which was consistent with his own inclinations. Unlike the other first ladies and unlike her advice on the 1964 race, Lady Bird did *not* follow the typical inner circle pattern of advocating running regardless of health considerations.

PRESIDENTS' WIVES AND HEALTH ADVICE: THE PATTERN

Those close to ambitious people tend to share in the goals of those persons for both emotional and material reasons. For many people, particularly the ambitious, losing their job is like losing their life. They are not likely to want to hear a recommendation for withdrawal, even if they ask for candor, and their advisers are not likely to make such a recommendation. We also know that although there may be heavy costs in being close to a president, most seek that closeness and few want to relinquish it. The emotional, symbolic, and material rewards of the Oval Office are very high. At least as important, those close to the president typically like and admire him and believe that he is by far the best leader for the country.

With the possible exception of Harding, each of the presidents examined here appeared to want very much to be president. Again excepting Harding, in each of the cases the leader was willing to put aside the question as to whether the stress of the office would damage his health in order to achieve and to retain the office. Their political intimates undoubtedly sensed that desire, and acceded to it. In each case, moreover, there was no firm medical opinion to the contrary. Finally, close associates often do not recognize changes in behavior or appearance; they see the president so often, and the change may be so gradual.

It is possible, however, that the position of the president's wife would be different enough to result in different advice. Typically, the marital relationship is longer than that of others and far more inti-mate. The emotional bond is likely to be stronger, and unlike that of other members of the inner circle, the first lady's relationship to the president will continue after he leaves office. That is, she will not lose her job quite in the same way as other members of the inner circle would.

We looked at the role of five first ladies regarding health-related political advice to their spouses. We wanted five in the twentieth century, so that the medical context would be roughly similar, and selected only among the deceased presidents, so that the records would be more nearly complete. From that group, those presidencies for which the scholarship was the strongest were chosen. Uninten-tionally, the resultant list produced five distinct types of first lady role: as protector (Edith Wilson), as manager (Florence Harding), as adviser (Eleanor Roosevelt), as supporter (Mamie Eisenhower), and as colleague and friend (Lady Bird Johnson).

To repeat: the pattern of inner circle health advice as demonstrated in Post and Robins, *When Illness Strikes the Leader*, was one of encouragement to the leader to seek and to stay in office, largely regardless of the state of, or the consequences to, the leader's health. That analysis mostly looked at political advisers and healthcare givers.

The first question that arises is whether the first lady's opinion was given and whether it mattered significantly to the president. It is possible that the first lady might be a member of the political inner circle, but not someone who would offer health advice or whom the president would listen to in health matters. This varied. Edith Wilson, though acting as president in many respects during her husband's stroke-induced disability, cared little for policy matters, but she certainly was at the center of determining whether her husband's medical condition would be made public and whether he would be fully apprised of his own condition. Florence Harding seems to have largely lost interest in her husband's career once he became president, and had little interest in his health after the first years of their marriage. Harding's psychological problems, and possibly his physical ones as well, were almost surely exacerbated by her pressure on him. Eleanor Roosevelt's influence on her husband, especially in his final years, is not clear. More than any other first lady, she was a public political influence in her own right. On the other hand, there is good reason to believe that her husband was not always among her followers. What we do know, however, is that she was among those who supported, or by her own words would have supported, the evidently ill Roosevelt's running again in 1944, though we do not know whether she was sufficiently close to FDR for that advice to matter. Mamie Eisenhower was a close and worried observer of her husband's health, though probably not always with positive results. She made no effort to advise her husband on purely political matters. She recommended that Eisenhower run in both elections, though Eisenhower was almost certainly most influenced by the advice of his long-time political and family friends. Lady Bird Johnson, who was a very close personal adviser to LBJ, stands alone as recommending that her husband not run a second time for reasons of health. Among first ladies, Lady Bird appears best at balancing her spouse's health needs, the country's needs, and her husband's ambition.

The pattern is not completely uniform, though it has a clear tendency. Different first ladies have given different reasons to a medically weak president for seeking and staying in office, and this advice has probably been the product of a variety of motivations, most probably mixed. Reasons offered by first ladies have been the same as those of other presidential intimates: principally that leaving the presidency would be bad for the president's health and/or the country. The bottom line is that, with only one exception, presidents have heard only one advice from their spouses: get in office and stay there as long as you can.

THE TWENTY-FIFTH AMENDMENT: THE PRESIDENT'S SPOUSE AND A CONTESTED "REMOVAL"

Experience suggests that a first lady is not likely to be a supporter in removing her husband from office. Nor, we would assume, would a first gentleman. But all generalizations can be modified by circumstances. Let us examine five contested presidential "removal" scenarios with reference to the spouse's behavior. That behavior will be substantially driven by what the spouse sees as her role.

Contested Removal with a First Spouse as Protector

This was the role that Edith Wilson assumed. Here the wife (extension the husband) will see her duty to be to subordinate all other considerations to the emotional well-being of her husband. Because the removal is being contested by, among others, the president, the wife will fully join in whatever deceptions or maneuvers are necessary for the continuation of the president in office. It is possible that the spouse may try privately to persuade the president, or have others persuade the president, to relinquish office. But as long as the president himself chooses to fight removal, she will stand by him.

Contested Removal with a First Spouse as Manager

This was how Florence Harding saw her relationship to her husband. The spouse will be independent, considering the wishes of the president as only one factor in coming to a decision. Perhaps she will consider the president's desires and interests in the light of how he would consider them "if he were really himself." Perhaps her personal interests will dominate; perhaps those of the country; or perhaps that of some group. Whatever her policy may be, she will attempt to direct the outcome.

Contested Removal with a First Spouse as Adviser

Eleanor Roosevelt filled this role. Advisers are not partners. Unless they are in fact covert managers, they are manipulators. They give their opinions based on whatever knowledge and values they have. The influence of advisers, including first spouses as advisers, depends on their wisdom and their relationship to the person advised. As has been shown here, the wisdom of the spouse and the access to the president has varied greatly. A first lady like Lady Bird Johnson will have great influence; one like Mamie Eisenhower will not. Of course, the president may not be in a condition to receive advice. A spouse accustomed to being an adviser may not be willing to make public statements, though the principal example here, Eleanor Roosevelt, would likely have done so.

Contested Removal with a First Spouse as Supporter

Mamie Eisenhower exemplified the first spouse as supporter. This is different from a protector (for example, Edith Wilson) in that the supporter's relationship is direct but limited; more passive than active when it comes to political matters, but more active than passive in matters dealing directly with the president's personal well-being, especially his health. Though Mamie Eisenhower was not as assertive in political matters as Edith Wilson was, she was very involved with her husband's health. It is much easier to imagine Mrs. Eisenhower's advocating the removal of her dangerously ill husband against his wishes than Mrs. Wilson's.

Contested Removal with a First Spouse as Partner

Lady Bird Johnson was her husband's partner more than any other president's wife we have examined. As with all the instances cited, the details of the circumstances will be important. How strongly does the president feel about the removal? What is the nature of the disability? What are the opinions of other confidants? Her opinions, however, will likely be closer to those of her husband than those of any other first spouse because they probably jointly came to the decision to resist. If, however, the problem involves a sudden and major change in presidential personality (as due to stroke or brain trauma), then her influence will likely be closer to what the "real" president would have wanted than what the "acting" one seeks.

CONCLUSION

Any effort to remove a resisting sitting president will be fraught with high conflict and high drama. All the players—in Congress, in the judiciary, and in the White House—will have influence. Only the president's spouse will be able to claim a special relationship to the chief. That relationship and that person will be powerful, even decisive.

Do any policy recommendations flow from this analysis? No, in terms of constitutional or legal change. Yes, in terms of public awareness. The president/spouse relationship is so variable and intimate that any law attempting to govern it would be both ineffective and unpredictable in its consequences. The election of a president, however, generally involves the "election" of a first spouse. Thus, it is appropriate that the public be informed, to the extent possible, as to the working arrangement between president and spouse. That relationship can be decisive in a variety of situations, including a health crisis involving the possible removal of a president from the exercise of power.

NOTES

1. The leading sources on presidential wives are Carl S. Anthony, *First Ladies: The Saga of the Presidents' Wives*, 2 vols. (New York: William Morrow, 1991); Betty Boyd Caroli, *First Ladies* (New York: Oxford University Press, 1993); L. Gould, "Modern First Ladies and the Presidency," *Presidential Studies Quarterly*, 20 (1990), 677–83; Peter Hay, *All the Presidents' Ladies: Anecdotes of the Women Behind the Men in the White House* (New York: Penguin Books, 1988); Nancy E. McGlen and Karen O'Connor, *Women, Politics, and American Society* (Englewood Cliffs, N.J.: Prentice-Hall, 1995); Karen O'Connor, Bernadette Nye, and Laura Van Assendelft, "Wives in the White House: The Political Influence of First Ladies," *Presi-*

dential Studies Quarterly, 26, No. 3 (Summer 1996), 835–53; James S. Rose-bush, *First Lady, Public Wife: A Behind-the-Scenes History of the Evolving Role of First Ladies in American Public Life* (Lanham, Md.: Madison Books, 1987); I. W. Scobie, "American First Ladies and the Question of Identity," *Journal of Women's History*, 7 (Winter 1995), 137–50; Margaret Truman, *First Ladies* (New York: Random House, 1995).

Leading sources on illness in the presidency are Kenneth R. Crispell and Carlos F. Gomez, *Hidden Illness in the White House* (Durham, N.C.: Duke University Press, 1988); Robert H. Ferrell, *Ill-Advised: Presidential Health and Public Trust* (Columbia: University of Missouri Press, 1992); Robert E. Gilbert, *The Mortal Presidency*, 2nd ed. (New York: Fordham University Press, 1998); Bert E. Park, *The Impact of Illness on World Leaders* (Philadelphia: University of Pennsylvania Press, 1986); Jerrold Post, M.D., and Robert S. Robins, *When Illness Strikes the Leader: The Dilemma of the Captive King* (New Haven, Conn.: Yale University Press, 1993).

2. B. Rensberger, "Amphetamines Used by a Physician to Lift Moods of Famous Patients," *New York Times*, December 4, 1972. See also the discussion in Post and Robins, *When Illness Strikes the Leader*, pp. 69, 70.

3. For concealments, see especially Ferrell, *Ill-Advised*, and Gilbert, *Mortal Presidency*.

4. Gilbert, *Mortal Presidency*; and especially Robert E. Gilbert, "The Political Effects of Presidential Illness: The Case of Lyndon B. Johnson," *Political Psychology*, 16, No. 4 (December 1995), 761–76.

5. Clarence. G. Lasby, *Eisenhower's Heart Attack: How Ike Beat Heart Disease and Held On to the Presidency* (Lawrence: University Press of Kansas, 1997).

6. See Robert E. Gilbert, "Personality, Stress and Achievements: Keys to Presidential Longevity," *Presidential Studies Quarterly*, 15 (Winter 1985), 33–50; and Robert. S. Robins and Robert M. Dorn, "Stress and Political Leadership" *Politics and the Life Sciences*, 12, No. 1 (February 1993), 3–17.

7. Anastasia Kucharski, "On Being Sick and Famous," *Political Psychology*, 5 (1984), 69–82; Anastasia Kucharski, "Medical Management of Political Patients," *Perspectives in Biology and Medicine*, 22 (1978), 115–26.

8. See the sections on political leader care in Post and Robins, *When Illness Strikes the Leader*, pp. 64–77.

9. Ibid., pp. 78–120.

10. A good example of a parallel situation is described in Hugh Berrington, "When Does Personality Make a Difference? Lord Cherwell and the Area Bombing of Germany," *International Political Science Review*, 10, No. 1 (1989), 9–34. Berrington notes (p. 9), "If you are going to have a scientist in a position of isolated power, the only scientist among non-scientists, is dangerous *whoever he is.*" See also C. P. Snow, *Science and Government* (Oxford: Oxford University Press, 1961).

11. For a discussion of the question of ethics regarding the president's health care, see Robert S. Robins and Henry Rothschild, "Ethical Dilemmas of the President's Physician," *Politics and the Life Sciences*, 7 (1988) 3–11; and Post and Robins, *When Illness Strikes the Leader*, pp. 206–209.

12. As quoted in O'Connor, Nye, and Van Assendelft, "Wives in the White House," 836.

13. As quoted in Caroli, *First Ladies*, p. 150.

14. The argument of this chapter is that the behavior of the first ladies regarding the presidents' health was largely the same as that of other members of the inner circle—they wanted, above everything else, to make and then to keep the president, president. In this respect, the office of the first lady is different from that of the vice president, with which it has been usefully compared. O'Connor, Nye, and Van Assendelft, "Wives in the White House."

15. This section relies not only on the sources listed in note 1, but also on Alexander L. George and Juliette L. George, *Woodrow Wilson and Colonel House: A Personality Study* (New York: John Day, 1956); Cary Grayson, *Woodrow Wilson: An Intimate Memoir* (New York: Holt, Rinehart, and Winston, 1960); Alden Hatch, *Edith Bolling Wilson: First Lady Extraordinary* (New York: Dodd, Mead, 1961); A. Link et al., *The Papers of Woodrow Wilson*, vol. 64 (Princeton, N.J.: Princeton University Press, 1991); Joseph P. Tumulty, *Woodrow Wilson as I Know Him* (Garden City, N.Y.: Doubleday, 1921); Judith L. Weaver, "Edith Bolling Wilson as First Lady: A Study in the Power of Personality," *Presidential Studies Quarterly*, 15, No. 1 (Winter 1985), 51–76; Edwin A. Weinstein, *Woodrow Wilson: A Medical and Psychological Biography* (Princeton, N.J.: Princeton University Press, 1981); Edith Bolling Wilson, *My Memoir* Indianapolis: Bobbs-Merrill, 1939).

16. Weaver, "Edith Bolling Wilson as First Lady."

17. Chauncey D. Leake, "Presidential Responsibility, Succession, and Tragedy: Woodrow Wilson, 1856–1924," *Military Medicine*, 30 (February 1965), 129–36.

18. Ibid., 132.

19. Ray S. Baker, *Woodrow Wilson: Life and Letters*, vol. 6 (New York: Doubleday, Doran, and Company, 1940), pp. 292–93.

20. Edwin A. Weinstein, "Denial of Presidential Disability: A Case Study of Woodrow Wilson," *Psychiatry*, 30 (November 1967), 380.

21. Link et al., eds., *Papers of Woodrow Wilson*, p. 363.

22. John B. Moses and Wilbur Cross, *Presidential Courage* (New York: W. W. Norton, 1980), p. 161.

23. Bert E. Park, "Presidential Disability," *Politics and the Life Sciences*, 7 (August 1988), 50–66.

24. Tumulty, *Woodrow Wilson as I Know Him*.

25. Grayson, *Woodrow Wilson*, p. 53.
26. Weinstein, "Denial of Presidential Disability," 376–91; Weinstein, *Woodrow Wilson*.
27. Weinstein, "Denial of Presidential Disability," 379.
28. George and George, *Woodrow Wilson and Colonel House*.
29. Robins and Dorn, "Stress and Political Leadership."
30. This section relies not only on the sources listed in note 1 but princi-pally on Carl S. Anthony, *Florence Harding: The First Lady, the Jazz Age, and the Death of America's Most Scandalous President* (New York: William Morrow, 1998) and also on Samuel H. Adams, *Incredible Era: The Life and Times of Warren Gamaliel Harding* (Boston: Houghton-Mifflin, 1939); Nan Britten, *The President's Daughter* (New York: Elizabeth Ann Guild, 1927); Robert H. Ferrell, *The Strange Deaths of President Harding* (Columbia: Uni-versity of Missouri Press, 1996); Evalyn Walsh McLean, *Father Struck It Rich* (Boston: Little, Brown, 1936); Francis Russell, *The Shadow of Bloom-ing Grove: Warren G. Harding in His Times* (New York: McGraw-Hill, 1968); H. M. Daugherty and Thomas Dixon, *The Inside Story of the Harding Trag-edy* (New York: The Churchill Company, 1932); Alice Roosevelt Longworth, *Crowded Hours* (New York: Charles Scribner's Sons, 1933).
31. Russell, *Shadow of Blooming Grove*, p. 588.
32. Ferrell, *Ill-Advised*, p. 27.
33. Anthony, *Florence Harding*, pp. 453–76.
34. Ibid., pp. 36, 37.
35. Ibid., p. 340.
36. O'Connor, Nye, and Van Assendelft, "Wives in the White House," 839.
37. Anthony, *Florence Harding*, p. 48.
38. Ibid., p. 54.
39. Ibid., p. 126
40. Ibid., p. 129.
41. Ibid., p. 59. Anthony and Farrell, *Ill-Advised*, differ substantially on the amount of Harding's womanizing and the relative extent of corruption in his administration. The question of degree aside, it appears that sexual promiscuity by Harding and corruption among some of his associates were prominent features of his life and his administration.
42. Caroli, *First Ladies*, p. 159.
43. As quoted in ibid., p. 153.
44. Anthony, *Florence Harding*, p. 137.
45. Caroli, *First Ladies*, p. 159.
46. Anthony, *Florence Harding*, p. 340.
47. Ibid., p. 218.
48. Ibid., p. 163.

49. As quoted in ibid., p. 261.

50. As quoted in ibid., p. 267.

51. As quoted in ibid., p. 351.

52. As quoted in ibid., pp. 284, 285.

53. Gilbert, *Mortal Presidency*, p. 12.

54. This section relies not only on the sources listed in note 1 but also on Maurine Beaseley, *Eleanor Roosevelt and the Media: The Quest for Self-Fulfillment* (Chicago: The University of Chicago Press, 1987); Doris Kearns Goodwin, *No Ordinary Time: Franklin and Eleanor Roosevelt—The Home Front in World War II* (New York: Simon & Schuster, 1994); Lorena A. Hickok, *Eleanor Roosevelt: Reluctant First Lady* (New York: Dodd, Mead, 1962); Joseph P. Lash, *Eleanor and Franklin* (New York: W. W. Norton, 1971); Joseph P. Lash, *Love, Eleanor* (Garden City, N.Y.: Doubleday, 1982); Eleanor Roosevelt, *Autobiography* (New York: McGraw-Hill, 1961); James Roosevelt, *My Parents: A Differing View* (Chicago: Playboy Press, 1976); Susan Ware, *Holding Their Own: American Women in the 1930s* (Boston: Twayne, 1982).

55. Caroli, *First Ladies*, p. 188; Lash, *Love, Eleanor*, esp. pp. ix–xvi.

56. Roosevelt, *My Parents*, p. 178.

57. Caroli, *First Ladies*, p. 193.

58. Roosevelt, *My Parents*, pp. 240, 241.

59. Winifred D. Wandersee, "ER and American Youth," in Joan Hoff-Wilson and Marjorie Lightman, eds., *Without Precedent: Politics and Personality in a Bureaucratic Age* (Bloomington: Indiana University Press, 1984), pp. 61–87, makes this argument, as do other essays in the volume.

60. Goodwin, *No Ordinary Time*, pp. 628, 629.

61. Ibid., p. 504.

62. Ibid., p. 503.

63. Ibid., p. 373.

64. O'Connor, Nye, and Van Assendelft, "Wives in the White House."

65. Howard G. Bruenn, "Clinical Notes on the Illness and Death of President Franklin D. Roosevelt," *Annals of Internal Medicine*, 72 (April 1970), 579–91.

66. Baron Moran, *Churchill Taken from the Diaries of Lord Moran: The Struggle for Survival, 1940–1965* (Boston: Houghton-Mifflin, 1966), pp. 218, 223, 226.

67. Roosevelt, *My Parents*, p. 281.

68. Lawrence K. Altman, "Surgeon Asserts Roosevelt May Have Had Cancer Before 4th Term," *New York Times*, December 2, 1979, p. 66.

69. Gilbert, *Mortal Presidency*, p. 57.

70. Roosevelt, *My Parents*, p. 59.

71. Ibid., pp. 59, 60.

72. Goodwin, *No Ordinary Time*, p. 525.

73. This section relies not only on the sources listed in note 1 but also on Stephen Ambrose, *Eisenhower* (New York: Simon & Schuster, 1990); Lester David and Irene David, *Ike and Mamie: The Story of the General and His Lady* (New York: Putnam, 1981); Fred I. Greenstein, *The Hidden-Hand Presidency: Eisenhower as Leader* (New York: Basic Books, 1982); Lasby, *Eisenhower's Heart Attack*; Steve Neal, *The Eisenhowers* (Lawrence: University Press of Kansas, 1984).

74. Ferrell, *Ill-Advised*.

75. Lasby, *Eisenhower's Heart Attack*.

76. Greenstein, *Hidden-Hand Presidency*, p. 39.

77. Ambrose, *Eisenhower*, pp. 29, 30.

78. Ibid., pp. 31, 32.

79. Truman, *First Ladies*, p. 212.

80. Caroli, *First Ladies*, p. 216.

81. Ferrell, *Ill-Advised*, pp. 60, 61.

82. Lasby, *Eisenhower's Heart Attack*, pp. 272, 273.

83. Gilbert, *Mortal Presidency*, p. 101.

84. Ibid., p. 115.

85. Personal communication from Robert Gilbert to Robert Robins. October 8, 1998.

86. Ferrell, *Ill-Advised*, p. 142.

87. Truman, *First Ladies*, p. 215.

88. Ferrell, *Ill-Advised*, p. 111.

89. Lasby, *Eisenhower's Heart Attack*, p. 174.

90. This section relies not only on the sources listed in note 1 but also on Birch Bayh, *One Heartbeat Away: Presidential Disability and Succession* (Indianapolis: Bobbs-Merrill, 1968); Liz Carpenter, *Ruffles and Flourishes* (Garden City, N.Y.: Doubleday, 1964); Gilbert, "Political Effects of Presidential Illness"; Lady Bird Johnson, *A White House Diary* (New York: Holt, Rinehart, and Winston, 1970); Lyndon B. Johnson, *The Vantage Point: Perspectives of the Presidency, 1963–1969* (New York: Holt, Rinehart, and Winston, 1971); Marie D. Smith, *The President's Lady: An Intimate Biography of Mrs. Lyndon B. Johnson* (New York: Random House, 1964).

91. Caroli, *First Ladies*, p. 297.

92. Ibid., p. 417. Jacqueline Kennedy was ranked eighth, below Edith Wilson and above Martha Washington. Lyndon was ranked fourteenth among presidents.

93. Caroli, *First Ladies*, p. 235.

94. Ibid., p. 353.

95. Johnson, *Vantage Point*, p. 93.

96. Johnson, *White House Diary*, pp. 138–40.

    97. Ibid., p. 139. The full text of the memorandum is printed in Johnson,
Vantage Point, pp. 93, 94.
    98. Ibid., p. 98.
    99. Ibid., pp. 95, 96.
    100. Gilbert, "Political Effects of Presidential Illness," p. 770.
    101. Johnson, *Vantage Point*, p. 425.
    102. Ibid.
    103. Johnson, *White House Diary*, pp. 583, 584.
    104. Johnson, *Vantage Point*, p. 425.
    105. Johnson, *White House Diary*, p. 612.

9

The Vice Presidency and the Twenty-Fifth Amendment: The Power of Reciprocal Relationships

Joel K. Goldstein

The Twenty-Fifth Amendment and the vice presidency reciprocally reinforce each other in a variety of relationships. They have an historical relationship in that the growth of the vice presidency made the solutions in the Twenty-Fifth Amendment possible. They have a constitutional relationship in that the Amendment articulates a new vision of the office. Finally, they have a functional relationship in that the Amendment cannot operate without the vice presidency. The fact of these relationships suggests that reform of either the Amendment or the office will impact the other. The vision of the vice presidency implicit in the Amendment calls for continued development of the office. Continued development of the vice presidency provides the best insurance that presidential inability will be handled as the Amendment prescribes.

It is impossible adequately to assess the Twenty-Fifth Amendment without considering the American vice presidency. To be sure, the Amendment is not about the vice presidency per se. Rather, it addresses the critical, and historically troublesome, question of how to ensure that the presidency is always filled with a functioning chief

I wish to acknowledge the insightful comments of John D. Feerick, Robert E. Gilbert, and Milton I. Goldstein, which improved this chapter, the patient and valuable help of Mary Dougherty, and the institutional support of Saint Louis University School of Law. All faults and shortcomings are my responsibility.

executive. But neither does the vice presidency make simply a passing appearance in the Amendment's provisions. On the contrary,
those who produced the Twenty-Fifth Amendment cast the office in
a starring role. The vice presidency may not be the Amendment's
subject, but it is the solution to the problems addressed.

Even a superficial reader of the Amendment would be challenged
to overlook the vice president's central role. The limelight shines on
that officer in each of the Amendment's four parts. Section 1 confirms
that upon a permanent presidential vacancy the vice president *becomes*, rather than simply *acts* as, chief executive. Section 2 specifies
procedures to fill a vice-presidential vacancy. Sections 3 and 4 confirm that the vice president acts as president when the chief executive is disabled and provide procedures to transfer power which
assign the second officer a critical role.

This quick review suggests the close functional or operational relationship between Amendment and office. The Amendment clearly
could not *operate* without the vice presidency. For an office that has
long endured more than its share of insults, such eminence provides
a new experience. But this functional relationship does not exhaust
the interconnections between office and Amendment. On the contrary, a larger, multifaceted relationship binds the two.

In addition to the functional relationship, an historical relationship
connects the vice presidency and the Twenty-Fifth Amendment. It is
common, but unfair, to castigate the founders for leaving gaps in
procedures for handling presidential succession and inability. The
Amendment's solutions made sense in 1967 when ratified but were
hardly transparent when the founders did their work in 1787. It is
not surprising that the original Constitution failed to address satisfactorily problems of presidential succession and inability. The founders
had a very limited conception of the vice presidency which prevented them from relying on it to solve totally these problems. Lacking that option, the founders could find no good remedy.
Accordingly, they largely punted those vexing issues to future gener-
ations. But the development of the vice presidency during the twentieth century, especially its latter half, made the arrangements found
in the Twenty-Fifth Amendment possible, indeed compelling. But
for the evolution of the vice presidency prior to 1967, the Twenty-
Fifth Amendment would have made little sense. Resolving presidential succession would have required a different fix, another hero.

In addition to the *functional* and *historical* relationships between office and Amendment, a constitutional relationship links the two. At one level, the Amendment assigns the office certain constitutional powers, duties, and privileges. It states, as a matter of constitutional law, who may do what, when, and with what consequence. But the Twenty-Fifth Amendment does not simply provide solutions for vexing problems of presidential succession and inability. It also articulates a new constitutional vision of the vice-presidential office,[1] a far grander, more optimistic conception than the founders dared advance. It *describes* the vice presidency as it appeared in the mid-1960s and *prescribes* how the Amendment's framers imagined the office ought to function. The premises and ideas, descriptions and prescriptions, associated with the Amendment help form the Constitution's architecture and contribute structural ideas that help shape constitutional reasoning.[2] This underlying vision assumes constitutional status and offers norms that should guide behavior regarding selection and use of vice presidents. This vision has largely been realized in recent years.

The relationship between the vice presidency and the Twenty-Fifth Amendment thus exists on an *historical, constitutional,* and *functional* (or *operational*) level. Exploring these connections helps us better understand and appreciate the office and the Amendment. But this inquiry is not simply another esoteric academic exercise bereft of practical application. To be sure, neither the vice presidency nor the Twenty-Fifth Amendment is the cynosure of American politics or government. But both play a vital role in providing effective executive leadership and in ensuring that America can handle well vexing problems of presidential succession and inability. This truth alone lends some importance to considering how they operate and their potential for growth. Their multidimensional relationship has implications for both the vice presidency and the Twenty-Fifth Amendment; exploring that interaction enhances our understandings of the prospects and limitations of the office and Amendment. Moreover, the linkages suggest that those who would tamper with either should proceed with some caution. Future change in one, positive or negative, will likely impact the other.

This chapter first sketches basic ideas in the Twenty-Fifth Amendment and in the original constitutional design in order to establish the context for exploring relationships between the vice presidency and the Amendment. It then reviews the historical relationship, showing how the development of the vice presidency set the stage for the Amendment. The chapter identifies the constitutional relationship by examining the vision of the vice presidency implicit in the Amendment and explains how that vision has been realized by historical developments following the Amendment's ratification. It then explores the functional relationship. These discussions provide the basis for the chapter's conclusions.

An Overview

The Amendment's text is available in the Appendix and will not be repeated here. But it is important to note that it includes four central ideas and that all four relate to the vice president. Section 1 makes clear that following a permanent presidential vacancy due to death, resignation, or removal, the vice president does not simply act as president; he becomes president. As such, Section 1 separates the contingencies of permanent presidential vacancy from inability, which may be temporary. As president, not simply acting president, the vice president assumes the full political and constitutional powers of the office. Section 2 reflects a constitutional judgment that the vice president is indispensable. This conclusion is implicit in the decision not only to fill a vacancy in that office, but to do so through expenditure of significant governmental resources.[3] Section 3 confirms that a president, for the period of his disability, should have discretion to delegate his powers to the vice president while retaining the right to reclaim them. Finally, Section 4 suggests that the vice president, with support from the president's top official advisers and subject to various checks, can act to displace a disabled president for the period of his incapacity. Although Congress is empowered to resolve a conflict once the president is relieved of his powers, the authority to initiate such a determination is lodged wholly in the executive branch.

The Original Design

These ideas are at once flattering to the vice presidency and foreign to the original Constitution. The founders were unable to offer solutions to problems of presidential succession and inability in part because of their modest view of the vice presidency. The original Constitution addresses succession and inability in the most tentative fashion. First, it conceived of the vice president as acting president, not president, upon the death, resignation, removal, or inability of the president. The Constitution provides:

> In Case of the Removal of the President from Office, or of his Death, Resignation, or Inability to discharge the Powers and Duties of the said Office, the same shall devolve on the Vice President, and the Congress may by Law, provide for the Case of Removal, Death, Resignation or Inability, both of the President and Vice President, declaring what Officer shall then act as President, and such Officer shall act accordingly, until the Disability be removed, or a President shall be elected.[4]

The clause is ambiguous. Under it, "the same" devolves on the vice president. But to what does "the same" refer? To the presidential office or simply to the powers and duties of "the said office"? If the former, the vice president *becomes* president; if the latter, he simply *acts as* chief executive. The text presents a grammarian's conundrum that supports arguments pointing both ways.[5]

Although relying on obscure rules of grammar to expose constitutional meaning seems dubious and in any event unhelpful here, other parts of the text assist in interpreting the original clause. The text does not separate the contingencies of death, resignation, or removal from inability. It implies that whatever devolves on the vice president in the case of death also devolves in the other three. The first three events, by definition, produce permanent vacancy. The prior chief executive is not coming back. But inability may be temporary. The president may recover his health or resume consciousness. What then? Should he lose his office simply because some passing illness or injury debilitated him for a few hours or days? Yet, once the *office* passes to the vice president, the original Constitution contains no provision for tossing it back. Of course, the same might be said if the powers and duties devolve; the original Constitution does not specify how or when they would return to the President. Yet, if the vice president assumes only the powers and duties, the office remains with the president. It is not so difficult to conceive of presidential action to reunite the powers and duties with the office. Perhaps Congress, under the Necessary and Proper Clause,[6] could have provided a mechanism to restore power to the chief executive. But a constitutional quandary results if the vice president becomes president; the Constitution does not allow for two presidents. If the vice president *becomes* president, presumably the chief executive relinquishes office.

It seems odd to divest the president of his office due to a transient illness or injury, a result so idiosyncratic as to impeach itself. The final clause quoted above reinforces these misgivings. In the absence of both the president and the vice president, Congress may identify an officer to act as president "until the Disability be removed, or a President shall be elected." Two things are striking about this clause. First, any such "Officer" has the same status in all four contingencies. No distinction is made between inability and death, etc. The designated officer simply "acts" as president whether the vacancy is permanent or temporary; he does not become chief executive. Second, the Constitution makes clear that the officer's service as acting president ends when the disability is removed, thereby returning the president or vice president to power.

It would seem anomalous that the officer Congress designates would fill in only until the president's health is restored but the vice president would permanently supplant the president. This interpretation could have produced absurd results. For instance, imagine if under the original regime (a) first the president, then the vice president becomes disabled, (b) an officer Congress designates steps in to act as president, and (c) the president then regains his health. Under the approach being reviewed, the president could presumably not recover his office, having relinquished it to the vice president. The designated "Officer" would have superior title to discharge presidential powers and duties to the elected chief executive who lost his office to the vice president. The officer's claim would not trump that of the vice president, however,[7] since the officer acts as president only until "the Disability be removed." The president would be out, the vice president in. On the other hand, if the vice president's disability preceded that of the president, or if the vice presidency was unoccupied, the chief executive would presumably not forfeit his office. The officer Congress designates would "act as President . . . until the Disability be removed," at which point the president accordingly could reclaim his powers and duties. Of course, if the vice president healed first, arguably he would bump both the president and the officer since his "Disability [was] removed." Presidential tenure should not turn on who comes off the disabled list first. These bizarre results ensue only if the *office* devolves in event of disability. If only the powers and duties pass, we avoid these hypothetical follies. Accordingly, the language specifying that the "Officer" (designated in the absence of a president and vice president) acts only until the "Disability be removed" supports a similar treatment of a vice president who steps up when the president is disabled.

Study of the framers' intent suggests they meant the vice president to serve only temporarily.[8] Drafts at the Constitutional Convention clearly conceived the vice president as an interim successor.[9] On September 4, 1787, the Committee of Eleven issued its report, which provided that in case of removal of the president or of his "death, absence, resignation or inability to discharge the powers or duties of his office the Vice President shall exercise those powers and duties until another President be chosen, or until the inability of the President be removed."[10] Under this formulation, the vice president would act as, not become, president. Indeed, the limit "until another President be chosen" implies that a special election might be held. The final clause—"until the inability of the President be removed"— separated "inability" from contingencies involving permanent vacancy. During floor discussions, a further clause was added that provided, in essence, that Congress could, in case of a double vacancy, designate an officer to act as president "until such disability be removed, or a President shall be elected."[11] The Convention appointed a Committee on Style that, as its name suggests, was to refine the text's language without changing its meaning.[12] It made two changes that contributed to much of the historical confusion. It replaced "powers and duties" with "the same"; it also included the phrase referring to removal of the disability only once, at the end of both clauses, rather than twice.[13] The vague language that emerged wound up in the Constitution.

The text and the framers' intent suggest that the original Constitution saw the vice president as simply discharging the powers and duties of the office, without becoming the new president. This conclusion is consistent with the founders' modest view of the vice presidency.[14] They harbored no grandiose ambitions for the vice presidency. For them, the office was an afterthought, invented in the waning days of the Constitutional Convention primarily as an expedient to enable the initial presidential electoral system to function. The framers feared that parochial loyalties would frustrate efforts to choose a national president as electors backed their state's favorite son. They designed a system in which each elector had two votes, one of which had to be cast for an out-of-stater. To attach significance to the second vote, they created the second office.[15] Some questioned the need for the office. "[S]uch an officer as vice-President was not wanted," opined Hugh Williamson.[16] Alexander Hamilton observed that some viewed "appointment of an extraordinary person" to be vice president as "superfluous, if not mischievous."[17]

The founders' diffidence regarding succession and inability becomes manifest in a second way—they did not identify a successor beyond the elected vice president. They signaled their misgivings about the vice presidency by making no arrangements to fill a vice-presidential vacancy. If the office was unoccupied, the vice president's rather modest duties would simply be reassigned. The Senate would elect a Senate President pro tempore in his absence; Congress could designate some officer to act as president when the second office was empty. The implications of that omission are striking. The founders simply did not see the vice presidency as an office important enough to merit filling. The station itself was expendable. The second Congress, a body including many framers and ratifiers, considered many possibilities for the "Officer" to be designated to act as president absent a president or vice president.[18] It did not suggest filling the vice presidency.

Finally, the founders did little about the difficult problem of presidential inability. "What is the extent of the term 'disability' & who is to be the judge of it?" asked John Dickinson at the Constitutional Convention.[19] The framers did provide that the vice president would act as president during a presidential inability. Much later, many thought the vice president himself would need to determine if such a situation existed.[20] But there is no indication the framers reached this conclusion.[21] None of Dickinson's colleagues ventured a response that has been recorded for posterity. Thus, the original Constitution was silent regarding these critical topics.

Interpreting that silence presents its own set of challenges. No doubt, the delegates were hot and tired and homesick. They may have decided that these problems were not sufficiently urgent or weighty to keep them in Philadelphia still longer. Alternatively, they may have considered some possible approaches and, based on their discussions, deemed the problems intractable. Perhaps any solution seemed likely to draw more opposition to, than support for, the proposed Constitution. The immediate costs may have exceeded future benefits. The framers may have deemed it expedient or appropriate to leave Dickinson's query for another day or a different generation. It is possible, though not likely, that they simply overlooked these problems.

If the framers did think or talk much about the issues Dickinson raised, it is unlikely that the formulation in Sections 3 and 4 of the Twenty-Fifth Amendment would have excited them. These two disability sections rely on the vice presidency in ways quite foreign to their approach. Both sections presume that the vice president is compatible with the chief executive and his administration. Yet, the founders had no reason to entertain that assumption. Under the original electoral system, the president and vice president were chosen in a single election. They were not partners who ran on a ticket together; on the contrary, they were competitors, vying for the same job. That history would be unlikely to breed cooperation or collegiality. Moreover, the vice president's only ongoing duty was to act as the Senate's president. As such, he was a *legislative* officer. Since the founders worried about mixing executive and legislative functions, the idea of the president's transferring power to the vice president might well have been controversial.[22] Finally, Section 4 would have gone beyond anything the founders endorsed. They provided for legislative impeachment and removal of the president and civil officers.[23] They accepted the idea that the president could remove subordinates.[24] They may have assumed that by default the successor would need to decide disability. But there is no indication they harbored this expectation; it contradicted their generally negative view of the vice presidency and raised a host of other problems, particularly if the two top officers were not compatible. There is no indication that the idea of the vice president and the cabinet acting together to force the president to relinquish powers would have resonated with the framers.

The founders' conception of the vice presidency included the following features.[25] First, they did not view the office as indispensable to governing; indeed, some viewed the office with ambivalence, even antipathy.[26] Instead, they saw it as an expedient to achieve the election of a national president. Second, they conceived the vice presidency as essentially a legislative office. As delegate Roger Sherman observed, but for the role as Senate president, the vice president "would be without employment."[27] Had the framers not given him this legislative role, he would have received federal money without providing any service, the first welfare recipient. Third, the founders apparently did not value highly compatibility between the two top officers since they structured the office in a way unlikely to promote harmony. The one positive aspect of the initial design was that the vice president, as the presidential runner-up, might be someone of stature. But even this attribute was not secure. The electoral scheme gave the vice presidency to the electoral vote runner-up but did not require him to receive a majority or anywhere close to one. If the electoral vote was badly split, he might be a regional figure with only a limited following.[28]

This view of the vice presidency made it difficult for the founders to address problems of presidential succession and inability in any but a provisional way. The vice president was not part of the chief executive's team, so his succession would not necessarily offer continuity or stability. The vice presidency was not structured to provide a long-term successor. He did not share in the president's popularity since he was elected separately. Accordingly, special elections might be desirable to produce a new leader with a national mandate. Nor could the founders anticipate that in a disability situation the vice president would be received hospitably by others in the administration.

The low regard in which the framers held the vice presidency contrasted with the assessment of those who conceived the Twenty-Fifth Amendment nearly 180 years later. They valued the vice presidency highly. For them, the vice presidency was not a form of electoral engineering. It was an office that would contribute to the success of the administration and ensure proper succession.

The Twenty-Fifth Amendment was in many respects inconsistent with the original Constitution. Yet, it was adopted by overwhelming majorities in the House of Representatives and Senate[29] in 1965 and was ratified by forty-seven states in short order.[30] How did the nation progress from the founders' misgivings about the vice presidency to the evident enthusiasm of those who drafted the Twenty-Fifth Amendment?

THE HISTORICAL RELATIONSHIP:
THE EVOLUTION OF THE VICE PRESIDENCY

It is not surprising, for an office conceived in such doubt, that its early years were not promising.[31] The first vice president, John Adams, found it "the most insignificant office that ever the invention of man contrived or his imagination conceived."[32] The best his successor, Thomas Jefferson, could say about the office was that it was "honorable and easy."[33] As humble as these beginnings were, they did not represent the vice presidency's nadir. The journey from original Constitution to the Twenty-Fifth Amendment was not a simple march forward. The founders at least created a system that might produce a competent successor. The first vice presidents—Adams, Jefferson, and Aaron Burr—were eminent leaders of their day.

That lone attractive prospect vanished with the ratification of the Twelfth Amendment in 1804, which changed the method of electing presidents and vice presidents. The development of political parties had impacted the framers' design. Parties had begun fielding slates with designated candidates for the two offices. At least one elector was to withhold his vote from the vice-presidential candidate to guarantee the presidential standard-bearer a higher total. Although Thomas Jefferson was the intended presidential nominee in 1800, he and his running mate, Aaron Burr, polled the same number of votes. The deadlock persisted through thirty-six ballots in the House of Representatives.[34] The experience brought the demise of the initial electoral system. Its replacement, set forth in the Twelfth Amendment, called for separate elections of president and vice president. Opponents of the new system had predicted that it would diminish the vice presidency. They anticipated that the prestige of the office would decline, that the new electoral system would make the office less attractive to able figures, and that the second spot on the ticket would be used for partisan purposes rather than to attract able servants.[35]

Each fear proved prophetic. John Calhoun and Martin Van Buren did later serve, but they were exceptions. The vice presidents of the nineteenth century were essentially historical nonentities, relative to their high office "a virtual rogues' gallery of personal and political failures."[36] Often they were plucked from obscurity. Except for four who exercised presidential powers upon the death of their predecessor,[37] they returned to oblivion following their term.[38] Chosen by party leaders, not the presidential nominee, to balance the ticket, not mirror the standard bearer, vice presidents often were not personally or politically compatible with the presidents under whom they served.[39]

During the remainder of the nineteenth century, one development did enhance the status of the vice presidency. When John Tyler insisted that he was president, not simply discharging presidential powers and duties as vice president after William Henry Harrison's death in 1841, his claim was controversial and inconsistent with the framers' view of the vice president as a temporary solution to presidential vacancy. Yet, Congress accepted his stance, and three other nineteenth-century vice presidents imitated it upon the death of the chief executive.

Tyler's experience illustrated the political weakness of the nineteenth-century vice president. Tyler lacked standing with the dominant wing of his party, coming as he did from a rival faction and lacking personal eminence of his own. He could not govern effectively and was not elected to a term of his own. The three nineteenth-century vice presidents who shared Tyler's fortune of following a deceased president—Millard Fillmore, Andrew Johnson, and Chester A. Arthur—experienced similar problems and fates.

The Tyler precedent, the idea that a vice president becomes president for the remainder of the term, added prestige to the office, but at a price. It complicated greatly handling problems of presidential inability. Since the Constitution did not distinguish disability from death, resignation, or removal in terms of what devolved on the vice president, the text suggested that whatever passed to the vice president in case of permanent vacancy also did so when a president was disabled. But if the presidency passed to the vice president whenever a president was disabled, what became of the disabled chief executive? Since the Constitution lodged executive power in *a* president, not multiple presidents, the president must lose the office if the vice president assumed it. This conclusion seemed particularly persuasive to some since the Constitution provided no way for a president to return to the presidency other than election.

Not surprisingly, the framers' Constitution and the political system that supported it handled situations of presidential inability poorly. During President Garfield's eighty-day disability, the cabinet unanimously thought that Vice President Arthur, who was from a rival wing of the Republican Party, should assume executive powers. Yet, no transfer of power occurred until Garfield died. The lengthy disability of Woodrow Wilson nearly four decades later was handled no better. Wilson was no fan of his vice president, Thomas Marshall. He had opposed his selection, viewing Marshall as "a small-calibre man."[40] Much government business required presidential leadership, which Wilson was physically unable to provide. Yet, no transfer occurred. Again, the lack of procedures and the constitutional issues impeded action.[41]

Wilson had no higher assessment of the office of vice presidency than he had of Marshall. Near the end of the nineteenth century, then a political scientist, he had devoted only a few lines of his book *Congressional Government* to the vice presidency since "the chief embarrassment in discussing [the] office is, that in explaining how little there is to be said about it one has evidently said all there is to say."[42] Wilson, no doubt, accurately depicted the sorry state of the office as it existed in 1885, eight decades after the Twelfth Amendment. Yet, eight decades later, when Congress overwhelmingly sent the proposed Twenty-Fifth Amendment to the states, the vice presidency and impressions of it had changed greatly. That transformation made the Twenty-Fifth Amendment possible. It is important to appreciate what happened, and why it occurred, in order to understand the Amendment.

The metamorphosis of the vice presidency occurred over time. Although scholars differ on the length of the period, the key dates, and the weight to attach to particular events, it seems clear that the evolution began during the twentieth century and accelerated sometime after World War II. Vice presidents began to find some work in the *executive* branch. Wilson's vice president, Thomas Marshall, and his successor, Calvin Coolidge, attended some cabinet meetings. Although that practice was interrupted during the presidencies of Coolidge and Herbert Hoover, it resumed when John Nance Garner became vice president in 1933 and has continued since that time.

Garner and Henry Wallace assumed some executive duties as legislative liaison, foreign emissary, and commission head. These involvements gave vice presidents some opportunity to influence decisions and their implementation. More important, they symbolized a migration of the office to the executive branch. In part because of the enhanced prestige of the office, it began to attract more able occupants. Several vice presidents during the first part of the twentieth century had served as legislative leaders. Virtually all were considered serious presidential candidates after their term.

Relations between the president and the vice president were still not particularly close, however. Several factors may have contributed to the distance; a principal cause was certainly the fact that the presidential candidates had little, if anything, to do with the choice of their running mates until 1940. The vice president, therefore, had no reason to feel grateful to the presidential candidate for his station; the president had no cause to feel responsible for the vice president's plight.

Although the new contours of the vice presidency were becoming evident during the first half of the twentieth century, the changes in the office were still relatively modest. The vice presidency was the beneficiary of larger developments in American politics and government which by mid-century had changed national government and the presidency.[43] The New Deal and World War II had brought new prominence to the national government. Increasingly, Washington was expected to remedy the nation's domestic problems. The enhanced international role of the United States became a permanent reality during the Cold War. The president was best equipped to address the nation's domestic problems by proposing programmatic solutions. He also assumed new prominence as the primary voice on foreign policy and the commander in chief of the military. Technological change contributed to his stature. The increasingly sophisticated machinery of war multiplied the burdens on the presidency. Increased air travel and communications gave the president easier access to multiple markets. These changes not only fortified the presidency; they also sapped power from the local political parties. As Washington, not local political machines, began to dispense benefits, the local machines lost their political clout. As technology eased communications directly to voters, presidential candidates were able to communicate independent of the old political machines.

These changes transformed the vice presidency as well. First, the nationalization of government and concomitant growth of the presidency also had the effect of pulling the vice presidency into the executive branch. Technological innovation encouraged this migration. The president was expected to address more issues, see more foreign leaders and countries, attend more events, than one person could possibly manage. The vice president became an acceptable surrogate. Vice presidents were assigned to head commissions dealing with problems large and small and were used as administration spokesmen on issues of the day. They were sent overseas on good will trips and to represent America at funerals. They cut ribbons, campaigned for administration supporters, and appeared at party events to arouse the enthusiasm of, and raise money from, the party faithful. Increasingly, the vice president became part of the executive branch.

Second, as presidential candidates began to choose their own running mates, the degree of political and personal compatibility between president and vice president increased. The two were not invariably bosom buddies, but they now had greater reason to identify with, and be loyal to, each other. Presidents gained a stake in the success of their vice president's tenure. If the vice president seemed not up to the task, voters knew whom to blame. Vice presidents had reason to be loyal to the chief executive—he had chosen them once and, they hoped, would do so again.

Third, the stature of vice presidents began to increase. The demands of the nuclear age, and the greater public scrutiny electronic media allowed, gave presidential candidates incentives to choose running mates of some substance. Parties could no longer hide an inept vice president.

The vice presidency of Richard M. Nixon first illustrated the modern American vice presidency.[44] Nixon functioned essentially as a member of the executive branch. He met with the cabinet and the National Security Council, presiding over both bodies in Eisenhower's absence. He chaired administration commissions, traveled as the president's representative, acted as a legislative liaison, served as a prominent administration spokesman, and assumed the partisan role of party leader to protect Eisenhower's image as a statesman above unseemly political battles. To be sure, relations with Eisenhower were not perfect. Eisenhower considered dumping him from the 1952 ticket owing to the Checkers scandal, wanted to drop him in

1956, and made comments that were less than helpful in 1960. Still, Nixon enjoyed much more eminence within the executive branch than virtually any vice president since Martin Van Buren. It is not surprising, then, that in March 1958 Eisenhower released an agreement with Nixon regarding any future presidential inabilities.[45]

By 1965, when both houses of Congress proposed the Twenty-Fifth Amendment to the states, the vice presidency had been elevated. The change did not trace to any formal constitutional amendment but rather to the different way governmental and political institutions then did their business. As previously noted, presidential nominees, not parties, chose the running mate; vice presidents acted as part of the executive branch, discharging various executive roles rather than tending to the Senate's business. Courts have recognized that constitutional change can occur through repeated practice that gains long acquiescence.[46] As such, the status of the vice presidency as a part of the executive branch had received constitutional recognition of sorts by long-standing practice.

THE CONSTITUTIONAL RELATIONSHIP: THE NEW CONSTITUTIONAL VICE PRESIDENCY

Had history not produced this new conception of the vice presidency, the Constitution would not likely have advanced beyond its original text with respect to problems of presidential succession and inability. It certainly would not have included the provisions of the Twenty-Fifth Amendment. That Amendment reflects a new perception that the vice presidency represents an efficacious solution to problems of presidential succession and inability. Accordingly, the office was deemed worth filling whenever vacant. By providing a new mechanism to fill a vice-presidential vacancy, the Constitution sought to make relatively remote the possibility that anyone other than a vice president would ever succeed to the presidential office.

The framers of the Twenty-Fifth Amendment certainly had misgivings about other possible successors. When Lyndon Johnson succeeded to the presidency, Speaker of the House John McCormack and Senate President pro tempore Carl Hayden were next in line to be president. Their ages[47] and limitations made the podium picture at Johnson's early speeches to Congress an unnerving sight.[48] Those who rise to these positions may be skilled legislative technicians but may come from unrepresentative electorates and may lack a national constituency. Similarly, cabinet succession, though preferred by some who drafted the Twenty-Fifth Amendment,[49] was no panacea. Cabinet officers might never have sought elective office. Their political antennae may not be sufficiently sensitive to register currents in public opinion and they may not be well versed in political folkways. Moreover, their expertise may be excessively narrow.

But the decision to fill vice-presidential vacancies did not reflect the view that the vice presidency was the best card in a bad hand. On the contrary, the office was viewed as indispensable on its own merits. "I remind Senators that the office of Vice President has gone through a period of development, perhaps to a greater degree than any other office in the history of the country," Senator Birch Bayh, sponsor of the measure, told his colleagues. Bayh described the vice presidency as a "full-time, highly responsible office"; Senator Hiram Fong thought it an office of "paramount importance."[50] President Johnson declared that "its occupancy on a full-time basis is imperative."[51]

Bayh and his colleagues viewed the vice president as part of the executive branch.[52] They saw him as undertaking significant executive assignments in domestic and international spheres. They saw him as participating in high-level councils that produced executive policy-making, as an adviser to, and troubleshooter for, the president.

In order for the vice president to succeed in this role, the framers of the Twenty-Fifth Amendment believed that he should be personally and politically compatible with the president. A "close relationship" must exist between president and vice president, argued Bayh, an aspiration other framers shared.[53] The vice president would receive important duties if he enjoyed the president's confidence. To encourage an harmonious relationship, the president was given the primary role in selecting the new vice president if a vacancy in the office should occur. Proposals that Congress initiate the selection or choose from a panel were rejected since they would undermine the close relationship the Amendment's framers sought to foster.[54] Confirmation by each house of Congress conferred a semblance of a popular endorsement. It also helped ensure that only highly competent people would be chosen.[55]

These features would, of course, increase the likelihood that the vice president would receive significant assignments, that he would be in the loop. But their purpose was not simply to enhance the quality of his daily life. Rather, the vice president's ability to perform as a successor depended in part on the extent to which he was involved. "One of the principal reasons for filling the office of Vice President when it becomes vacant is to permit the person next in line to become familiar with the problems he will face should he be called upon to act as President," explained the 1965 Report of the Senate committee on the Judiciary.[56] Particularly "in a hydrogen age, when decisions have to be made within split seconds," it was critical that the Vice President be up to speed.[57]

Section 3 reflects the idea that the president can pass executive powers temporarily to the vice president. That arrangement would be awkward if the vice president is a legislative officer independent of, and with relatively little contact with, the executive branch or its personnel. But perceptions of the office had evolved, so that the vice president was seen as a member of the executive branch chosen by the president to work with him and his administration. The idea of passing powers temporarily to him seemed neither odd nor constitutionally problematic. On the contrary, what could be more natural than to transfer power to the president's right hand man, his own chosen successor, his political personal representative?

Similarly, Section 4, which allows the vice president and the cabinet to determine that the president is unable to discharge his office, seems consonant with these understandings of the office. Indeed, the Eisenhower–Nixon agreement allowed the vice president, after appropriate consultation, to act. The vice president, like the cabinet, was part of the official family.

To some extent, the Twenty-Fifth Amendment describes the new reality of the vice president as its framers appreciated it. They had read their history and understood that the office had come a long way from the days when it was a sinecure occupied by mediocrities.[58] They operated in an age when there was reason to view the office favorably. After all, Nixon had recently completed a successful vice presidency that had helped catapult him within a few disputed electoral votes of the White House. He had emphasized his vice-presidential service as a prime credential on his political résumé. Lyndon B. Johnson had responded magnificently when the assassination of John F. Kennedy elevated him to the presidency. In his quest to don the Kennedy mantle, he celebrated his vice-presidential service, largely hiding until later the misery he had felt.[59] The framers of the Twenty-Fifth Amendment believed the office had risen to new heights. Birch Bayh's words are instructive. He wrote in 1968:

> In addition to making the government function again, two of Lyndon Johnson's most important tasks during those dark days were to gain America's confidence and to soothe the fears of a nation shaken by the trauma of an assassination. He was admirably equipped to do so—as Vice President, he had been given more responsibility than anyone else in that office in modern times—but the fact remained that he was working without a Vice President of his own. There was no one to carry the burden that he himself had borne under John Kennedy.[60]

Johnson's choice of Hubert H. Humphrey, a widely respected long-time ally, seemed likely to raise the office much further. Ironically, at the time the Twenty-Fifth Amendment, with its celebration of, and reliance on, the vice presidency, was being sent to the states, Johnson was injuring the office. After having promised Humphrey important new responsibilities, Johnson was in the process of denying him any significant role. Only days into his vice presidency, Humphrey committed the tactical blunder of opposing in a meeting the recommendation of the president's top advisers to bomb North Vietnam. Humphrey compounded his transgression by following his oral advice with a written memorandum to the president.[61] Johnson took offense at Humphrey's two steps. He disliked the oral advice, which violated their understanding that Humphrey would not oppose Johnson before others. He was furious about the writing, too. Johnson could imagine only two motives for Humphrey to commit his view to paper: to provide a document that Humphrey could leak to embarrass Johnson or to preserve the historical record in Humphrey's favor in case the war went badly. Neither pleased Johnson. He excluded Humphrey for months.[62]

To the extent that it sought to *describe* the vice presidency, the Twenty-Fifth Amendment exaggerated reality in the mid-1960s. The vice presidency had not quite reached the heights the Amendment's framers then suggested. Subsequent accounts of the Johnson vice presidency[63] and Humphrey's painful experience demonstrated that, the office's significant advance notwithstanding, the picture was not so rosy as thought. But the Amendment's account of the vice presidency served an additional purpose: it articulated aspirations for the office; it *prescribed* how the vice presidency should be.

Bayh and the other framers thought the vice presidency *should* be an important office in the executive branch. The vice president should be a close presidential adviser, someone in the inner circle. He would be most likely to achieve that status if the president had substantial leeway to select his political heir. The president should choose his understudy, subject to some check, to provide legitimacy and to ensure competency. Those exercising that check should do so, however, with the understanding that the president is entitled to a surrogate with whom he is politically and personally compatible. The vice president would become knowledgeable about the problems the nation faced. As Dwight Eisenhower put it:

> But the replacement provision does more than simply settle the question of succession; it additionally ensures that there will be brought into the Presidency, in case of necessity, an individual who has had full opportunity to learn much about all of the critical problems then facing the nation. In this manner there will always be available a man well prepared to carry out the job of President who will be in accord with the President's views. The President will be able to train, teach, and work with him. In short, they can develop the relationship necessary for a smooth executive transition which is so vital to the country in times of crises. The structure of this part of the amendment, to my mind, will provide a great added benefit to the nation.[64]

He would be able to step in on short notice to help guarantee informed leadership and continuity of policy and personnel. As the president's close colleague, he would help the administration succeed. As a model understudy, he would solve the dilemma of succession and disability.

The Vision Achieved

The constitutional vision of the vice presidency lay dormant from the Amendment's ratification in 1967 until 1973. The vice presidency was something of a mixed bag. During this period, Vice President Humphrey and his successor, Spiro T. Agnew, did emerge as visible administration spokesmen, at times for controversial programs. Both experienced the benefits of the office as a political springboard— Humphrey became his party's 1968 presidential nominee and Agnew topped polls for the Republican nomination in 1976. But neither emerged as the president's "very close confidant,"[65] his companion,"[66] or the beneficiary of "an intimacy of connection" with the "closest possible rapport" with the president,[67] as called for by the vision. Far from it. I have alluded to Humphrey's agony above and discussed it in more detail elsewhere.[68] Agnew's experience, deservedly so, was worse. "Thanks to his refusal to be politic, Agnew was simply cut out of the policy loop before his term of office was two years old," historian John Robert Greene reports.[69] Late in his tenure, Agnew acknowledged that Nixon had still not defined his role; the lack of definition was not inadvertent.[70] Of course, Agnew's problems were just beginning. On October 10, 1973 he resigned as vice president and pleaded *nolo contendere* to income tax evasion to avoid indictment for more serious offenses.

By Agnew's second term, the disparity between the real and the ideal vice presidency could hardly have been greater. Soon, the noted scholar Arthur M. Schlesinger, Jr. began calling for abolition of the vice presidency.[71] Yet, Agnew's resignation, coupled with the cloud of impeachment hovering over President Nixon, provided an opportunity for the vice presidency to begin to realize the vision the Twenty-Fifth Amendment expressed. The Amendment provided occasion for the office to justify itself.[72]

Agnew's resignation provided the first opportunity to use any part of the Amendment, fortuitously Section 2. The need to fill the vice presidency afforded the opportunity to recall and reiterate the Amendment's vision of the office. Although some Democrats initially advocated applying partisan tests,[73] Bayh urged that "we should find someone who's going to be a good Vice President and a good President"[74] and "a Vice President who would be compatible and could work harmoniously with the President."[75]

In short order, the Amendment and the vice presidency collaborated to demonstrate the merit of each. In October 1973 impeachment seemed increasingly likely. Under the Presidential Succession Act of 1947, two Democrats, Speaker of the House Carl Albert and Senate President pro tempore James Eastland stood next in line. Section 2 allowed installation of Gerald Ford, a Republican politically compatible with Nixon, thereby obviating the risk that impeachment would shift partisan control of the executive branch. In so doing, it spotlighted the political strengths of the vice presidency and the weaknesses of alternative ways of handling succession. When Nixon resigned in August 1974, Ford became president under Section 1, demonstrating the advantages of the vice presidency as a solution for succession. Finally, the selection of Nelson A. Rockefeller as Ford's vice president, though controversial, provided an opportunity to reassert an ambitious vision of the office. Rockefeller was an imposing public servant who answered Ford's summons in response to promises of important responsibilities. The Rockefeller vice presidency did not succeed, in large part due to tactical mistakes, the clash of administration personalities, and the vagaries of internal Republican Party politics. But it dusted off the vision the Twenty-Fifth Amendment articulated.

Perhaps the framers of the Twenty-Fifth Amendment were simply optimistic historians who presciently anticipated the further evolution of the vice presidency. As political theorists, they had articulated a compelling vision of the institution. The office they imagined became reality in short order. Vice presidents became even more identified with the executive branch. The vice presidencies of Walter F. Mondale and Al Gore best met the Twenty-Fifth Amendment's vision of the office. Both enjoyed close relationships with the president and his staff, which maximized their influence. Both were intimately involved in administration decision-making. Neither may have prevailed on all policy issues; no one does. But both managed to preserve influence and remain involved throughout their terms.[76] George Bush became an important figure during the Reagan Administration, especially in foreign policy. This achievement was significant in view of his earlier rivalry with Reagan and his identification with a different wing of the Republican Party. Even Dan Quayle's tenure, though less successful than those of other recent incumbents, approximated more closely the new constitutional vision of this office than had earlier vice presidencies.

The transformation related largely to certain informal changes initiated by one administration which became precedents that successors followed. Indeed, beginning with Mondale, every vice president has had an office in the White House.[77] Having space down the hall from the Oval Office has symbolic importance. More significantly, physical proximity to the president and his primary assistants puts the vice president in position to exert influence. In addition to space in the president's office suite, the vice president has also won regular

time on the president's schedule. Vice presidents beginning with
Rockefeller have had a standing private weekly meeting with the
President. Vice presidents since Mondale have had easy access to
Oval Office meetings and have received presidential security
briefings. These opportunities to discuss policy and politics give the
vice president a chance to exert influence. Increased staff support
allows the vice president to participate constructively. Moreover, the
vice president's guaranteed time with the president provides the vice
president an asset to enhance his power with other officials. Other
political players, in and outside the administration, have found new
reason to take the vice president seriously. It has become worthwhile
to try to influence the vice president, given his access to the chief
executive.[78]

THE FUNCTIONAL RELATIONSHIP

Finally, an *operational* relationship exists between the vice president
and the Twenty-Fifth Amendment. Each section reflects the functional dependence of the Amendment on the office. For instance,
Section 1 confirms that the vice president *becomes* president following the death, resignation, or removal of the chief executive. The vice
president not simply is an acting or interim president, but becomes
president for the remainder of the term of the former chief executive.
It is tempting to dismiss Section 1 as simply being concerned with
constitutional housekeeping, as elevating the Tyler precedent from
constitutional practice to text with respect to three contingencies and
distinguishing them from the case of inability. By so doing, it helps
the Amendment resolve one of the constitutional questions that complicated prior disabilities: could a vice president act as president
without permanently supplanting the disabled chief executive?

But Section 1 also reflects the conviction that the vice presidency
provides the most efficacious solution to the problem of presidential
succession. The framers of the Twenty-Fifth Amendment believed
that, given the evolution of the vice presidency and the political realities that shaped it, vice-presidential succession afforded the best
chance of providing continuity and stability in policy and personnel.
"It is generally agreed that the Vice-President is the official in the
best position to succeed to the Presidency and insure the contin-

uum," wrote John D. Feerick, who played an instrumental role in helping to craft the Twenty-Fifth Amendment.[79] Moreover, the Amendment's framers viewed the vice presidency as the optimal station for an official to prepare to assume office on short notice, to become proficient on issues of war and peace that might require immediate decisions. Finally, the consensus that the vice president was the preferred successor owed something to an appreciation of the fatal flaws in all other courses.

In one sense, Section 2 is anomalous. Whereas Sections 1, 3, and 4 deal with ensuring the continuity of presidential leadership, Section 2 ostensibly addresses the less pressing (yet more frequent) problem of vice-presidential vacancy.[80] Yet, Section 2 also reflects the dependence of the Amendment on the office, in some sense, most powerfully. It reflects an acceptance of the novel proposition that the vice presidency must always be occupied, that it is worth cranking up the costly and cumbersome unique double confirmation process to make sure that a vice president is always on call. Section 2 has largely accomplished this mission. Prior to 1973, the vice presidency had been vacant for thirty-seven years, 20 percent of our history until that time. Since then, two vacancies have left the office open for only six months, roughly 2 percent of this twenty-six–year period.

The commitment here rests largely on an appreciation of the advantages the vice presidency offers for handling problems of presidential succession and inability. In the three contingencies under Section 1, where the chief executive clearly will not return to office, vice-presidential succession offers the advantages discussed above—continuity, a trained successor, legitimacy—and avoids the problems inherent in any alternative solution. The case for the vice presidency is perhaps more compelling regarding disability, the domain of Sections 3 and 4. As noted, both sections specifically empower the vice president as transferee of presidential powers; Section 4 designates him as the indispensable decision-maker. Without a vice president, Sections 3 and 4 cannot operate; they provide only material to formulate analogous constitutional and political solutions. Section 2 virtually eliminates instances in which the three other sections of the Amendment are inoperative for want of a vice president.

The vice president plays a crucial role in the disability provisions contained in Section 3 and 4. The Amendment provides separate procedures for voluntary and involuntary transfers of power. With respect to voluntary transfers of power, the topic of Section 3, the framers essentially wrote into the text of the Constitution the Eisenhower–Nixon understanding—the president is authorized to transfer, and reclaim, presidential powers in anticipation or realization of a disability. That the Amendment borrowed an existing formula in no way diminishes the magnitude of its contribution. By virtue of the Amendment, the propriety of transferring power to the vice president no longer depends on an agreement between transferor and transferee but rather carries constitutional sanction. The constitutional questions that once paralyzed decision-makers have been answered.

Significantly, Section 3 authorizes transfer only to the vice president. No provision is made for delegating presidential powers to another officer. It would be incorrect to conclude definitively that the Constitution prohibits such a transfer absent a functioning vice president. Congress could probably make some provision for that contingency under Article II, section 1, clause 6 subject to constitutional restraint. A long pattern of executive practice might also suffice.[81] But the specific authorization to transfer power just to the vice president fit the new vision the framers of the Amendment had of the Vice Presidency. Since the vice president is his hand-picked associate, the president need have no concern about delegating power to him in case of his disability. The president need anticipate no political self-dealing or other shenanigans while he is incapacitated. Since the vice president shares the president's electoral mandate, his political legitimacy as acting president is unassailable. Since the vice president would have worked intimately with the president and his top advisers, he would be able to govern consistent with administration policy.

Compared to procedures under Section 4, voluntary transfer under Section 3, where possible, offers clear advantage for the president, vice president, and system of government. The president avoids the stigma of being relieved by others of his duties. The vice president avoids the risk of appearing to usurp the chief executive's prerogatives. Instead, he acts with presidential benediction. The presidential blessing is always comforting for a vice president. No doubt, it would be especially cherished when the vice president sought to exercise presidential powers and duties. The governmental system avoids the friction that would likely accompany an involuntary transfer.

The framers of the Twenty-Fifth Amendment provided two types of incentives for presidents to invoke Section 3 where appropriate. First, as suggested above, the close political and personal relationship between president and vice president reduces the risk of delegation. The president would not be empowering some enemy, rival, or independent operator, but his chosen heir, his guy. Second, Section 3 allows the President to reclaim powers immediately upon his unilateral declaration of his ability to do so.[82]

The framers intended Section 3 to allow a president wide latitude to transfer power. It applies, John D. Feerick has concluded, to "all cases in which some condition or circumstance prevents the President from discharging his powers and duties and the public business requires that the Vice President discharge them."[83] Transfer under Section 3 has occurred only once—when President Ronald Reagan, in anticipation of surgery for colon cancer, shifted power to Vice President George Bush for nearly eight hours on July 13, 1985. Unfortunately, President Reagan at the time claimed he was acting not under Section three but under his private understanding with the vice president. In fact, President Reagan followed the procedures of Section 3 precisely in shifting and reclaiming power, and the section provided the only legal basis for so doing. At the time he was rightly criticized for obfuscating the issue.[84] More recently, several thoughtful scholars have correctly recognized Section 3 as the basis for his action.[85]

Vice President as Section 4 Decision-Maker

The vice president's role under Section 4 is far more complicated. Under Section 3, the vice president is simply a recipient of power the president has revocably bestowed. Transfer under Section 4 comes without presidential sanction. Section 4 authorizes involuntary transfer of power to the vice president under a range of circumstances. On occasions, the transfer would come without the president's opposition. If, for instance, the chief executive was unconscious, he would not approve the conveyance of powers, as under Section 3, but neither would he voice his displeasure (until later perhaps). In other instances, say if the president was mentally unbalanced, a transfer might encounter the president's strenuous protest.

In either Section 4 paradigm, the vice president's position is far more precarious than under Section 3. A vice president who exercises powers the president gives him under Section 3 may not be immune from criticism or second-guessing for decisions he makes, but it is hard to imagine anyone's accusing him of improperly seizing the presidential powers he is given (or lent). Administration officials take their cues from the president. His support would help ensure the cooperation of his subordinates. The president's letter transferring power would shield the vice president unless the latter begins to act inappropriately, figuratively pounding his chest and proclaiming that he is the boss.

Action under Section 4 could be far more controversial. The vice president might find himself at odds with the chief executive, his erstwhile patron, over an issue of paramount sensitivity to the chief executive—whether the president can do his job. Even if the president is unable to voice a protest, the presidential spouse, family, chief of staff, or others could undermine the vice president's status with a public rebuke or a few whispered comments to Geraldo or Bob Woodward. Public business did not necessitate the transfer, they might say; "Yond [vice president] has a lean and hungry look."[86] Alternatively, the vice president might be subject to public criticism for attempting to act as president. The prospects for an acrimonious encounter with the president would, of course, be greatest when the proposed transfer encounters the president's opposition. But even when a transfer responds to a clear presidential disability—an unconscious president, for instance—the chief executive might later complain that no pressing events mandated the transfer.

The delicacy comes largely from the fact that Section 4 assigns the vice president a critical role as decision-maker. It empowers "the Vice President and a majority of either the principal officers of the executive departments or of such other body as Congress may by law provide" to determine the president's inability to discharge the powers and duties of his office. Several aspects of this arrangement are noteworthy. First, Section 4 lodges the sobering decision whether to transfer presidential powers in members of the executive branch. The phrase "principal officers of the executive departments" refers to the cabinet.[87] The president chose the vice president and cabinet; many presumably are his close colleagues. To be sure, the Amendment provides that Congress may supplant the cabinet as a decision-maker by substituting some other body to act with the vice president. But this escape valve diminishes only slightly the Amendment's view that the decision to push the president aside is one for the executive branch. The Amendment makes clear its preference for executive control of the initiation of the decision by choosing the vice president and the cabinet over any other possible decision-makers. Unless Congress acts to the contrary, the cabinet remains part of the process. Congressional action is, by design, discouraged. Replacing the cabinet would require complying with both the bicameralism clause[88] (that is, the House and the Senate must pass the identical measure) and the presentment clause[89] (the president could veto any such legislation subject to a two-thirds override). Consistent with the founders' intent,[90] these arrangements make lawmaking difficult. The "such other body" alternative does offer an escape, but the framers of the Twenty-Fifth Amendment left the hatch barely ajar.

The Amendment further emphasizes the executive nature of the issue by making the vice president an indispensable decision-maker. Congress cannot replace him by mere legislation. And, in the unlikely event that Congress should designate some other body, that entity would have to act with the vice president. The vice president need not initiate the process under Section 4, but no transfer can occur if he is unwilling to concur that the president is disabled.

The decision to vest the vice president with this essential role is particularly significant, because it clashes with an important constitutional principle. The Rule of Law,[91] which *Marbury v. Madison*[92] recognizes as an important tenet of constitutional democracy, includes the teaching that no person should be judge in his own case. That precept, strictly applied, would most clearly exclude the president from any significant decision-making role regarding his disability. But it would seem to preclude the vice president, too. After all, a decision that the president cannot discharge his powers and duties results in their transfer to the vice president. The vice president has a conflict of interest in making such a decision.

The role Section 4 assigns the vice president is all the more intriguing when viewed in the larger context of other constitutional arrangements. The Constitution provides two mechanisms for involuntarily separating the president from the powers and duties of his office: (*a*) impeachment and removal, which permanently dislodges the president from office for treason, bribery, or other high crimes and misdemeanors;[93] and (*b*) Section 4 disability, which relieves him of his powers and duties until he can discharge them. In the case of presidential impeachment, the Constitution specifically provides that the chief justice, not the vice president, preside over the Senate trial.[94] Presumably, the vice president is disqualified to avoid injecting bias, or even its appearance, into the proceeding. In the case of involuntary removal under Section 4, however, the vice president's participation is mandated, not as a presiding officer, but as the decision-maker for relieving the president. The vice president need not be the prime advocate to relieve the chief executive, but he must at least acquiesce in the judgment of his colleagues. He is the one official who alone can effectively veto an attempt to relieve the president. Although the decision of the vice president and the cabinet to transfer power can be reversed by one-third plus one of either the House or the Senate, his decision not to transfer power is not subject to legislative or judicial review.

By conferring this constitutionally anomalous role on the vice president, Section 4 acknowledges the unique functional virtues of the vice presidency in disability determinations. The advantages of the office were sufficient to override any constitutional aversion to conflicts of interest and to deviate from the legislative model of decision-making used in impeachment and removal. The architects of the Twenty-Fifth Amendment sought to draft a provision that would at once allow the nation to arrange alternative executive leadership when truly necessary without subjecting the presidency or any president to undue risk of usurpation. They sought to ensure executive leadership while protecting the presidency. The vice presidency plays a crucial role. The vice president and members of the cabinet would, presumably, be familiar with the president's condition from their interaction with him.[95] Moreover, they would understand whether international and domestic exigencies made formal transfer of power necessary. Although these assumptions may be questionable regarding some cabinet members—how often does the secretary of veterans affairs receive an Oval Office audience? what does the secretary of agriculture know about threats to American security interests?—they describe the vice presidency as the office has evolved. The vice president not only has access to much of the president's time but also is exposed to the range of issues on the public agenda. He can observe whether the president is erratic or incoherent at daily security briefings or at lunch; he knows the risks of executive paralysis or incapacity. Knowledge of the condition of the president and the world would provide two critical sets of data to determine disability.

Moreover, assigning the vice president the pivotal role in deciding disability served the objective of protecting the presidency in at least two respects. The vice president was likely to be a close colleague of the chief executive's; the vice president would not take on the chief except for manifest cause. Moreover, because of the vice president's conflict of interest—the powers and duties transferred from the president would come to him—he was unlikely to move except in clear cases of disability. History had suggested that vice-presidential timidity was a greater problem than vice-presidential aggression. Logic would confirm that intuition. A politically ambitious vice president would seem unlikely to risk his political future by seeking to supplant the president improvidently.[96]

As a Section 4 decision-maker, the vice president presented something of a paradox. His identification with, and knowledge of, the chief executive and his perspective on public affairs afforded him unique qualifications to make the assessment when the president himself did not transfer powers. The extra-constitutional agreements between earlier presidents and their potential successors accorded him such a role. A further consideration argues for vice-presidential involvement, too. Suppose some other decision-maker authoritatively concluded that the chief executive was disabled, but the vice president, disagreeing, refused to assume the powers and duties. Little would be achieved. As a practical matter, before acting to separate the president from his powers and duties for awhile, it would be comforting to know that the vice president would take the controls.[97] All these considerations argued strongly for vice-presidential involvement in the decision. On the other hand, the vice president's apparent conflict of interest might impede him from acting when objectively he should.[98]

The vice president needed cover from the charge that his action was opportunistic. Even a credible suggestion that the Vice President seemed too anxious to act could mark him as an ingrate and a usurper, characterizations unlikely to enhance either his image or his reputation. Action by the president's adversaries obviously could not confer that legitimacy. The vice president would be best able to move if the president's allies ran interference for him. For that reason, including the cabinet as the other decision-maker seemed prudent. The conclusion of the president's own appointees that the chief executive was disabled gave the vice president cover to the extent needed. The vice president need not initiate the decision. He could acquiesce to a cabinet summons to act under Section 4.[99]

Including the cabinet not only protected the vice president by affording him cover, it also guarded the president from an overthrow if the vice president could act alone or with some body independent of, or not friendly to, the chief executive. To calm those worried about a vice-presidential coup, the framers imposed two checks on the vice president. He could not move to assume presidential powers without the support of a majority of the cabinet. And even if he obtained that endorsement, he could not hold onto those powers against the president's opposition if one vote more than one-third of either house of Congress dissented from his diagnosis that the president was disabled. Congress was empowered not in its conventional role of checking and balancing the president but rather to umpire a dispute between the vice president and cabinet on the one hand and the president on the other regarding the latter's fitness to lead. It was hoped, then, that the vice president would act when appropriate but not when the case was subject to doubt.

Occasions for Transfer

Predicting the circumstances under which future decision-makers will take particular political actions, like invoking Section 3 or 4, is a hazardous enterprise engaged in by fools and academics (no doubt groups with some overlap). Nonetheless, assessing the merits of a procedure to which recourse is seldom made inevitably must depend in part on some reasonable estimate of its likely use. Resort to Section 3 seems most likely when a president anticipates that he will undergo a medical procedure while unconscious. Although Section 3 might be invoked in other situations to which it applies, the president under general anesthesia is the most likely paradigm. In that situation, it is obvious that the president could not act if called upon to do so. Given the opportunity to transfer power before anesthesia is administered, failure to do so could subject the president to well-deserved criticism and encourage the inference that he lacked confidence in the vice president.

Presidents might invoke Section 3 under a range of other situations, following a serious injury or illness or during debilitating treatment. Whether they will do so will depend on a variety of factors including (a) their relationship with the vice president, (b) the severity of their anticipated condition, (c) the likelihood that they will have to take action when their judgment would be impaired, and (d) the political context.

It seems likely that vice presidents and cabinets will use Section 4 sparingly. They are most likely to invoke Section 4 when the disability is most evident and when doing so will not be seen as a rebuke to the chief executive's judgment. Under these circumstances, the propriety of the decision is most likely to be accepted and the political risk to the administration is slightest. These criteria presumably would be met if the president becomes unconscious and is likely to remain so for a long period of time. Convincing criticism of the vice president for acting would be unlikely. Moreover, one could not fault the president for failing to transfer power when he was unable to do so. Even so, absent some exigent circumstances, it seems unlikely that Section 4 will be used immediately when the president suffers some acute illness or injury—a heart attack or is shot. Unless there is need to take some prompt action that only a president can take—for instance, the nation is at war or attack seems imminent—a vice president and cabinet will be inclined to sit tight for a few hours or days to see how the chief fares and/or whether any crisis warrants a transfer. Unless the president's condition is critical or some emergency dominates the news, it seems unlikely that Section 4 will be used in these situations, although Section 3 might be.

When a president could have, but does not, declare himself disabled, the vice president and cabinet are unlikely to do so absent extenuating circumstances. Section 4 becomes more compelling if (a) the situation persists for a sufficiently long time to arouse intense media or public criticism, (b) the president becomes unconscious and seems likely to remain so for a long period of time, (c) some action urgently must be taken which the president cannot or will not take, or (d) the president is mentally or emotionally compromised to an extent that leaves no grounds for controversy. In these situations, invoking Section 4 may reflect adversely on the chief executive—after all, presumably he might have done right under Section 3—but the risks of not acting may outweigh those of transferring power.

If we apply these tests to historical situations, Section 4 might have been invoked to declare Garfield disabled but probably would not have been when Eisenhower had his heart attack or stroke, and certainly not when Grover Cleveland had cancer surgery, Franklin Roosevelt had coronary disease, or Kennedy had Addison's disease, even if the vice president and cabinet had been informed in each instance.[100]

The Wilson disability presents the most difficult case. The Twenty-Fifth Amendment certainly would have made it easier to declare the president disabled. Section 3 or 4 provides definite procedures and the assurance that the transfer would be only temporary. Wilson would not be "ousted" from office, as he feared. Moreover, with the development of the vice presidency, Wilson might have had an understudy whom he viewed as a big-caliber man, with whom he was compatible. Moreover, public opinion might have insisted on action if the president could not leave his room for months on end. If the president was isolated from leading officials and unable even to wave from his window, it is difficult to imagine that the vice president and cabinet would take no action. Surely, the media would be saturated with reports of a paralyzed government. No doubt, the airwaves would be dominated with talking heads speculating why no transfer occurred. Television would make the issue more immediate than it was eighty years ago. The pressure on the vice president would be intense in a modern Wilson situation. The very presence of Sections 3 and 4 in the Constitution would impose incentives for action that Wilson and Marshall did not encounter.

On the other hand, Wilson's intransigence, if repeated today, would present a formidable barrier for the vice president and his fellow decision-makers. Transfer under Section 4 would be far less appealing than under Section 3. The president's determination to retain presidential powers and duties might polarize the administration, greatly raising the stakes of vice-presidential action. The prospect of a public fight with the chief would at least give most vice presidents and cabinets pause, especially if the president's condition was improving and some would attest to his mental acuity.

Too many uncertainties remain to resolve this modern-day Wilson hypothetical. Timing might also be a factor. Late in the second term, a vice president who hoped to become the heir apparent might act differently from the way he would in the first few months of his incumbency. It does seem clear, however, that the procedures Section

3 and 4 provide, the growth in the vice presidency, and the pressures technological change have brought would make transfer of presidential power far more likely than it was in 1919–20.

The Vice President as Acting President

In considering the circumstances under which presidential power should be transferred, it is worth thinking about how vice presidents are likely to function as acting president, the second role the Amendment assigns them, under various scenarios. Such speculation has its perils, but no alternative exists (other than dodging the inquiry) until history furnishes data to assess.

As a matter of constitutional law, a vice president acting as president under Section 3 or 4 has the same powers and duties as the chief executive does under whom he serves. As a practical matter, in most situations, the vice president is much constrained. The limits are imposed in part by the knowledge that the president, not the vice president, was elected to do the job. A much greater restraint comes from the transitory nature of the vice president's status as acting president. Absent some crisis that makes action imperative before the president returns, his authority, *as a practical matter*, is much diminished.

One can imagine a range of possibilities. Suppose the president, following some trauma or disease, lapses into unconsciousness from which medical specialists agree he will never recover. As long as he remains on life support, he retains the title "president." But the vice president, once Section 4 is invoked, has constitutional authority to exercise presidential powers and duties. As a practical matter, the common realization that the president is not coming back frees the vice president to act across a wide range. He need not feel inhibited by the specter that the president will return and second-guess his actions. He might move the troops, report on the State of the Union, propose a new budget, send judicial nominees to the Senate for confirmation, remove the secretary of treasury, do virtually all the things that presidents do. He might even prepare to control his national party apparatus and to secure its presidential nomination. To be sure, the vice president's prestige may be somewhat less than if he became president under Section 1. He lacks the title and some of the trappings. It probably would be imprudent to move into the White House (especially if the grieving first spouse is still there) or to begin using the Oval Office or Air Force One or helicopter up to Camp David. He would not have a vice president (since he remains vice president) to shield him from some partisan chores. But the knowledge that he will possess presidential powers for the remainder of the term free of presidential rebuke confers political power to wield his constitutional authority.

Quite different contingencies lurk at the opposite end of the disability spectrum. Suppose a president transfers power to the vice president just before he has his wisdom teeth removed under general anesthesia or because he is running a fever of 105 or because she is on maternity leave. The vice president's constitutional power is the same—he/she is acting president—but as a practical matter, that authority is substantially reduced. Now, all these situations do not present the same problem. But, in each, it is unlikely that the vice president will take any action unless events force his hand. He may respond to a nuclear attack on the United States or veto a bill if the time will expire before the president returns (although the president would probably have done so before going to the dentist or delivery room), but it is virtually inconceivable that she would nominate a new chief justice, remove the chief of staff, or start issuing executive orders. She might receive a head of state or preside over a White House meeting but she could (and does) do these things as vice president. She would probably communicate with the chief executive if possible. She would not take any other action as acting president that she could not take as vice president. Her power, as a practical matter, is much reduced under these circumstances.

If the president was comatose, the vice president might have to respond to an emergency. But if the president was conscious but simply indisposed, the vice president would face greater constraint. It is unlikely that a vice president would act, or that the president would let him act, even in an emergency, if the president himself could decide and utter a command or drag a pen across paper.

Some have proposed that Section 3 generally be invoked due to death or serious illness in the president's family.[101] Proper sentiments motivate this suggestion, but, as a practical matter, it seems unrealistic. Let us suppose that a president transfers power to the vice president to allow the chief executive time to grieve for a deceased

relative. The vice president might perform ceremonial or other duties that he could handle without a transfer of power, such as chairing
a White House conference or discussing some issues with advisers.
But it is hard to imagine that if an emergency arose the president
would not resume. At least the vice president would ring him at
Camp David to get instructions. Otherwise the vice president under
such a Section 3 transfer would be in an untenable position when
Russian troops seal off Berlin, or the North Vietnamese reportedly
fire on an American patrol boat, or Iraq invades Kuwait. His ability
to act would be compromised by the common realization that the
president may reappear and reverse course. Even if he circumvented
that hazard, he still would confront the unpleasant prospect that
credit for a successful response will likely go to the team and policy
the president put in place, while blame for failure may rest at the
vice president's door. It is not clear what is achieved by the transfer
in this situation.

The eminent political scientist Clinton Rossiter grasped this point
forty years ago, before the consensus for the Twenty-Fifth Amendment existed. In discussing the Eisenhower disabilities, he wrote:

> Putting aside the plain fact that Eisenhower was not disabled except
> for a few hours or days, that not a single piece of routine business
> failed to get done, we might ask just what it was that Nixon could have
> done any better or would have done any differently during the weeks
> in which, on each of these occasions, the President was recovering.
> And the answer is: exactly nothing. As acting President he would have
> done just what he and the other members of the Eisenhower team did
> so well in so painful a pause: he would have kept the shop. Let us be
> entirely clear on this point: the only thing a Vice President can do, so
> long as there is the slightest chance that the President will recover, is
> to keep the shop. All the machinery in the world cannot alter that fact,
> which is inherent in the status and functions of all great offices of state,
> and most especially in the unique case of the American Presidency.[102]

The transformation of the vice presidency since Rossiter wrote probably stretches the possibilities somewhat. Nonetheless, his insight
remains valid today in many situations that may arise. If the vice
president will simply keep shop as acting president in situations
where the president is ill but capable of decision, why transfer
power?

It probably is a good idea for presidents to transfer power before operations under general anesthetic as President Reagan did, however ambiguously, in 1985. Such a step avoids any period when emergency action cannot be taken if necessary. It also is no doubt important to use Section 4 when the president is in a permanent coma or mentally unstable or in the advanced stages of a terminal illness. No doubt there are other situations where transfers under Section 3 or 4 will be prudent.

Yet, considering the realities of the vice president's position should make us more cautious about prescribing situations in which presidential power should be transferred. Simply because the president is sick or recovering or grieving does not mean that Section 3 or 4 should be invoked if, as a practical matter, the vice president will do nothing that he cannot already do.

CONCLUSIONS

Appreciating the connections between the Amendment and the vice presidency should prove helpful in structuring the operation of the two. Students of government frequently lament the unanticipated consequences of various reforms, the frequency with which ideas that once seemed destined to cure some social ill unhappily spawn unforeseen disasters. This phenomenon may be less common if those interested in improving government explore connections between various institutions before insisting upon remedies. Having explored the relationship between the Amendment and the office, it seems plausible to conclude that reforms in one will have ramifications for the other. We may at least filter out some bad ideas for change in one if we consider how they might affect the other.

For instance, some distinguished students of American government have suggested that the vice presidency would be improved if its occupant was chosen separately from the chief executive.[103] They conclude that the office would attract abler people who would better serve America if they enjoyed a separate mandate. I have already explained too often why I believe these suggestions are misguided and would diminish, not enhance, the vice presidency, presidency, and American government.[104] I will spare any current readers another such general discussion. My purpose here is simply to suggest that such a change, whatever its other credits and debits, would impact the arrangements the Twenty-Fifth Amendment provides for addressing presidential succession and inability. A vice president not chosen by the president would be less likely to be personally and politically compatible with him. Accordingly, he would probably be less intimately involved in the administration, less knowledgeable regarding the current status of pressing issues and programs, less able to succeed on short notice. Presidents would be less likely to transfer power to an independent vice president under Section 3, and the cabinet would be more reluctant to shunt the president aside under Section 4.

Just as reforms of the vice presidency could imperil the Twenty-Fifth Amendment, so, too, proposed reforms of the Twenty-Fifth Amendment could undermine the Vice Presidency. Take the legitimate issue of providing medical input to the disability determination, for instance. Some rightly point out that in some situations, access to the president's medical information may be important for political decision-makers to determine whether a President is disabled. They worry that maintaining total confidentiality regarding the president's medical information might prevent a determination of presidential inability. Contrary to the claims of some critics of the Amendment, those who drafted it recognized the need for the vice president and cabinet to have access to medical information. The legislative reports from the House and Senate that accompanied the proposed Amendment stated that "It is assumed that such decision [by the vice president and cabinet] would be made only after adequate consultation with medical experts who were intricately familiar with the president's physical and mental condition."[105] Critics of the Amendment, one hopes, will refrain from the false suggestion that its framers did not contemplate medical input where appropriate. But two remedies are problematic.

First, some suggest that Congress create an independent medical commission to administer annual exams to the president.[106] There are many reasons why this is a bad idea, a discussion of which is beyond the scope of this paper. Some insightful scholars have elaborated the defects in the proposal both in this volume and elsewhere.[107] One demerit within my topic is the negative impact on the vice presidency. If the medical commission was an "other body" to replace the cabinet, it would undermine the vice president's position by removing his political cover.[108] No disrespect to the medical profession intended, but a vice president would be more likely to invoke Section 4 with the cabinet on his side than surrounded by an eminent group of medical practitioners. Even if the medical panel was merely advisory to the vice president and cabinet, it is not likely to be helpful. In many cases, other reputable medical professionals would be marshaled to give contrary conclusions. The vice president would then be caught between competing groups of medical experts.

A second more modest proposal is also problematic. Some suggest that the president's physician be instructed routinely to share the president's medical records with the vice president. This well-intentioned suggestion might have the effect of occasionally bringing to the vice president's attention some presidential illness. On balance, it is a horrible idea. Unless one supposes that presidents should routinely relinquish or be stripped of their powers and duties whenever they suffer some malady (for example, a morose Calvin Coolidge depressed by the death of his teenage son, a hypertensive Franklin D. Roosevelt, a John Kennedy receiving steroid injections to deal with the Addison's disease he had sought to conceal),[109] disclosing the information would produce some action in only the remotest circumstance. Even if such presidents should be relieved of their responsibilities, a judgment I resist, as a practical matter it is unlikely that such information would often induce a vice president to take any such action. It is hard to imagine even one as bold as Vice President Harry S. Truman suggesting that FDR should take a break from being commander in chief before the war was won. In other words, the benefit from such a reform is likely to be slight.

Any such ephemeral benefits would, however, come at a cost to the vice presidency. Vice-presidential significance stems largely from the relationship the vice president develops with the chief executive. That relationship must overcome certain inherent awkward features: the fact that president and vice president are often rivals before forming their political partnership, the dependence of the latter on the former, and the mutual realization that the understudy's ambitions would be realized by the premature demise of the principal. Fortunately, for a variety of reasons, recent presidents and vice presidents have managed to overcome those obstacles in impressive fashion. Giving the vice president access to personal information a president may share with his physician would complicate a tenuous relationship.

Thinking about the historical, constitutional, and functional relationships between the Amendment and office may contribute to the future performance and development of both. The historical evolution of the vice presidency teaches the importance of informal developments in shaping political institutions. Although reformers proposed many statutory and constitutional changes in the vice presidency, these have not propelled the vice presidency to the new heights to which it has risen. Vice-presidential power has not depended upon separate election, giving the vice president a cabinet post or making him chief of staff, or other misguided suggestions for formal constitutional or statutory changes. On the contrary, a series of informal practices have largely transformed the office—allowing the presidential nominee to designate the vice-presidential candidate, inviting him to cabinet meetings, sending him on overseas missions, using him as an administration spokesman and party leader, giving him executive assignments, giving him a White House office, assigning him standing slots on the president's calendar, including him at presidential briefings and meetings, and so on. The statutory changes that have contributed to this development, most notably appropriations to provide a residence and official staff of advisers, have been supportive of changes otherwise under way.

The realities of modern political life give power to these practices. It becomes difficult, virtually impossible, to deviate from these developments which have enhanced the modern vice presidency. To be sure, no statute says the president must invite the vice president to Thursday lunch, give him the big office down the hall, or allow him the other goodies that have helped transform the office. But imagine the political consequences of exiling the vice president to the Executive Office Building or denying him his soup and salad in the dining room off the Oval. No President would give Sam Donaldson or Maureen Dowd such fodder, not to mention the political consultants, the Carvilles and Matalins, who craft the opposing party's rhetoric. The actions taken by one administration create precedents compulsory on those that follow. This dynamic has transformed the vice presidency into the more robust office it now is.

The inadequacies of proposals for legislating change regarding disability need not be cause for despair. Just as the vice presidency grew from repetition of new practices, so too might an evolutionary approach enhance the procedures the Twenty-Fifth Amendment provides for dealing with presidential succession and inability. After botching its first disability, the Reagan Administration did transfer power in 1985. Bush was prepared to follow suit in 1991, even though doing so might have been politically costly, given the widespread misgivings about Vice President Quayle. Apparently, the Bush Administration concluded that these costs did not justify disregarding the constitutional procedure. These historical precedents will make it difficult for future presidents to retain executive power when they undergo procedures under general anesthesia.

Other practices may also create constructive patterns. For example, the contingency plans developed by the Bush and Clinton Administrations for handling possible scenarios under Sections 3 and 4 are clearly useful precedents. Another possibility for informal change is that each president should identify to his vice president, cabinet, chief of staff, and spouse situations in which he would expect Section 4 to be invoked. The president should make clear that he expects compliance with the spirit of the Amendment. If he does so, his associates will likely comply. Such action, if taken in an appropriate public manner, would be difficult for successor administrations to resist. After repetition it would become part of our settled constitutional understandings.

What are the implications of the constitutional relationship? Most obviously, the new constitutional vision of the vice presidency that is embodied in the Twenty-Fifth Amendment gives the office an enhanced constitutional status. The Twenty-Fifth Amendment articulates an appreciation of the office as an essential institution, integral to the executive branch and crucial to solving problems of presidential succession and inability. Picking an incompetent vice president or excluding him from the loop not simply is bad practice but now offends the spirit of the Constitution.

But the new constitutional vision of the Vice Presidency does not simply enhance the office. It also has implications for the operation of the Twenty-Fifth Amendment. To the extent this new vision is embraced in practice, transfer of power under Section 3 and 4 should become more comfortable. As presidents and vice presidents become closer, as the Twenty-Fifth Amendment anticipates, transfer of power should become far less threatening. Perhaps no development would strengthen Section 3 or 4 more than the continued development of the vice presidency consistent with the Amendment's vision.

Moreover, appreciating the constitutional vision of the Twenty-Fifth Amendment may help assess some proposed reforms. In addition to its conception of the vice presidency, the Amendment also reflects a strong preference that the executive branch initiate any decision to transfer power. This preference rests upon a desire to protect primarily the president and secondarily the vice president. It is instructive that the decision to transfer presidential powers and duties can be initiated only by those close to the chief executive. To some extent, including the cabinet provides a check on a vice president overly anxious to relieve his superior. But the more basic purpose of that arrangement is to protect the vice president from political criticism. This constitutional arrangement should give pause to those seeking to empower some non-executive decision-makers to initiate, either formally or informally, the process.

Finally, appreciating the functional relationship should lead students of the Amendment to develop a more sophisticated understanding of the way it will operate in practice. The text of the Amendment gives the vice president certain powers and duties—it makes him a potential decision-maker regarding presidential inability and a potential acting president. But these words have meaning only relative to the context in which vice presidents operate. It promotes neither the operation of the Amendment nor the office to proceed from unrealistic expectations of the vice president in either role. The action of vice presidents will necessarily reflect certain limitations inherent in the situation. It is naïve to ignore these.

This is not an indictment of the vice presidency or of the Twenty-Fifth Amendment. The development of the former, and conception and ratification of the latter, afford far more protection against the hazards of presidential inability than previously existed. Indeed, the prospects that presidential inability will be handled well are far greater now than they have ever been.

Surely, gaps remain. But their existence hardly impeaches the office or the Amendment. Rather, they testify to the intractable nature of the problem of presidential inability. Most scholars eventually recognize limits on their ability to engineer solutions to the most vexing problems of government and politics. Few problems in American government are so immune to a perfect cure; in few areas do lawyers and doctors and others have such reason for humility when measuring the efficacy of their proposed remedies against the dimensions of the problem.

As the drafters of the Twenty-Fifth Amendment appreciated, presidential inability raises to some extent a legal problem which often raises medical issues. The Twenty-Fifth Amendment addresses both—by providing procedures and encouraging appropriate medical consultation. But its framers recognized that no formal procedure can itself guarantee that the problems of succession and inability will always be well handled.

For, ultimately, presidential inability poses a political problem. At some point the solution must rely on the interplay of political institutions and must anticipate that responsible officials will act in patriotic fashion, will honor their oaths or else endure the consequences. There are no guarantees, but constitutional democracy promises none.

The vice presidency and the Twenty-Fifth Amendment are linked in a variety of ways. Indeed, the two have reciprocally reinforced each other. Over time, the vice presidency has grown though informal change, from an object of derision to a position of substance. Its continued development, which the Amendment recognizes, will best promote the proper use of the Twenty-Fifth Amendment. The vision of the vice presidency implicit in the Twenty-Fifth Amendment provides a model for the further development of the office.

NOTES

1. See, generally, Joel K. Goldstein, "The New Constitutional Vice Presidency," *Wake Forest Law Review*, 30, No 3 (Fall 1995), p. 505.

2. See Charles Black, *Structure and Relationship in Constitutional Law* (Baton Rouge: Louisiana State University Press, 1969).

3. See, generally, John D. Feerick, *The Twenty-Fifth Amendment: Its Complete History and Applications* (New York: Fordham University Press, 1976; repr. 1992), pp. 117–90; Joel K. Goldstein, *The Modern American Vice Presidency: The Transformation of a Political Institution* (Princeton, N.J.: Princeton University Press, 1982), pp. 228–48.

4. U.S. Constitution, Article II, section 1, clause 6.

5. John Feerick, *From Failing Hands: The Story of Presidential Succession* (New York: Fordham University Press, 1965), p. 50. Ruth C. Silva, *Presidential Succession* (New York: Greenwood Press, 1968), pp. 10–11; Michael

Nelson, *A Heartbeat Away* (New York: Priority Press Publications, 1988), pp. 80–87.

6. U.S. Constitution, Article I, section 8, clause 18 ("The Congress shall have power . . . to make all Laws which shall be necessary and proper for carrying into Execution the foregoing Powers, and all other Powers vested by this Constitution in the Government of the United States, or in any Department or Officer thereof").

7. See Feerick, *From Failing Hands*, p. 51.

8. See ibid., pp. 50–51; Silva, *Presidential Succession*, pp. 8–13.

9. Max Farrand, ed., *Records of the Federal Convention of 1787*, vol. 2 (New Haven, Conn.: Yale University Press, 1911; repr.1937), pp. 163 and n.17, 172, 427.

10. Ibid., pp. 493, 495.

11. Ibid., p. 535.

12. Silva, *Presidential Succession*, p. 8. Feerick, *From Failing Hands*, p. 48.

13. See, generally, Feerick, *From Failing Hands*, pp. 48–51; Silva, *Presidential Succession*, pp. 8–10.

14. See, generally, Goldstein, "New Constitutional Vice Presidency," 515–18.

15. See ibid., 512–13; Lucius Wilmerding, Jr., "The Vice Presidency," *Political Science Quarterly*, 68 (1953), 17–41.

16. Farrand, ed., *Records*, p. 537.

17. Clinton Rossiter, ed., *The Federalist Papers*, No. 68 (New York: New American Library, 1961), p. 414.

18. See David P. Currie, *The Constitution in Congress, 1789–1801* (Chicago: The University of Chicago Press, 1997), pp. 139–46.

19. Farrand, ed., *Records*, p. 427.

20. Silva, *Presidential Succession*, p. 100 (referring to time of Garfield inability in 1881).

21. See ibid. (records of constitutional convention do not reveal framers' intent).

22. Of course, others might not have been bothered by the suggestion. After all, the vice president was next in line. The Succession Law of 1792 designated the Senate's President pro tempore as the officer who would act as president absent a president or vice president.

23. U.S. Constitution, Article I, section 2, clause 5; Article I, section 3, clause 6; Article II, section 4.

24. See, generally, Currie, *Constitution in Congress*, pp. 36–41.

25. These ideas are developed at greater length in Goldstein, "New Constitutional Vice Presidency."

26. See Rossiter, ed., *Federalist Papers*, No. 68, p. 414 (Hamilton).

27. Farrand, ed., *Records*, p. 537.

28. See U.S. Constitution, Article II, section 1, clause 3.

29. The House approved H.R. J. Res. 1, 368 to 29; the Senate approved S.J. Res. 1 72 to 0. After a conference committee harmonized differences, the House approved by voice vote; the Senate, 68 to 5.

30. Only Georgia, South Carolina, and North Dakota failed to ratify.

31. "[T]he Vice Presidency was a failure, and was recognized as such, almost from the outset," wrote presidential scholar Clinton Rossiter. Rossiter, *The American Presidency* (New York: New American Library, 1960), p. 129. Professor Rossiter appears to ascribe to the founders a more optimistic view of the vice presidency than I believe warranted.

32. Charles F. Adams, ed., I *The Works of John Adams*, vol. 1 (1856), p. 460.

33. P. L. Ford, ed., *The Writings of Thomas Jefferson* , vol. 7 (1896), p. 120.

34. See, generally, Tadahisa Kuroda, *The Origins of the Twelfth Amendment: The Electoral College in the Early Republic, 1787–1804* (Westport, Conn.: Greenwood Press, 1994).

35. See Goldstein, "New Constitutional Vice Presidency," 520–21.

36. Nelson, *A Heartbeat Away*, p. 30.

37. John Tyler, Millard Fillmore, Andrew Johnson, and Chester A. Arthur.

38. Except for six who died as vice president—George Clinton, Elbridge Gerry, William R. King, Henry Wilson, Thomas A. Hendricks, and Garret A. Hobart.

39. Quoted in Feerick, *From Failing Hands*, p. 163.

40. Quoted in ibid.

41. Ibid., pp. 162–80.

42. Woodrow Wilson, *Congressional Government: A Study in American Politics* (Boston: Houghton Mifflin, 1885; repr. Gloucester, Mass.: Peter Smith, 1973), p. 162.

43. See, generally, Goldstein, *Modern American Vice Presidency* where this thesis is developed.

44. See, generally Stephen E. Ambrose, *Nixon: The Education of a Politician, 1913–1962* (New York: Simon & Schuster, 1987); Richard Norton Smith, " 'You Can Be President Someday': Richard M. Nixon as Vice President" in *At the President's Side*, ed. Timothy Walch (Columbia: University of Missouri Press, 1997), pp. 79–87.

45. "Agreement Between the President and the Vice President as to Procedures in the Event of Presidential Disability," in *Public Papers of the Presidents of the United States, Dwight D. Eisenhower, 1958* (Washington, D.C.: Government Printing Office, 1959), p. 196.

46. See, for example, *McCulloch v. Maryland*, 4 Wheat. 316 (U.S. 1819); *United States v. Midwest Oil Co.*, 236 U.S. 459 (1915); *Youngstown Sheet & Tube Co. v. Sawyer*, 343 U.S. 579 (1952) (Frankfurter, J. concurring).

47. McCormack was seventy-one and Hayden eighty-six when Johnson became president; neither had been considered presidential timber.

48. As Senator Bayh observed later, "Public concern over who would serve as President in the event of Lyndon Johnson's death had been increased even more by the telecasting of his special message to Congress on November 27. During the speech, the television cameras focused repeatedly on . . . McCormack and . . . Hayden." Bayh, *One Heartbeat Away: Presidential Disability and Succession* (Indianapolis: Bobbs-Merrill, 1968), pp. 8–9.

49. Early versions included provisions for cabinet succession after the vice presidency. These were dropped since they seemed likely to alienate some key legislators.

50. 110 Cong. Rec. 22, 986 (Sen. Birch Bayh), 22987 (Bayh), 22993 (Sen. Hiram Fong) (1964).

51. "Special Message to the Congress on Presidential Disability and Related Matters," in *Public Papers of the Presidents of the United States, Lyndon B. Johnson, 1965* (Washington, D.C.: Government Printing Office, 1966), pp. 100, 102.

52. See, for example, 110 Cong. Rec. 22993–94 (1964) (Sen. Hiram Fong); 111 Cong Rec. 7937 (1965) (Rep. Emanuel Celler) (vice president is "part of the official family of the President.") See, generally, Goldstein, "New Constitutional Vice Presidency," 530–32.

53. 110 Cong Rec. 22994 (1964) (Sen. Birch Bayh). See also 111 Cong Rec. 7960, 7963 (1965) (remarks of Rep. Emanuel Celler); 111 Cong. Rec. 3262 (remarks of Senator Hiram Fong). See, generally, Goldstein, "New Constitutional Vice Presidency," 532–33.

54. See Goldstein, *Modern American Vice Presidency*, pp. 233–34. See also U.S. Congress, Senate Subcommittee on Constitutional Amendments of the Committee on the Judiciary, *Hearing on Presidential Inability and Vacancies in the Office of Vice President*, 88th Cong., 2d Sess., 1964, pp. 130–31 (testimony of Professor Paul Freund).

55. See, generally, Goldstein, "New Constitutional Vice Presidency," 533–34.

56. "Presidential Inability and Vacancies in the Office of the Vice President," S. Rep. No. 66, 89th Cong. 1st Sess. (1965), pp. 11–12; "Presidential Inability and Vacancies in the Office of the Vice President," H.R. Rep. 203, 89th Cong. 1st Sess. (1965), p. 11.

57. 111 Cong. Rec. 7961–62 (1965) (remarks of Rep. John V. Lindsay).

58. S. Rep. No. 66, pp. 10, 14–15; H. R. Rep. 203, pp. 14–15.

59. See, generally, Robert Dallek, "Frustration and Pain: Lyndon B.

Johnson as Vice President," in *At the President's Side*, ed. Walch, pp. 88–100.

60. Bayh, *One Heartbeat Away*, pp. 7–8.

61. See Hubert H. Humphrey, *The Education of a Public Man* (Garden City, N.Y.: Doubleday, 1976), pp. 320–24.

62. See Joel K. Goldstein, "More Agony than Ecstasy: Hubert H. Humphrey as Vice President," in *At the President's Side*, ed. Walch, pp. 103–23.

63. See, for example, Doris Kearns Goodwin, *Lyndon Johnson and the American Dream* (New York: New American Library, 1976), pp. 167–76; Robert Dallek, *Flawed Giant: Lyndon Johnson and His Times, 1961–1973* (New York: Oxford University Press, 1998), pp. 3–46.

64. Dwight D. Eisenhower, "Preface," in Bayh, *One Heartbeat Away*, p. vii.

65. 111 Cong. Rec. 3262 (1965) (remarks of Sen. Hiram Fong).

66. 111 Cong. Rec. 7963 (1965) (remarks of Rep. Emanuel Celler).

67. See also Senate Subcommittee, *Presidential Inability and Vacancies in the Office of Vice President*, p. 79 (1964) (statement of Sen. Frank Church).

68. Goldstein, "More Agony Than Ecstasy," pp. 103–23.

69. John Robert Greene, " 'I'll Continue to Speak Out': Spiro T. Agnew as Vice President," in *At the President's Side*, ed. Walch, p. 127.

70. See *ibid.*, pp. 124–30; Goldstein, *Modern American Vice Presidency*, p. 171.

71. See Arthur M. Schlesinger, Jr., "On the Presidential Succession," *Political Science Quarterly*, 89 (1974), 475–505.

72. See, generally, Feerick, *Twenty-Fifth Amendment*, pp. 117–90. Goldstein, *Modern American Vice Presidency*, pp. 228–48.

73. Indeed, some advised Nixon that his presumed first choice, John Connally, would attract opposition.

74. *Washington Post*, October 12, 1973, p. A10.

75. U.S. Congress, Senate Committee on Rules and Administration, *Hearings on Nomination of Gerald R. Ford of Michigan to Be Vice President of the United States*, 93d Cong., 1st Sess. (1973), p. 148.

76. On Mondale, see Paul C. Light, *Vice-Presidential Power* (Baltimore: The Johns Hopkins University Press, 1984), and Steven M. Gillon, *The Democrat's Dilemma: Walter F. Mondale and the Liberal Legacy* (New York: Columbia University Press, 1992), pp. 179–293. Gillon demonstrates that despite Mondale's unprecedented role his vice presidency was not free of strain. On Gore, see, for example, Bob Woodward, *The Agenda: Inside the Clinton White House* (New York: Simon & Schuster, 1994); Joseph A. Pika, "The Vice Presidency: New Opportunities, Old Constraints," in *The Presidency and the Political System*, ed. Michael Nelson, 5th ed., (Washington, D.C.: Congressional Quarterly Press, 1998).

77. Agnew had a West Wing office, which he vacated after a brief time. See Light, *Vice-Presidential Power*, pp. 76–77.

78. On these recent developments, see, generally, Goldstein, *Modern American Vice Presidency*, pp. 172–75, 318–19; Light, *Vice-Presidential Power*, pp. 63–100; Nelson, *A Heartbeat Away*, pp. 74–78.

79. John D. Feerick, "The Vice-Presidency and the Problems of Presidential Succession and Inability," *Fordham Law Review*, 32 (1964), 486.

80. Whereas the presidency has fallen vacant 9 times due to death or resignation, the vice presidency has been vacant on 18 occasions totaling 37 years, 9 months. See Goldstein, *Modern American Vice Presidency*, p. 229.

81. For instance, if absent a vice president, several presidents delegated power during disability to the officer Congress designated as successor and this action won acquiescence, it might establish a constitutional precedent. See cases cited at note 49 above.

82. 111 Cong. Rec. 7941 (1965) (remarks of Rep. Richard H. Poff).

83. Feerick, *Twenty-Fifth Amendment*, pp. 197–98.

84. I was among the critics; see Joel K. Goldstein, "First Test for the 25th Amendment," *St. Louis Post-Dispatch*, July 21, 1985.

85. See, for example, Feerick, *Twenty-Fifth Amendment*, p. xvi; Robert E. Gilbert, "Presidential Disability in Law and Politics," *Miller Center Journal*, 5 (Spring 1998), 3, 11.

86. William Shakespeare, *Julius Caesar*, Act I, scene 2, line 194.

87. See Feerick, *Twenty-Fifth Amendment*, p. 202.

88. U.S. Constitution, Article I, section 7, clause 2.

89. Ibid., clause 3.

90. Rossiter, ed., *Federalist Papers*, Nos. 62 (Madison), 73 (Hamilton), pp. 378–82, 442–47.

91. See, generally, Richard H. Fallon, Jr., "The 'Rule of Law' as a Concept in Constitutional Discourse," *Columbia Law Review*, 97 (1997), 1.

92. 5 U.S. (1 Cranch) 137 (1803).

93. U.S. Constitution, Article II, section 4.

94. Ibid., Article I, section 3, clause 6.

95. S. Rep. No. 66, p. 13; H. R. Rep. 203, p. 13.

96. See Gilbert, "Presidential Disability in Law and Politics," 12.

97. As Senator Bayh later explained, "It does not do any good to have a provision unless the people who are going to play the game are willing to suit up and go out on the field. We didn't want a [Thomas] Marshall hiding under the bed someplace saying that even if Mrs. Wilson asks me, I'm not going to accept the responsibility." Kenneth W. Thompson, ed. *Papers on Presidential Disability and the Twenty-Fifth Amendment* (Lanham, Md.: University Press of America, 1988), p. 90.

98. Senate Subcommittee, *Presidential Inability and Vacancies in the Of-*

fice of Vice President, p. 129. See also pp. 151 (statement of John Feerick) (stating that the vice president's apparent self-interest could cause inaction); 184 (statement of Sidney Hyman) (testifying of the danger that the vice president will not act, due to fear he would be accused of usurpation); and 212 (statement of Rep. Louis C. Wyman) (expressing concern that the vice president will not act).

99. 111 Cong. Rec. 5385 (1965) (comments of Sen. Birch Bayh, Sen. Jacob Javits).

100. Cleveland's surgery would, however, have been a classic Section 3 case. Had the vice president and cabinet been aware of the situation and had the Twenty-Fifth Amendment existed, Cleveland would probably have been spared the spectacle of surgery on a boat afloat.

101. See, for example, Abrams, *The President Has Been Shot: Confusion, Disability, and the Twenty-Fifth Amendment in the Aftermath of the Attempted Assassination of Ronald Reagan* (New York: W. W. Norton, 1992), p. 224; Herbert L. Abrams, "The Vulnerable President and the Twenty-Fifth Amendment, with Observations on Guidelines, a Health Commission, and the Role of the President's Physician," *Wake Forest Law Review*, 30, No. 3 (Fall 1995), pp. 453, 463.

102. Rossiter, *American Presidency*, p. 214.

103. See, for example, Akhil Reed Amar and Vik Amar, "President Quayle?," *Virginia Law Review*, 78 (1992), 913–47; Richard D. Friedman, "Some Modest Proposals on the Vice Presidency," *Michigan Law Review*, 86 (1988), 1703.

104. See Goldstein, *Modern American Vice Presidency*, pp. 271–99; Goldstein, "New Constitutional Vice Presidency," 549–59.

105. See Sen. Rep. No. 66; H. Rep. No. 203.

106. See, for example, Abrams, "Vulnerable President," 465; Bert E. Park, "Protecting the National Interest: A Strategy for Assessing Presidential Impairment Within the Context of the Twenty-Fifth Amendment," *Wake Forest Law Review*, 30, No. 3 (Fall 1995), 596–606.

107. Robert E. Gilbert, *The Mortal Presidency: Illness and Anguish in the White House*, 2nd ed. (New York: Fordham University Press, 1998), pp. 240–41; Birch Bayh, "The Twenty-Fifth Amendment: Dealing with Presidential Disability," *Wake Forest Law Review*, 30, No. 3 (Fall 1995), 447; John Feerick, "The Twenty-Fifth Amendment: An Explanation and Defense," *Wake Forest Law Review*, 30, No. 3 (Fall 1995), 499–501; Edwin M. Yoder, Jr. "Determining Presidential Health Under the Twenty-Fifth Amendment," *Wake Forest Law Review*, 30 No. 3 (Fall 1995), 612–15.

108. See Richard Neustadt, "The Twenty-Fifth Amendment and Its Achilles' Heel," *Wake Forest Law Review*, 30, No. 3 (Fall 1995), 433.

109. See, generally, Gilbert, *Mortal Presidency*.

10

The Imperfect but Useful Twenty-Fifth Amendment

Tom Wicker

In the 1960s, I was one of those who opposed the Twenty-Fifth Amendment, largely because it afforded another constitutional means by which a president could be removed from office. I still have fears that the Amendment could be abused but, as explained here, I now see it in a different—and more favorable—light.

History has established the real possibility of a presidential disability—either physical or mental—as one that constitutes a weak link in the American system of government.[1] Whether that same history demands a new remedy beyond the present Twenty-Fifth Amendment, as some urge, is far more open to question.

As other authors have discussed earlier in this volume, at least four presidents in the twentieth century (Wilson, Franklin Roosevelt, Eisenhower, and Reagan) suffered disabilities that were either severely or somewhat incapacitating. In the most recent instance, Ronald Reagan virtually began his presidency by surviving an assassination attempt that easily could have left him physically or mentally too impaired to perform his duties. As it was, his wounds hospitalized him for a substantial period. Already seventy-eight when he left office in 1989, Reagan developed Alzheimer's disease soon thereafter, raising the possibility that, as an elderly man, he might have been stricken while he was still serving. If known at the time, this situation might have caused the vice president to try to take over under the Twenty-Fifth Amendment or at least to be urged to do so.

Of the seventeen twentieth-century presidents, then, four—nearly 25 percent—vividly dramatize the potential disability problem. That only one of them, Wilson, actually was unable to govern was largely a matter of luck. Mostly partisan debate continues, in fact, on the question whether in the last years of FDR's third term, and in his brief fourth, he was fully capable of the important efforts he was called upon to make.

The death of a president in office—Harding, Roosevelt, John F. Kennedy—is sad and could, of course, be disastrous, but in such cases, well-established precedent, and now the Twenty-Fifth Amendment to the Constitution, puts the vice president in office for the remainder of the term. It is when a president may be too sick to exercise his powers and duties, particularly if he or she cannot or will not admit it, that the most grievous problem arises. For that frightening eventuality, the Twenty-Fifth Amendment is probably the best, but by no means a flawless, response to a complex problem for which, almost certainly, no perfect solution exists.

A major contribution of the Amendment is that it makes clear, for the first time in our history, that when a vice president assumes the powers and duties of the presidential office because of some presidential inability, it is only as an acting president. The president continues to hold his title and office. This would be the only circumstance under which the United States would have a president and an acting president at the same time, at least in a formal sense. It would not, however, have two presidents.

Whether the transfer of powers be temporary or permanent, the president may reclaim them under procedures that the Twenty-Fifth specifies forthrightly and in some detail. Once again, therefore, the Amendment clarifies a process that, in our past, was indefinite and troublesome. This is all to the good.

On its face, therefore, the Twenty-Fifth Amendment seems to solve the disability problem, except that, for it to work properly, everyone involved has to act honorably and with selfless disregard for his or her own personal or political interest. Human nature, alas, is seldom so inclined to dispassion, and might well not be so when the most powerful political office in the world is at stake.

For that reason, when Congress passed the Twenty-Fifth Amendment in 1965, a number of historians and commentators (including me) opposed it on several grounds. First, as I wrote at the time, since the Amendment provided a constitutional means of "removing" a president from office, someone, someday, would try to use that means to usurp the presidency. Until the Twenty-Fifth Amendment was ratified in 1967, the only constitutional means of taking the presidency away from a president had been to impeach him or her in the House of Representatives, followed by conviction in the Senate—in itself, an unclear and highly difficult course of action. Now there is a new method of "removal," even though it, too, is difficult to implement.

Second, the Amendment aroused fear among some observers that when a president refused to admit that he was disabled but was nonetheless supplanted by an acting president, the Amendment could lead to paralysis and pose a danger to orderly government. Although Congress is empowered to settle the issue within twenty-one days, there would be terrible confusion during that period with two different individuals both claiming presidential powers. Congress and the people would be torn between them, and foreign governments would observe the spectacle with either trepidation or glee. Even after Congress resolved the matter, the final "winner" would surely be a president or acting president functioning under a considerable cloud.

Third, the possibility of an untoward congressional influence over the presidency seemed inherent in the Amendment. A president who has had to bargain with Congress to get the person he wants into the vice presidency, a president or an acting president who is in the White House only after a congressional vote on disability, and thus only by sufferance of Congress, and even a vice president who has been confirmed in office by Congress and who then succeeds to the White House, might someday find himself or herself more beholden to an overbearing Congress than a Chief Executive ought to be, particularly in a system based on separation of powers.[2]

The amendment aroused opposition for other reasons as well, including a president's probable reluctance to give up his office under any circumstances and the obvious difficulty of getting a vice president and the cabinet to act even when a president might be truly disabled. Contemporary critics of the Amendment still share some of these concerns.

Because of this, the effort to find a better response to the problem of presidential disability has continued. Presidents Bush and Clinton, for instance, entered into agreements with their vice presidents on procedures to be followed in the event of disability. To what extent these procedures, if necessarily carried out, would be convincing to Congress and the public—particularly if a president, once supplanted, tried to reclaim his powers—has not been tested (and might never be, if the nation's luck holds).

Outside groups also have suggested possible courses of action, including, for example, the appointment of a legally constituted body of medical persons empowered to conduct periodic physical and mental evaluations of the president. This proposition, even though such check-ups undoubtedly would be useful medically and might sometimes be reassuring to the public, also has its drawbacks.

One, the panel could be subject to scary publicity and/or malicious or inaccurate "leaks" that might cause undue pressures on a president, as well as public worries about his or her well-being, and thus undermine confidence in the national leadership. Two, the possibility exists that if the panel recommended the "removal" of the president on medical grounds, he or she might disagree and refuse to relinquish power. No matter what the legal role of the panel, the president and his supporters could at least deadlock government; and his or her legitimacy surely would be tainted at home and abroad.

With all due respect, moreover, to the integrity of the medical persons so empowered, still another legitimate means for the removal of a president from office, in addition to the Twenty-Fifth Amendment and to impeachment for high crimes and misdemeanors, would be established. That would raise again the specter of usurpation, or political crisis, or both.

These are not fanciful problems. Woodrow Wilson's incapacity was real; behind the scenes, his wife and his staff essentially took over and a cabinet officer who questioned the arrangement was fired. More than thirty years later, when Eisenhower was suffering from ileitis, Vice President Richard Nixon—no doubt with the Wilson precedent in mind—literally feared to discuss with Secretary of State John Foster Dulles the possibility that the president might have to be removed. Nixon did not hesitate, however, during his own presidential campaign in 1960 to make the exaggerated claim that he had been a sort of assistant president.

Suppose that in the 1940s Vice President Henry Wallace, with the support of the cabinet, had believed Franklin Roosevelt too sick to govern. The Twenty-Fifth Amendment was not yet in effect, and Wallace and the cabinet would have had no legal means of action. If they had had, would the nation, let alone the Roosevelt cabinet, have accepted Wallace as President? In wartime? Few would argue now, or would have then, that he was preferable even to a weakened FDR.

Or suppose publicity about Roosevelt's real or supposed illness, perhaps leaked by one of those who had believed him incapacitated, had resulted in the election of Thomas E. Dewey to the presidency in 1944. History undoubtedly would have been changed, whether for better or worse perhaps only partisans would be willing to judge.

After the Reagan assassination attempt in 1981, would Vice President George Bush (not a popular figure among Reagan's conservative supporters) have been willing to certify that the president was unfit to serve, even if Bush believed that to be the case? And could he have persuaded a majority of the Reagan cabinet to go along even if those Reagan appointees also considered their patron disabled? Or might a different vice president with less scruple have tried to use the episode for an illicit takeover of the presidency? Even if such a shady effort had failed, might it not have been politically disastrous for the administration and damaging to the nation?

As we begin a new century, and as the final months of the Clinton Administration run out, one of the great distinctions of American politics and government—its stability—probably has already been undermined. Unlike a parliamentary system, in which prime ministers and governing parties can rise and fall with unpredictable frequency, the American constitutional regime has guaranteed any national government a fixed period in which to exert its leadership, largely free from the threat of removal or reduced tenure.

In the first century of the republic, only one (Andrew Johnson) out of thirty-four presidents was impeached, and he was acquitted. In the last quarter-century, however, two (Bill Clinton and Richard Nixon) of six presidents have been impeached, though Nixon officially resigned before the House could cast an impeachment vote he knew it would approve.

The count nearly became three of six. The so-called Iran-Contra scandal in Reagan's second term so threatened his impeachment that the late Arthur Liman, the Democrats' chief counsel in the case, predicted to me that Reagan, like Nixon, ultimately would have to go.

Three presidents under threat of forced removal from office (one actually ousted) in the six presidential terms since the 1972 election calls into question what was once the general American assumption that any president of either party would serve four statutory years,

probably eight, in the most stable of offices. That new uncertainty is
bound also to affect presidents themselves, which means that in the
future they will not feel or be as secure in office as they and the
public once believed.

In addition to impeachment and the Twenty-Fifth Amendment,
would it make sense now to add still another route, as some students
of the disability problem would have us do, by which a president
might suffer separation from his or her powers and duties? Particularly since recent precedents make impeachment more likely than in
the past, a partisan threat is likely to shadow the mind of any future
chief executive faced with a disputed political or diplomatic decision.

At least three factors are already at work to heighten presidential
insecurity. First, the desire for political revenge. Long memories of
the Nixon and Reagan investigations obviously influenced the impeachment of Bill Clinton and, conversely, his acquittal. Human and
political nature being what they are, the Democrats, in return, may
well go for the jugular of the next Republican president, and so on
and on.

Second, hardening partisanship. Civility and tolerance for those of
opposing views and party seem to be declining, perhaps influenced
by the increased visibility of politicians in the age of television.

Third, pocketbook rewards. Those Republicans who took the lead
in impeaching Bill Clinton, and those Democrats most active in his
defense, are reported to be reaping large financial returns in campaign funds.

To the increased possibility of impeachment must already be
added the concrete presence in the Constitution of the Twenty-Fifth
Amendment. Carefully worked out by a Senate subcommittee that
had made a thorough study of the disability problem and possible
responses, the Amendment may well be the best possible safeguard
against presidential disability, despite the flaw that it indisputably
offers a means other than impeachment for effectively removing a
president from office.

An unlikely means? Perhaps. But the temptation for someone or
some group to take advantage of it sooner or later may be too great
for highly partisan politicians—or even for one of the same party and
persuasion as the President—to resist. Too great, surely, to add still
another, even theoretical, route to usurpation in the name of protec-

tion against the threat of presidential disability. Luck, though capricious, seems a less dangerous alternative.

As stated earlier, I did not always think so and I still fear the possible misuse of the Amendment. But after years of contemplation, and after studying various options, I have come to the conclusion that the Amendment is as near a solution as men of good will are likely to find. I reached this conclusion because of factors that have acquired increased potency over the years.

First, the Amendment permits quick and orderly action when a president is *clearly* disabled. Second, the Amendment provides constitutional legitimacy to a vice president and cabinet who take the initiative in operating the government during periods of presidential incapacity. Third, the Amendment gives Congress the prerogative to act if the cabinet refuses to co-operate with the vice president, either out of fear of public opinion or out of loyalty to a stricken leader, by creating another body to replace the cabinet. Fourth, in providing for the filling of a vacant vice presidency, the Amendment gives the American people more of a voice in the selection—through their elected representatives in Congress—than they have now when the vice-presidential candidate is chosen by the presidential nominee of the party and then simply ratified by convention delegates. Fifth, the Amendment, over time, might actually give the American people better and more carefully selected vice presidents. No presidential nominee will be tempted to carelessly bargain away the vice-presidential nomination solely for political gain when he or she knows that there is now a constitutional provision that might be perverted by a malicious or ambitious vice president attempting to seize power.

Finally, as I indicated earlier, the Amendment makes clear that, whenever its disability provisions are invoked, the powers and duties of the presidency are passed on to an acting president, not the office itself. This is an important, and very helpful, distinction. It might well make protracted conflicts between a president and an acting president considerably less likely because, after all, the president remains president, and the title alone gives authority and stature.

With the passage of time, the advantages of the Twenty-Fifth Amendment have emerged clearly as outweighing its disadvantages. It should not be subjected to any constitutional change. Although the Amendment is not foolproof, further efforts to perfect it may only verify the old saying that "the perfect is the enemy of the good."

NOTES

1. Brief sections of this chapter have appeared in altered form in the biweekly publication *Earth Times*.

2. Tom Wicker, "Washington: Defining the Disability Amendment," *New York Times*, July 4, 1965, sec. 4, p. 6.

11

Report of the Working Group on Disability in U.S. Presidents

Edited by Robert J. Joynt, M.D., and James F. Toole, M.D.

The Twenty-Fifth Amendment to the Constitution raises a number of salient questions. Is the Amendment adequate to ensure continuity of presidential leadership? Should it be changed? How is disability to be determined and by whom? Will the public understand and support the process? These, and other, questions were discussed in detail by members of the Working Group on Presidential Disability in several multiple-day meetings beginning in November 1995 and concluding in December 1996 when its recommendations were presented to President Clinton at the White House. While no changes in the Amendment itself are recommended, steps are suggested that will facilitate its implementation in the future.

EDITORS' INTRODUCTION

The Working Group on Presidential Disability was established in 1994 at the urging of former President Jimmy Carter and with the active assistance of the Bowman Gray School of Medicine at Wake Forest University. The group consisted of some fifty persons prominent in the fields of medicine, law, history, political science, journalism, and government who had an interest and/or expertise in the issue of presidential disability and the best way to control and minimize its effects. Some sessions of the Working Group were open to the public, and several sessions were televised on C-Span. Former

President Carter attended the first meeting at the Carter Center in Atlanta, Georgia, and former President Ford attended the second meeting at Wake Forest University in Winston-Salem, North Carolina. Both addressed the meeting and took an active part in the discussion; both recommended against trying to change the content of the Amendment. Former Senator Birch Bayh, a key figure in the adoption of the Twenty-Fifth Amendment, who also participated in the deliberations of the Working Group, shared this view.

Among the physicians who participated as members of the Working Group, there were several who were serving or had served in the White House as White House Physician or as Physician to the President. Their intimate knowledge about the relationship of the medical staff to the president and to the executive branch added greatly to the discussion.

The co-chairs of the Working Group were Professor Arthur S. Link and Dr. James F. Toole. Arthur Link, now deceased, was professor of history at Princeton University, the premier Woodrow Wilson scholar and editor of Wilson's voluminous papers. In the course of his work, he became intimately familiar with Wilson's long period of disability at a critical stage in national history. It was during this period that the president's most important issue, the Treaty of Versailles, which would have enabled the United States to join the League of Nations, was defeated in the Senate, in part because he could not supply his strong advocacy. James F. Toole is professor of neurology at the Bowman Gray School of Medicine at Wake Forest University. He is an acknowledged leader in the area of cerebral vascular disease. In his own practice and research, he sees the effect of various types of strokes and other diseases on the functioning of individuals. He, like many physicians, has to make clinical judgments about the ability of someone afflicted with brain disease to carry on in a position of responsibility. For presidents of the United States, this is a critically important consideration.

In May 1994, Professor Link and Dr. Toole made a presentation to the American Academy of Neurology and then published a paper in the *Journal of the American Medical Association* in which they raised concerns over the current procedures dealing with presidential disability set forth in the Twenty-Fifth Amendment.[1] In that same JAMA issue are a graphic description of the assassination attempt on President Reagan written by Aaron and Rockoff,[2] a perspective on the

Twenty-Fifth Amendment written by former President Carter,[3] and an editorial comment on these three articles authored by Joynt.[4]

The description by Drs. Aaron and Rockoff, two physicians involved in the care of President Reagan at the time of the attempted assassination, emphasized the very precarious condition of the president as a result of his injury. The perspective of former President Carter indicated his own concern about the process to ensure stable and healthy leadership and his recommendation that members of the medical community offer their suggestions on the way the procedure should be modified. The editorial comment by Joynt considers the factors that make leadership, particularly presidential leadership, so vulnerable. These risk factors include advanced age, lack of retirement restrictions, lack of a temporary substitute, stress, protection by others, poor medical advice, poor medical care, and assassination attempts. Many of these risks have been closely studied and are discussed in books on the subject, most notably by Post and Robins,[5] Gilbert,[6] and Park.[7]

The concern about ensuring healthy leadership in the White House has waxed and waned during our national history. It receives much attention and debate at times of leadership crisis, but there is less interest and discussion when things are going well. The original provision for transition of leadership as presented in the Constitution of 1787 may have seemed straightforward to a casual reader, but various events in our national history soon revealed its inadequacies. In 1841, Vice President John Tyler seemed to resolve at least one inadequacy when he successfully claimed the presidency—and not just its powers and duties—upon President Harrison's death. However, it should be noted that Tyler's action established a *political*, but not necessarily a *legal*, precedent.

The assassination of Abraham Lincoln imposed no serious problem in transition as he lived only some eight hours after being shot, and Vice President Andrew Johnson, following the Tyler precedent, became president immediately thereafter. However, the serious inadequacy of the disability provision of the original Constitution became very apparent on three occasions within the next fifty years or so: during the 80-day incapacitation of President Garfield, after he was shot by a disappointed office-seeker; during the 8-day incapacitation of President McKinley, after he was attacked by an anarchist; and during the 281-day period throughout which President Wilson absented himself from all public activity after he suffered a massive stroke.

Since the original Constitution had failed to establish any mechanism by which presidential inability might be determined, governmental paralysis of varying degrees ensued in each of these instances. Nevertheless, change came very slowly. In fact, almost half a century elapsed after Wilson left office before the Constitution was amended to clarify issues of disability and succession. Some quarter of a century later, the Working Group on Presidential Disability was formed to revisit the disability provisions of the Amendment and to determine whether they needed improvement, either in language or in implementing mechanisms.

Although the Amendment contains four sections, the first (which deals with the filling of a permanent vacancy in the presidency) and the second (which deals with filling a permanent vacancy in the vice presidency) were not addressed in any formal way by the Working Group since both were outside its purview. It is worth noting, however, that both these sections contribute to an orderly transition in power, which is the ultimate objective of the Twenty-Fifth Amendment.

The focus of the Working Group's attention was clearly Sections 3 and 4 since they are designed to provide continuity of leadership when the president is disabled—whether or not he or she acknowledges the disability. An analysis of Sections 3 and 4 (see the Appendix for the complete text) immediately raises several questions. Is the language of the Twenty-Fifth Amendment so ambiguous that it should be changed? What physician or what group of physicians should be constituted to make medical judgments? What is the role of confidentiality between the patient–president and his or her physician? How should the spouse and family be involved? Whose role is it to make the judgment regarding the ability to discharge the powers of office? What is the role of a contingency plan in the transfer of power? Who is responsible for disclosure of information about the president's medical condition? How is the public going to accept the transfer of power from their elected president?

These and related questions were discussed in detail by members of the Working Group. Their final recommendations were offered as answers to many of them.[8] An edited Report of the Working Group, along with the commentaries and addenda, follow the references to this introductory statement. A complete compilation of the discussions of the Working Group has been collected and is being published by the University of Rochester Press.

NOTES

1. Arthur S. Link and James F. Toole, "Presidential Disability and the Twenty-Fifth Amendment," *Journal of the American Medical Association*, 272 (1994), 1694.
2. Benjamin L. Aaron and Samuel D. Rockoff, "The Attempted Assassination of President Reagan," ibid., 1689.
3. Jimmy Carter, "Presidential Disability and the Twenty-Fifth Amendment: A President's Perspective," ibid., 1698.
4. Robert J. Joynt, "Who Is Minding the World?" ibid., 1699.
5. Jerrold M. Post, M.D., and Robert S. Robins, *When Illness Strikes the Leader: The Dilemma of the Captive King* (New Haven, Conn.: Yale University Press, 1993).
6. Robert E. Gilbert, *The Mortal Presidency: Illness and Anguish in the White House*, 2nd ed. (New York: Fordham University Press, 1998).
7. Bert E. Park, *Ailing, Aging, Addicted: Studies of Compromised Leadership* (Lexington: University Press of Kentucky, 1991).
8. Working Group on Presidential Disability, *Disability in U.S. Presidents: Report, Recommendations, and Commentaries* (Winston-Salem, N.C.: Bowman Gray Scientific Press, 1997).

REPORT, RECOMMENDATIONS AND COMMENTARIES BY THE WORKING GROUP ON PRESIDENTIAL DISABILITY (1996)

PREFACE

If the president of the United States must decide within minutes how to respond to a dire emergency, the citizens of the United States expect him or her to be mentally competent and to act wisely. Because the presidency of the United States is now the world's most powerful office, should its incumbent become even temporarily unable to exercise its powers, or to recognize his or her incapacity, because of a brain disorder, the consequences for the world could be unimaginably far reaching.

The question of the temporary exercise of presidential power clearly arose in this century during the latter years of the incumbency of Franklin Delano Roosevelt. Stricken by poliomyelitis in 1921 and thereafter unable to walk, Roosevelt was impaired but able to serve in office. As commander in chief of the United States military, he met the challenges of the dictators of Germany and Italy and of the Japanese militarists. He had overall responsibility for a global war while suffering the complications of uncontrolled severe hypertension. He almost ignored medical advice, and, by the time of his fourth election in 1944, was in the very late stages of heart failure and cerebral vascular disease. There is considerable controversy about the degree to which these disorders affected his ability to "stand up" to Stalin at the Yalta Conference of February 4–11, 1945. However, there is some agreement that dementia may have affected Roosevelt's refusal to join British Prime Minister Winston Churchill in a military operation to occupy Berlin and Czechoslovakia in advance of the Russians during the last months of the war in Europe. Roosevelt died of hypertensive cerebral hemorrhage soon thereafter, on April 12, 1945.

With global deployment of nuclear weapons following World War II, the possibility that impulsive misjudgment could precipitate a catastrophic disaster increased exponentially. Harry S. Truman was in the pink of health during his incumbency, 1945–53. He and his able secretaries of state rallied the non-Communist nations in erecting a strong and effective barrier against Soviet expansion in Europe and East Asia. However, not only did Truman's successor, Dwight David Eisenhower, suffer several serious illnesses during his years in the White House but Eisenhower's secretary of state, John Foster Dulles, remained in office though dying of cancer.

Acknowledging that even the most short-lived lapse in a president's ability to exercise executive power is dangerous to the nation, President Lyndon Baines Johnson said in a special message to Congress on January 28, 1965:

> While we are prepared for the possibility of a President's death, we are all but defenseless against the probability of a President's incapacitation by injury, illness, senility or other afflictions. A nation bearing the responsibilities we are privileged to bear for our own security, and the security of the world, cannot justify the appalling gamble of entrusting its security to the immobilized hands or uncomprehending mind of a Commander-in-Chief unable to command.

Our nation's awareness of executive vulnerability increased exponentially thereafter. One result was the successful addition to the Constitution of the Twenty-Fifth Amendment.

Sections 1 and 2 of the Amendment deal with succession. No implementing legislation is necessary to either section, as was proven by the appointment of Gerald R. Ford, Jr., and Nelson Aldrich Rockefeller to the vice presidency in 1973 and 1974, respectively, and by the elevation of Gerald Ford to the presidency after the resignation of Richard Nixon in 1974. The latter transition did not depend on the Tyler precedent, as Section 1 had supplanted it.

Sections 3 and 4 are designed to maintain an active and empowered chief executive office if the president is so physically or mentally impaired that his or her advisers judge him or her to be unable to exercise its duties. However, its application has a potential Achilles' heel in the medical evaluations utilized for determining the president's incapacity. Therefore, its use may require guidelines established by enabling legislation or executive orders.

The Working Group on Presidential Disability, after extensive discussion and deliberation, approved overwhelmingly nine recommendations relative to Sections 3 and 4 of the Twenty-Fifth Amendment. They are presented here along with accompanying explanatory commentaries. The minority views expressed on two recommendations are presented in Addenda I and III of the Report.

The Working Group agreed that the Twenty-Fifth Amendment gives sufficient power to the executive and legislative branches to enable them to act in cases of inability of the president, particularly when disease prevents the President from recognizing the seriousness of the deficit. It also agreed that medical advice must be sought on a continuing basis for evaluating the president's health and degree of impairment, if any.

The Working Group recognized that the issues it was considering are of major importance and that the ideal use of the Twenty-Fifth Amendment will come only when the public is well-informed about its purpose and utility. The Working Group offers these recommendations in the hope that they, the commentaries, and minority opinions will be studied and discussed in many forums—schools, civic groups, and perhaps congressional hearings. As our population ages, the elderly may begin to fail in their cognitive function long before their physical being is similarly reduced. This leads to the dichotomy of healthy physique but impaired cognition which is not always apparent. This problem occurs at all levels of society, including local, corporate, national, and international arenas. People with failing minds who are in positions of responsibility may make faulty judgments without their cognitive disorder being recognized. Serious consequences can result and cause enormous and widespread harm. This could be avoided if mechanisms to identify cognitive decline had been in place. If, in the future, the disability provisions of the Twenty-Fifth Amendment must be used—as surely they will—an informed nation will evaluate its leaders by how well they use it for the good of the country.

Recommendation One:

The Twenty-Fifth Amendment is a powerful instrument which delineates the circumstances and methods for succession and transfer of the power of the presidency. It does not require revision or augmentation by another constitutional amendment. However, guidelines are needed to ensure its effective implementation.

Commentary:

Since its ratification in 1967, the Twenty-Fifth Amendment has enhanced America's ability to respond to presidential inability. The Amendment provides constitutional procedures for transferring power, voluntarily or involuntarily, from president to vice president. It makes clear that the vice president acts as, but does not become, president during the period of inability and that when the president is able to resume the powers and duties of the office, he or she can do so. It removes such constitutional questions as "Who decides when, or if, the president is unable to discharge his or her duties? What is the status of the president and vice president during the period of the inability? Can the President later resume office?" which before 1967 inhibited those responsible from appropriate transfers of presidential power. Moreover, by designating the cabinet to act along with the vice president as constitutional decision-makers, it increases the likelihood that vice presidents would act, when appropriate, by assuring the president's political associates against usurpation of the president's office while, at the same time, protecting the vice president from criticism. By providing that Congress would resolve any dispute between the vice president and cabinet on the one hand and the president on the other, it imposes a further check on improvident behavior while providing a mechanism for resolution by politically accountable individuals. Finally, by allowing Congress the option to substitute "such other body as Congress may by law provide" for the cabinet, the Amendment affords a means by which to change that feature in the light of experience.

Although its authors and the Working Group viewed the Amendment as imperfect, revision or augmentation by amendment appears to be impractical and might create greater problems than it sought to correct.

Recommendation Two:

The Twenty-Fifth Amendment has not been invoked in some circumstances envisioned by its founders. When substantial concern about the ability of the president to discharge the powers and duties of office arise, transfer of power under provisions of the Twenty-Fifth Amendment should be considered.

Commentary:

The Amendment provides a mechanism for transferring presidential power whenever appropriate constitutional decision-makers determine that the president "is unable to discharge the powers and duties of his office." The framers of the Amendment intended to address a wide range of situations involving temporary or permanent physical or mental illness which could prevent the president from exercising his or her powers and duties when public business requires presidential leadership. On at least two occasions, and for quite sufficient reason, the Reagan Administration could have set a precedent for clearly and unequivocally invoking the Amendment's disability provisions but did not do so.

Recommendation Three:

A formal contingency plan for the implementation of the Amendment should be in place before the inauguration of every president.

Commentary:

Documented guidelines are needed to ensure the consistent application of the Twenty-Fifth Amendment in appropriate situations. This can best be accomplished by a White House contingency plan that clearly delineates alterations of function, including cognitive, judgmental, behavioral, and communicative capacities, that should cause consideration of a transfer of power. The plan must define precise lines of authority and communication and specify exact procedures to be followed for implementing the provisions of Sections 3 and 4, respectively.

The contingency plan must be developed during the transition period and implemented at the time of inauguration. Every aspect should personally be approved by the president, be clearly understood by the president's spouse, the vice president, and all government officials and staff members who would be involved in its implementation. The plan should state explicitly that it constitutes an order by the president for specific actions to be taken in case of presidential inability to carry out the duties of office.

Furthermore, the plan should delineate those situations and medical conditions that would normally warrant a voluntary transfer of power under the provisions of Section 3 or an involuntary transfer of power under the provisions of Section 4. Approval of the plan by the president would constitute authorization for the release of all medical information to the vice president and principal officers of the executive departments in any situation where an involuntary transfer of power must be considered.

The contingency plan pertaining to presidential inability and continuity of government will contain highly sensitive information and should be classified. Nevertheless, an unclassified summary of the contingency plan, including its medical aspects, should be released to the public at the beginning of each presidential term.

Recommendation Four:

Determination of presidential impairment is a medical judgment based on evaluation and tests. Close associates, family, and consultants can provide valuable information that contributes to this medical judgment.

Commentary:

The assessment of impairment is a medical responsibility. The Senior Physician to the President is responsible, with the assistance of appropriate medical and non-medical consultants, for determining and documenting the extent to which impairment might affect the cognition, judgment, behavior, and communication abilities of the president. The Physician to the President should communicate and interpret these findings to the constitutionally designated decision-makers responsible for determining presidential inability under the provisions of the Twenty-Fifth Amendment.

While the determination of presidential inability is to be made by constitutionally empowered officials, conclusions concerning the degree of medical impairment should significantly inform their judgment. Some medical conditions, such as coma, severe dementia, massive trauma, general anesthesia for major surgery, major psychiatric disorders, and terminal cancer produce impairment of such severe degree as always to warrant consideration of invoking the Twenty-Fifth Amendment.

Recommendation Five:

The determination of presidential inability is a political judgment to be made by constitutional officials.

Commentary:

Working Group consensus was achieved by consideration of the following:

1. A clear distinction must be drawn between the terms "impairment" and "inability." Judging presidential impairment is a medical determination; certifying presidential inability relates to the powers and duties of the office he or she is unable to execute as a consequence of that impairment.

2. Determining impairment should rest solely with the Senior Physician in the White House and consulting medical specialists. Declaring inability pertains to constitutional, administrative, and political considerations as determined voluntarily by the president (Section 3 of the Twenty-Fifth Amendment), or by the vice president

and the principal officers of the executive departments should the president be unable—or unwilling—to do so (Section 4 of the Twenty-Fifth Amendment).

3. Issues such as the urgency of executive functions or perceived risks to the public interest must be considered before initiating disclosure and discovery procedures for either section.

4. In accordance with each administration's contingency plan, the president should agree that full disclosure of all medical information to the vice president and principal officers of the executive departments be made in order to assist in their determination.

Recommendation Six:

The President should appoint a physician, civil or military, to be Senior Physician in the White House and to assume responsibility for his or her medical care, direct the Military Medical Unit, and be the source of medical disclosure when considering imminent or existing impairment according to the provisions of the Twenty-Fifth Amendment.

Commentary:

The president must have full authority to choose his or her own physician. This medical doctor will be the focus for medical information about the president and will render personal care to the president and collect all needed medical information about the president's fitness for office. The Senior Physician in the White House must be the person to advise the president, vice president, cabinet, and others stipulated by the Twenty-Fifth Amendment when medical evaluation is required.

The Working Group, therefore, believes that it is necessary to create the office of Senior Physician in the White House, with clearly delineated responsibility and authority. This Senior Physician must meet the highest professional standards and enjoy the respect and esteem of the medical community.

While the Senior Physician in the White House might be either civilian or military, the office of Senior Physician should be formally separated from, and independent of, the White House Military Office. Whether civilian or military, the Senior Physician must have full military medical support. The Working Group recommends that the physician office be accorded the title and rank of Assistant to the President, Deputy Assistant to the President, or an equivalent military rank. In addition, the Senior Physician may retain additional titles or appointments, such as Senior Physician in the White House Medical Unit, as appropriate.

The current role of physicians assigned by the military branches to duty in the White House should remain in place. It is expected that the Senior Physician in the White House Medical Unit will carry the responsibility of the personal Physician to the President at the times when the office of Senior Physician to the President is vacant.

Recommendation Seven:

In evaluating the medical condition of the president, the Senior Physician in the White House should make use of the best consultants in relevant fields.

Commentary:

The Working Group recognized that there might be instances when medical consultation would be essential for optimal care and for the development of recommendations by the Senior Physician to the President. The Working Group considered ways for developing consultant(s) resources; (a) an established panel of distinguished consultants could be activated when needed by the Senior Physician in the White House; or (b) ad hoc consultants could be selected when need arose, perhaps drawn from a roster of recognized medical specialists.

After lengthy discussion, it was concluded that the best system would result from ad hoc selection of consultants by the Senior Physician in the White House, who must be able to select from any and all consultants appropriate to the specific medical issue(s) at hand.

Considerations included that no one can foresee which experts would be best for a medical crisis. Furthermore, there was concern that appointment to a standing commission could become a political process rather than one of merit.

Recommendation Eight:

Balancing the right of the public to be informed regarding presidential illness with the president's right to confidentiality presents dilemmas. While the Senior Physician to the President is the best source of information about the medical condition of the President, it is the responsibility of the president or designees to make accurate disclosure to the public.

Commentary:

Because the president must make critical decisions for the nation, the public must know enough about presidential mental and physical well-being to be confident of his or her judgment. The nation is clearly entitled to that information. But presidents are also patients and are entitled to privacy, which cannot be as encompassing as that of ordinary patients. Presidents tend to surround themselves with aides whose loyalty is primarily personal and who, at times, have concealed the gravity of presidential illnesses. The Working Group could not reach unanimity regarding methods for avoiding concealment.

The group acknowledged that even the most confidential evaluation might be made public and raise damaging political questions. This possibility might cause president and aides to evade or thwart the objectives of medical candor and confidentiality that is needed. Furthermore, presidents might invoke the doctrine of separation of powers and decline to submit to any congressionally mandated examiners. The dilemma is more easily delineated than solved.

Recommendation Nine:

The Twenty-Fifth Amendment provides a remarkably flexible framework for the determination of presidential inability and the implementation of the transfer of powers. Its provisions should be more widely publicized and its use destigmatized.

Commentary:

The presidency of the United States possesses unparalleled authority and power. Both have been guarded zealously by presidents and those around them. As a result, there have been times when, unknown to the American people, the chief executive was unable to perform the powers and duties of office.

The ratification of the Twenty-Fifth Amendment recognized that the national interest demanded an end to this dangerous practice. In two critical sections, the Amendment provides procedures for ensuring that the powers and duties of the Presidency will always reside— permanently or temporarily—with one capable of using them properly.

Section 3 provides for voluntary transfer of power from the president to the vice president, who will serve as acting president whenever the president believes his medical condition makes it impossible for him to perform. It provides that the president can resume his office when he or she recovers. The framers of the Twenty-Fifth Amendment believed that Section 3 would encourage presidents to act voluntarily and responsibly in disclosing and seeking treatment for illnesses. It was their belief that most incidents of presidential inability could be handled in this manner.

Section 4 provides for occurrences in which a president does not, for whatever reason, declare his or her inability to perform in office. In such circumstances, the vice president and a majority of the cabinet may determine that it is in the national interest for the vice president to serve as acting president. If the president regains the ability to perform, he or she may reclaim the powers of the presidency. Here, too, the provisions are specific.

The news media should have a major role in creating an environment in which the Twenty-Fifth Amendment can and will be implemented. They can help make the public aware of the Amendment's existence and predispose citizens to insist that it be implemented when appropriate. Those who are given the responsibility for governing must be made to understand that their failure to implement the Amendment in case of presidential impairment could put the nation in peril.

Addendum 1: Minority Opinion Regarding Recommendation Four

This opinion, signed by three members of the Working Group, is summarized by one member of the minority, John Feerick, in chapter 1. However, since addendum 1 to the Report has two other authors and makes reference to Recommendation Five as well as to Recommendation Four, the minority opinion is presented here in full:

This separate statement expresses our reservations regarding Recommendation Four and some of the commentary discussing "presidential impairment."

We have the following specific concerns. First, the distinction between "presidential impairment" and "presidential inability," is not likely to be understood by the public or the media, particularly if not considered in conjunction with Recommendation Five.

Second, that there will be a determination of presidential impairment separate from the constitutional determination of presidential inability implies that a two-threshold determination must take place when, in fact, the Constitution speaks of only one. This creates the misleading impression of two "determinations" with equal weight when, in fact, the Constitution stipulates one.

The legislative history and debates of the Twenty-Fifth Amendment leave no doubt that only the constitutional decision-makers are entrusted with the determination of presidential inability. Integral to that determination is whether there is an impairment of the president that prevents him or her from discharging the powers and duties of office. As Senator Birch Bayh made clear in the Senate debates of February 19, 1965:

> [T]he words "inability" and "unable" as used in [Section 4 of the Amendment] . . . , which refer to an impairment of the President's faculties, mean that he is unable either to make or communicate his decisions as to his own competency to execute the powers and duties of his office. I should like for the RECORD to include that as my definition of the words "inability" and "unable."

The dual track approach contained in Recommendations Four and Five, therefore, is not constitutionally based or wise.

Third, the notion of a "determination of presidential impairment" conveys an inaccurate picture of the proper role of medical advice in decisions under Section 3 and Section 4 of the Twenty-Fifth Amendment. Recommendation Four implies that the medical role will be limited to a single "determination"; in fact, in many instances the appropriate doctors will be involved in a less formal but continuing advisory role to the constitutional decision-makers. In many instances, the doctors will not be making a single "determination" but will be offering medical advice and responding to questions on a continuing basis.

Fourth, the implication that there will be a formal "determination" of presidential impairment in addition to the constitutionally required determination of presidential inability raises some concerns regarding the operation of Sections 3 and 4. Even information confidential in the White House is likely to leak. We are concerned that a determination that the president was impaired, if leaked, would be seen as a judgment that the president was unable to discharge his duties. This would have the effect either of compromising his ability to lead or of forcing the constitutional decision-makers to a decision they otherwise might not make.

In essence, we believe that the Constitution requires that "[t]he determination of presidential inability is a political judgement to be made by constitutional officials" (Recommendation Five). Constitutional decision-makers will generally require medical advice from appropriate medical experts (in accordance with Recommendations Six and Seven) regarding the president's condition in making decisions under Section 3 and 4 as to whether the president is able to discharge the powers and duties of his office. The legislative history surrounding the adoption of the Twenty-Fifth Amendment makes clear that its framers intended that constitutional decision-makers would solicit appropriate medical advice. Decisions regarding the exercise of executive power under the Twenty-Fifth Amendment, however, should be made by accountable constitutional officials, not by doctors, attorneys, or others who have not been elected by the people or confirmed by their representatives.

Addendum II (Report by Former and Current Military Physicians Assigned to the White House Regarding Recommendation VI) is included in chapter 4, written by James M. Young, M.D., who chaired the Physicians' Subcommittee and prepared its Report.

Addendum III

Minority Opinion regarding Recommendation Seven (signed by six members of the Working Group) relates directly to the proposal for an independent medical panel which is described in much more detail in the Editor's Introduction, pp. xviii–xix. Addendum III reads as follows:

1. We believe the president's physician is subject to such a power-

ful potential conflict of interest that it is impossible to ensure the prevention of cover-ups.

2. We, therefore, recommend the creation of a Consulting Commission on the Health of the President by Congressional resolution or statute.

3. Such a dispassionate group of expert physicians would be available to provide consultative advice and support to the president's physician and to report to the public on the state of the president's health in the event that the question of impairment arose.

4. Because they would not be subject to presidential pressure, or serve purely at the president's pleasure, as does the White House physician, they would enhance public confidence, allay suspicions of cover-up, and provide a solid base of medical information for the president, the vice president, and the cabinet if invocation of the Twenty-Fifth Amendment was under consideration.

12

Report of the Miller Center Commission on Presidential Disability and the Twenty-Fifth Amendment

Edited by Kenneth W. Thompson

The Miller Center Commission on Presidential Disability and the Twenty-Fifth Amendment was co-chaired by Herbert Brownell, attorney general during the Eisenhower Administration, and Birch Bayh, former United States senator from Indiana. In studying issues of presidential disability, they were joined by eleven other Commission members, including a former chief justice of the United States (Warren Burger), a second former United States senator (William Spong of Virginia) and a former United States representative from Virginia (Caldwell Butler).

EDITOR'S INTRODUCTION

The history of the Miller Center Commission on the Twenty-Fifth Amendment reflects the convergence of factors that made the Amendment's creation possible. Not only were the principal authors of the Amendment able to serve as the Commission's co-chairs but the leaders of several major national organizations, such as the League of Women Voters, the American Bar Association, and the American Medical Association, were also available to participate in the sessions and then assist in disseminating the final report. Legal research for the Commission was readily available and carried out by two professors at the University of Virginia Law School (Paul Stephan and Daniel Meador). A former political and diplomatic reporter for *The Washington Post* (Chalmers Roberts) agreed to serve as the main draftsman of the Commission's report. Beginning in 1985, the Miller Center Commission held approximately six working sessions, then issued its final report in 1988.

Among the more important topics the Commission discussed was the unique role played by the President's Physician, particularly within the context of the Twenty-Fifth Amendment. I would like to give attention here to the Commission's thoughts on this subject. It is worth noting at the start that Commission members were struck by the fact that in the 1981 *Congressional Directory*, the first issued during the Reagan Administration, the staff listing for the Executive Office of the president (that is, the White House office) contained fifty-five names. It began with the counselor to the president, the chief of staff, his deputy, a raft of varied assistants to the president, then deputy assistants and special assistants. The last name on the list was the chief usher; the name just before his—fifty-fourth of fifty-five—was that of the Physician to the President, preceded by the curator of White House artifacts.

The Commission was shocked at the low rank and the seemingly low esteem sometimes accorded the physician. Dr. Daniel Ruge, President Reagan's first White House Physician, told Commission members that "despite its glamorous name, the office of the White House physician is somewhat blue collar."

But it is far easier to say that the physician's job should be upgraded than to suggest how to do it. Each president has had his own relationship with his physician, and this has varied almost as greatly as have presidential foreign and domestic policies.

This led the Commission to conclude, first of all, that the president's physician must remain a person of the president's own choice, that he or she should not be subject to Senate confirmation or to approval by any other body, medical or otherwise. The president and his personal physician must have total mutual confidence and confidentiality, as a symbiotic relationship.

The Commission reached the following conclusions with regard to the president's physician:

(*a*) From the beginning of his or her appointment, the physician must know the history, medical and political implications, and use of the Twenty-Fifth Amendment.

(*b*) He or she should abide by the views of the American Medical

Association Council on Medical Ethics regarding patient–doctor confidentiality and those instances when it can be abridged. The Commission considered recommending a statute stating that the presidential physician had a positive duty to communicate details concerning the president's condition if it jeopardized the national interest, but decided that such a statute was not necessary and probably would be self-defeating.

(c) He or she should meet during the transition period with the president-elect regarding the potential use of the Twenty-Fifth Amendment's disability provisions. With the president-elect, the vice president–elect, and those who will become the president's chief of staff and legal counsel, the physician should undertake, during the transition, to establish, if possible, a written protocol regarding the use of these provisions.

(d) He or she should possess the knowledge, humility, and expertise to obtain consultation to ensure the best medical care for the president. Any presidential physician, if only because of the office itself, has easy access to any consultant or group of consultants that he or she wishes to have see the president, either to aid in treatment or to make the difficult decision of evaluating disability.

To reinforce the presidential physician's influence whenever the Twenty-Fifth Amendment might come into play, suggestions have been made at various times that an independent board of physicians be created to examine the president's physical and mental health periodically. The Commission and its medical advisory group discussed this concept. The general conclusion was that such a board would hinder or prevent the development of a real doctor–patient relationship between the president and his or her physician.

The political and world situation, the power of the White House staff and, most of all, the president's wishes will always determine when and how Section 3 of the Amendment will be used. Commission members came to the conclusion that, because of his or her unique status, the president's physician, with consultants if he or she desires, should play a major role. The physician should help the president make the decision to invoke Section 3 and to reassume office if the Amendment is used.

Because the physician's relationship with the president is so central to any examination of the Twenty-Fifth Amendment, this summary of the Commission's interpretation of that relationship, originally found in an appendix to its final report, serves here instead as a useful introduction to it.

REPORT OF THE MILLER CENTER COMMISSION (1988)

The recommendations of the Commission are presented here in summary form, then discussed in the narrative commentary that follows:

Recommendation 1: Problems of presidential disability and use of the Twenty-Fifth Amendment must be discussed and agreed upon through contingency planning by the new president, vice president, presidential physician, and White House chief of staff before the inauguration.

Recommendation 2: The presidential physician can and must play an increased role under provisions of the Twenty-Fifth Amendment.

Recommendation 3: No further constitutional changes should be made, but legislation should be considered by Congress and the president in order to bring current law into better harmony with the Twenty-Fifth Amendment and its intentions.

Recommendation 4: Any president receiving anesthesia should use Section 3 of the Amendment routinely so that the appearance of crisis will be avoided.

Recommendation 5: The transfer of power under Section 3 should extend beyond the period of time in the operating room to perhaps twenty-four hours or more.

Recommendation 6: Even in borderline cases, the president should take the precaution of using Section 3.

Recommendation 7: Delegations by the president of his Section 3 authority under certain specified conditions to the vice president are incompatible with Section 4 of the Twenty-Fifth Amendment and should not be contemplated.

Recommendation 8: The creation by Congress of another statutory body to replace the cabinet in applications of Section 4 of the Twenty-Fifth Amendment is not warranted.

Recommendation 9: No set of rules or codes of conduct for future presidential spouses are recommended, but each spouse should be brought into the preparatory transition discussions.

Recommendation 10: To protect the belief of the American public in the dependability of the American presidency, White House staff members must not act to prevent use of the Twenty-Fifth Amendment in instances when it is called for.

COMMENTARY

The Commission believes, overall, that under most circumstances, the Twenty-Fifth Amendment is clear, simple, and easily implemented.[1] Certain of the Amendment's provisions, however, are designed to respond to extremely complicated circumstances and could prove to be more difficult to implement. Hence, the Commission strongly urges steps to provide a guide for future applications of the Amendment—whether they be of a crisis nature or of a lesser nature—a guide intended to ensure prompt application in a manner faithful both to the spirit of the Constitution and to the intent of the framers of the Amendment.

Above all, the Commission believes this is a time to "seize the moment." Every four years Americans choose a president, who is inaugurated barely ten weeks later. During the critical and often frenetic transition period, many policy and personnel problems must be resolved. Along with them, the potential problems of presidential disability and the use of this Amendment must be discussed and, as far as humanly possible, agreed upon through contingency planning by the new president, vice president, presidential physician, and White House chief of staff. In all this, there surely will be a role for the president's spouse. Most emphatically, this contingency planning must be done not after inauguration but before.

Why the urgency? One example should suffice. Consider the testimony of Dr. Daniel Ruge, who was President Reagan's physician on

March 31, 1981, less than three months after his inauguration, when a would-be assassin seriously wounded the chief executive. Dr. Ruge was in the entourage that rushed with Reagan to the hospital. When the Commission asked about the possible use of the Twenty-Fifth Amendment, he responded:

> It was discussed. There is a big difference between Dan Ruge on March 30, 1981, after a shooting when he'd only been on the job two months for one thing, and what Dan Ruge would have been like four years later [at the time of Reagan's colon cancer operation] when he would have actually had time from April 1981 to July 1985 to think about it. I think very honestly in 1981, because of the speed of everything and the fact that we had a very sick president, that the Twenty-Fifth Amendment would never have entered my mind even though I probably had it in my little black bag. I carried it with me. The Twenty-Fifth Amendment never occurred to me.
>
> Q: You think it would have occurred to you if the shooting had happened four years later?
> Dr. Ruge: Yes.

Later, Dr. Ruge was asked:

> Could the President have signed a letter [making the vice president the acting president] after he got to the hospital and was in the operating room?

Dr. Ruge replied:

> Yes, he could have signed anything up until the time he went under anesthesia.

Clearly, there must be much greater public recognition that the Twenty-Fifth Amendment, among other things, offers excellent standard operating procedures for times of temporary presidential disability, such as the 1981 experience described above, and provides a simple method to get through such contingencies without government disruption or public alarm.

The Commission has been impressed by what it has learned of the advances, and complexities, of modern medicine, in part through our discussions with two former presidential physicians, who cared for five presidents. It is now obvious that the presidential physician can, and must, play an increased role. We view it as a dual role: first, the physician must uphold his or her role in the traditional, confidential doctor–patient relationship; second, and equally important in the unique presidential case, the physician must act as a representative, in strictly non-political terms, of the interests of the nation that elected the president.

The Commission does not recommend any further constitutional changes at this time, but it does point to some legislation it feels Congress and the president should consider in order to bring current law (for example, the Presidential Succession Law of 1947) into better harmony with the Twenty-Fifth Amendment and its intentions. It should be noted that, in studying the Twenty-Fifth Amendment, Congress considered a number of possible horror story scenarios. It concluded that the final language of the Amendment allowed the fewest malfunctions and that each effort to shore up potential weaknesses only made matters worse.

Throughout, the Commission has assumed that stability in time of crisis, or in any departure from what has been the norm, depends on the good judgment and the good sense of both our leaders and our citizens, regardless of their political associations. As the late Senate Republican leader Everett M. Dirksen put it during the deliberations about the Twenty-Fifth Amendment, "We must assume that, when confronted with monumental national crisis, when subjected to the white heat of political scrutiny, those charged with responsibility will do what is in the public interest."

THE TWENTY-FIFTH AMENDMENT'S DISABILITY PROVISIONS*

Section 3

Section 3 was a great leap forward, an effort to provide a method of continuity at the top of our government, that is, in the presidency. The president is the only person with the power and prerogative to invoke or not invoke Section 3. The section has, in the Commission's view, been used in a single instance: at the time of Reagan's hospitalization for colon cancer surgery, despite the fact that the president's letter at the time clouds the issue.

In his testimony to the Commission, Fred F. Fielding, then counsel to President Reagan, made the following comments:

---

*See Appendix for the complete text.

Let's go back to the week before the operation. We knew—some of us knew—and I forget when it became public, that the President was going to have his physical. We knew at the time that he was going to have a form of anesthesia, to have the procedure that occurred on Friday, if I recall my dates correctly. He was operated on Saturday, got a procedure on Friday. What was going to happen was that there was a possibility that if something was found that they would have to instantly put the President under. I used that as an opportunity the preceding week to schedule a meeting with the President and the Vice President and Don Regan (then chief of staff). We sat in the Oval Office and we discussed the whole situation: the National Command Authority plus the President's desires on passage of power temporarily if he were suddenly temporarily incapacitated. . . .

The decision was obvious that unless something unexpected occurred on Friday there would be no need for the Twenty-Fifth Amendment in any way, shape or form. But Don Regan called me down late afternoon on that Friday and said, "We've got some problems with the health exam." And we went through the whole drill—if you will—of what is to be done and where is the Vice President, and what is the press to be advised of and what is not to be told, and the normal procedures that you go through. One of the subjects obviously was the Twenty-Fifth Amendment. I can tell you, and I think it is important for the sake of history, that when we left, no decision of a recommendation to the President had been made although we knew the procedures. I drafted basically two letters: one was . . . very clear, that of exercise of the Twenty-Fifth Amendment, the other [optional letter] would accomplish the activation of the Twenty-Fifth Amendment but was more consistent with what I perceived to be the president's concerns. His concern mainly was that he didn't want to set a precedent for future presidents. But I can tell you in all candor there was no political reason why he didn't want to, which theoretically there could be as with someone who is having a power fight . . . with their vice president.[2]

Appropriate Uses

The Commission believes that any president receiving anesthesia should use Section 3 of the Twenty-Fifth Amendment. This mechanism should be made part of a routine course of action so that its invocation carries no implications of instability or crisis. Each president will have to make the decision, and circumstances will be different. However, the Commission believes that use rather than non-use will create the sense of routine.

It should be possible to identify in advance a fairly wide range of circumstances in which the president should almost automatically invoke Section 3. One situation involves elective surgery where a general anesthetic, narcotics, or other drugs that alter cerebral function will be used. Another involves a similarly debilitating disease or physical malfunction. Because anyone under anesthetic is unable to function both during the period of unconsciousness and afterward while disoriented, presidents should accept the inevitability of temporarily transferring power to the vice president beyond the immediate hours in the operating room, or even in the hospital—perhaps twenty-four or forty-eight hours. It would be wise for a president to state this publicly, so that the nation and the world are reassured and, importantly, so that the pressure is lessened on those White House officials fearful of some loss of power.

In short, let the president wave from his window to show he is up and around but convalescing, while the vice president, as acting president under Section 3, takes care of the day-to-day business. As Herbert Brownell noted, there is a substantial difference between the president's being able to wave to the crowd from a hospital window and being able to govern.

The Commission re-emphasizes that, during the transition period between electing and inaugurating the new president, the vice president, presidential physician, and chief of staff should consider what to do in contingencies of a medical nature. The Commission recommends written guidelines if possible, agreed upon in advance, under which Section 3 could or would be invoked for three levels of medical conditions: an emergency, a planned procedure, and treatment for a chronic ailment. Most certainly, it should be invoked for any surgical procedure involving the use of anesthesia, narcotics, or other drugs, that alter cerebral function. In judging the president's ability to resume the powers and duties of office, consideration must be given to anything that impairs mental capacities.

The advice of the presidential physician is especially important, because the president may otherwise not appreciate the extent to which particular medical situations may compromise his ability to function. As part of the periodic review of the president's health, he and his physician should consider whether any new situations should be added to the list of contingencies that may involve disability.

In cases of elective surgery and similar circumstances, the president will have no difficulty invoking Section 3. But situations may arise in which an unanticipated medical crisis places the president in a position where he, his vice president, chief of staff, and physician had previously agreed to rely on Section 3. President Reagan's surgery following the assassination attempt is just such a case. The president-elect, his vice president, chief of staff, and physician should, at the earliest possible date, try to design special rules to cover such a crisis if and when it occurs.

One possibility would be for the president-elect to prepare an appropriate letter for invoking Section 3. He could leave the letter unsigned and undated, but under agreed-upon conditions, such as an imminent general anesthetic or an injury resulting in impending shock or loss of consciousness, Secret Service personnel or others accompanying the president (as could well have been the case with Dr. Ruge, already discussed) could produce the letter for his signature. This plan of action can be used, of course, only in cases where the president remains conscious and competent at the time he signs the letter. Although this prospect of shifting presidential power under emergency conditions might strike some as unsettling, the Commission believes that such a formula is preferable to putting the vice president and the cabinet to the choice of invoking Section 4 or leaving the office of the president effectively unoccupied.

The Commission recognizes that a president facing a "gray area" medical situation—a case in which his inability is likely to be transitory—may prefer to do nothing, on the assumption that any transfer of power can erode the appearance of his authority even where it does not affect its actual exercise. In many cases, however, a wait-and-see attitude carries unacceptable risks. Even the most straightforward medical procedure, if conducted under general anesthesia, can lead to complications. The patient can suddenly stop breathing or undergo cardiac arrest, in response to the surgery itself or to the anesthesia. The patient may simply remain unconscious much longer than anticipated or remain confused after regaining consciousness. The Commission is concerned that instances have occurred in which officials in an administration have overestimated the president's ability to perform his duties without the proper interval following anesthesia.

The Commission recommends that, in borderline cases, the president, rather than run the risk of leaving a power vacuum, take the precaution of using Section 3 and designate the vice president as acting president. Once the public comes to accept this course as a normal way of doing business, the perception problem will disappear. By showing strong leadership here, a president could increase his stature in history as well as aid his successors in office. We believe that the president can count on the good sense and good judgment of the American people, the Congress, and his immediate colleagues in such situations.

Arguments Against Invocation

The Commission has heard four reasons for not invoking Section 3. The first is that a president who invokes its provisions would set a precedent for future presidents, a concern expressed in Reagan's letter of July 13, 1985. The second is that to invoke it would contribute to a crisis atmosphere that might alarm friends and allies abroad, mislead our adversaries, and cause serious reactions in the financial community, even a stock market crash. The third is that the casual use of Section 3 might tempt the vice president or others to undertake a coup by employing Section 4 to seize presidential powers. The fourth is the skepticism in political circles over whether medical information is or can be precise enough to determine with any degree of certainty the disability of the president.

The Commission examined these four viewpoints, in turn, and rejected each of them. First of all, Section 3 leaves to each president the determination of whether to invoke it. Its use is strictly voluntary. Second, the risk of a crisis atmosphere is proportionate to the degree to which a natural and orderly routine for the transfer of powers is institutionalized, that is, widely understood and generally accepted by the public. Thus, the more the provision is used by succeeding presidents, the more routine it becomes and the less sense of crisis there will be at home and abroad. Third, the fear of a coup by the vice president is based on a false analogy with other political systems. Historically the defects of the American vice presidency have not included the temptation to seize power, but the refusal to accept power inherent in the office. Fourth and finally, modern communications technology, and the media habits that have grown with it, make it far less likely that a president's physicians could successfully hide illnesses. This is not to say that the public no longer suspects medical cover-ups, but it surely lessens their suspicion. And as the public better understands the uses and reach of modern medicine, including anesthesia, the Commission has repeatedly been told, a cover-up will carry increasing political as well as physical risks to those who would opt for it.

Delegations of Section 3 Authority

One issue the Commission considered is the advisability of the president's and vice president's written agreements by which the president would in effect delegate his Section 3 authority under certain specified circumstances. Through such an agreement the president would declare his intent that if a particular situation should arise, as a result of which he lost his capacity to determine his ability to function, the vice president would have the authority to inform the Speaker of the House and the President pro tempore of the Senate that an inability existed and that he would serve as acting president until the president recovered. Before the adoption of the Twenty-Fifth Amendment, similar agreements existed between some presidents and their respective vice presidents, although no occasion arose to test their efficacy or validity.

Whatever the constitutional status of those agreements that predate the Twenty-Fifth Amendment, the Commission believes that such delegations no longer are appropriate. The Commission regards the constitutionality of such agreements as an open question in the sense that there is no definitive authority on the point. However, it seems likely that such an agreement would be inconsistent with the Twenty-Fifth Amendment. One could assert that the express authority of Section 3 carries with it implicit power to anticipate in advance when that power will be exercised. More persuasive to the Commission is the argument that Section 4 provides the exclusive means for determining a presidential inability once the president loses the capacity to make that determination for himself. When the Constitution so clearly and directly addresses an issue—here the mechanism for temporary transfers of power from the president to the vice president—efforts to find alternative, implicit resolutions seem forced.

Because the principal purpose of the Twenty-Fifth Amendment is to resolve all doubts about the status of the chief executive during periods of crisis or uncertainty, the Commission considers it unwise and contrary to the Amendment's spirit to rely on a method not clearly contemplated by the Amendment. In coming to this conclusion, the Commission offers no judgment on the binding effect of such agreements during the period before adoption of the Twenty-Fifth Amendment. The history of the Amendment indicates that its framers intended to create a mechanism that would supersede those prior strategies and that they did not intend either to repudiate or merely to supplement the earlier arrangements.

In short, Section 3 creates a constitutional mechanism within the Twenty-Fifth Amendment for a president to say, in effect, "I am unable to serve temporarily. Rather than resign the office, I will temporarily remove myself and have the vice president serve as acting president. When I am able again to serve I will reclaim the powers of the presidency." This is the pattern Reagan followed in July 1985 during his surgery, despite the disclaimer in his letter. The testimony to this Commission of his then counsel, Fred Fielding, shows invocation of Section 3 was his and his associates' clear intent. The disclaimer simply was a device, offered to the president as an alternative, to get him at least to start down the Section 3 route. And that is how it worked out.

Section 4

Section 4 is the most tantalizing and so far the only unused provision of the Twenty-Fifth Amendment. It deals with a crisis that our nation has never directly confronted, although, had the Amendment existed then, it probably could have applied to the final period of Woodrow Wilson's presidency or of Franklin D. Roosevelt's.

In brief, this provision involves a sick president who refuses, or is unable, to confront his disability. Put another way: this section was basically framed to apply to a president who is disabled but unwilling to step aside. He or she may be a "stubborn mule" or be in the hands of a powerful staff or a strong-willed spouse. Section 4 has inspired much criticism and many scenarios for endless mischief. The effect of modern medicine on human life certainly has increased the imaginable scenarios. For reasons such as these, Congress deliberated at great length before approving Section 4 in order to erect what might be called a large enough constitutional tent, with plenty of room inside to accommodate all possible cases, whether foreseen, completely unforeseen, or simply imagined.

In assessing this section's potential use, it is essential to remember that no mechanical or procedural solution would be fail-safe unless the public possesses, at such a time of crisis, a certain sense of "constitutional morality." Or, as another observer has put it, "In a word, the Amendment is only technically self-executing. Nonetheless, it contains all that a constitutional device should: a set of presumptions about the process of exercising power and an implicit expectation that it will be applied in a mood of restraint."[4]

Section 4 operates in two stages. First of all, there has to be the momentous decision to "remove" the president and make the vice president the acting president. This decision requires the declaration of the vice president and of a majority of the president's cabinet. A situation might also arise if the president, having temporarily transferred his powers to the vice president, sought to resume his powers by transmitting written declarations to the Senate and House, but was then prevented by the vice president and the cabinet declaring him unable to discharge his duties.

Alternatives to the Cabinet

Section 4 also has built into it the authority for Congress to create some other "body" to substitute for the cabinet. There is no limitation on who would serve in such a "body" other than the realities of American politics and public opinion and that sense of "constitutional morality" that is most essential at a time of national crisis. But if such other "body" were set up, a majority of the members of that body would need to take the initiative or concur with the vice president in order to temporarily transfer the powers and duties of the presidency to the vice president. The cabinet would play no role in this process if Congress were to enact a statute creating such a body. Thus, it lies within the power of Congress to consider whether the cabinet is the best decision-making group to be involved in a determination of presidential inability.

Various groups, other than the cabinet, were suggested during the hearings leading up to the formulation of the Twenty-Fifth Amendment, and they continue to be suggested. Suggestions for the "other body" include, for example, a group comprising the chief justice, the Speaker of the House, the President pro tempore of the Senate, and the minority leaders of both houses of Congress. Another suggestion is that this "other body" be composed of medical doctors, either appointed for terms of years or designated by office, such as the surgeon general. The concern underlying all these suggestions is that, while the cabinet members are apt to be loyal to the administration and have firsthand awareness of the president's condition, they are also likely to be overly reluctant to acknowledge publicly that the president has any deficiencies. Therefore, the argument goes, the public interest requires that the question of the president's ability to perform the duties of his office be evaluated by a group able to view the question in a more disinterested way.

The Commission has considered whether to propose that Congress exercise its power under Section 4 to create a body other than the cabinet for this purpose. In this process, the Commission has reviewed the various arguments and proposals made in the hearings leading up to the framing of the Amendment, as well as current proposals, and has concluded *not* to recommend the creation of some other statutory body. The Commission recognizes that, although the cabinet does suffer from the defects mentioned above and may not be an ideal group, it is unlikely that any other body could be designed that would be free of other difficulties or receive as much political acceptance. It would seem desirable that, whatever group is employed, consultation could usefully take place with the White House Physician who should solicit assistance from outside medical specialists.

Even if Congress does not create a permanent body of this sort, this provision in Section 4 is salutary in that it gives Congress power to act if, in a particular situation, the cabinet fails to do so when it is clear that the president is suffering from an inability. In that special situation, Congress could create another body to take action. That body would be temporary and tailor-made for a one-time–only assignment, leaving the cabinet in place as the body to deal with other situations thereafter.

The Commission strongly believes that the chief justice and other members of the Supreme Court should have no role in any such "body" or in any other fashion under terms of the Twenty-Fifth Amendment. During deliberations in Congress on the Amendment, former Chief Justice Earl Warren advised strongly against any such role, and former Chief Justice Warren Burger took the same position in speaking to the Commission. The Commission considers it essential to keep the judicial role separate lest, in a situation perhaps now unimaginable, the Supreme Court might be called on to rule on some application of the Twenty-Fifth Amendment. It is worth recalling the presidential election crisis of 1876, in which, just two days before inauguration day, Rutherford B. Hayes prevailed over Samuel J. Tilden and then only by the vote of a congressionally appointed electoral commission of seven Republicans, seven Democrats, and one "independent"—five of whom were senators, five representatives, and five justices of the Supreme Court. Four of the justices were selected by the Congress, and the fifth, the "independent," by the four. This fifth justice, Joseph P. Bradley, cast the deciding vote in the 8-to-7 ruling. It is true that concurrent political bargaining over the underlying post–Civil War issues provided the essential resolution of the crisis, but the Court was misused in the role it did play.

Future Uses of Section 4

Given current medical knowledge about the disabilities of older persons, the current prominence at all ages of psychiatric, as well as physical, illnesses, and the progressive impairment of mental functions including the so-far irreversible disease known as Alzheimer's, the scenarios to which Section 4 might some day apply can only be imagined. The Commission discussed such problem areas with both the former presidential physicians and other medical authorities. Knowledge has only reinforced the Commission's doubts that any new law, or even constitutional amendment, can adequately provide for the future. But some established regime might help, especially one involving the presidential physician.

It is obvious that the presidential physician would be a critical person should Section 4 ever have to be considered. A vice president and cabinet, or "other body," would be highly dependent on medical advice in reaching what would be, nonetheless, basically a political decision. Other persons should also be considered, notably the president's spouse and the White House chief of staff and entourage.

Thus far, many presidential spouses have been apolitical, several politically influential, and some powerful in terms, as they have seen it, of protecting their husbands' health and political fortunes. Sometimes this has led to hiding presidential illnesses.

Of course, voters do not elect presidential spouses, but first ladies have historically had differing roles and, in recent years, their own staffs and offices. The Commission cannot and does not suggest any set of rules or codes of conduct for future presidential spouses, but it does strongly recommend that each spouse be brought into the preparatory transition discussions, already noted, on the possible applications of the Twenty-Fifth Amendment. It is essential that spouses, like the other key personnel around the president, be mentally prepared for what could occur, and unfortunately so often has occurred, and be familiar with the Amendment's provisions. The vice president's spouse should also know about the Twenty-Fifth Amendment and its potential applications.

The presidential chief of staff, a post that President Eisenhower brought into the White House after his years of commanding allied forces in Europe during World War II, has become a critical cog in the executive branch. In recent years it has proved more important in certain respects than even the more senior of the cabinet departments, including state and defense.

The White House staff understandably sees an important role for itself in assessing presidential disability. Key staff members and, in particular, the chief of staff and immediate associates are in continual contact with the president. They consider themselves uniquely qualified in judging the president's capacity for exercising his powers and duties. They are conscious of their prerogatives, fearful of threats to the president's authority, and cognizant of the high stakes of political power. The White House staff has the most to lose if and when the president relinquishes his powers. Particularly in some presidencies, the staff carries major responsibility for the details of administering and managing the presidency. Top staffers are likely to worry that the vice president, in the role of acting president, is less likely than they to know and do what the president would have wanted if not disabled. The worst fate of all, in the view of the White House staff, would be for the acting president to bring in assistants from the vice-presidential staff.

Concluding Thoughts

Sure signs of the presidential office's unremitting responsibilities accompany the president wherever he goes. In these times, a president is never away from the means of instant communication with any department of the United States government and with the head of almost any foreign government. Always within reach is the "football" containing the secret codes that enable the president to signal this country's immediate response if ever it should face a nuclear attack. Even while asleep, a president is subject to call at any time, and his aides will be rightfully criticized if, upon learning of a major calamity or an alarming threat to the nation, they do not inform the president immediately.

The office's well-known aspects and the worldwide prestige the American presidency earns in advance for each new incumbent have given rise to extraordinary public expectations of what any person with the immense power of that office can and would do to cope with a sudden national emergency or world crisis. To keep and preserve the American public's respect for the capacity and dependability of the American presidency is an important reason for not deliberately permitting an official hiatus, however brief. If the president becomes unconscious or is otherwise disabled, and the vice president is not duly authorized to act and no person with the president's authority and power is present and capable of acting, then the importance and value of the presidency would be debased. Much more harmful, to be sure, would be the effect if a national emergency or world crisis were actually to erupt during a hiatus. Such considerations, among others, ought to convince every responsible presidential aide that, whenever or however a situation arises for applying the Twenty-Fifth Amendment, he or she must not dissemble about the president's health or otherwise fend off use of the constitutional remedy for a presidential illness. In addition, the American people must understand that their presidents, whoever they may be, are not superhuman. They are human beings subjected to enormous pressures and responsibilities and, like the average citizen, may face disabling infirmities. However, the Commission believes that the Twenty-Fifth Amendment provides the means of ensuring that the powers and duties of the presidency are always in the hands of someone able to perform them. And the Commission believes that this Amendment must be utilized whenever necessary as a normal ingredient in the governmental process.

NOTES

1. For the complete version, see *Report of the Commission on Presidential Disability and the Twenty-Fifth Amendment*, Miller Center Commission No. 4, (Charlottesville, Va.: White Burkett Miller Center of Public Policy, 1988).

2. Fred F. Fielding, Testimony to the Commission, September 30, 1986.

3. Logically, this would be an expanded version of the "emergency book" notes created by Fred Fielding in the early Reagan years.

4. Richard P. Longaker, "Presidential Continuity: The Twenty-Fifth Amendment," *UCLA Law Review*, 13 (1966), 560.

APPENDIX: TWENTY-FIFTH AMENDMENT TO THE CONSTITUTION OF THE UNITED STATES (Ratified on February 10, 1967)

SECTION 1. In case of the removal of the President from office or of his death or resignation, the Vice President shall become President.

SECTION 2. Whenever there is a vacancy in the office of the Vice President, the President shall nominate a Vice President who shall take office upon confirmation by a majority vote of both Houses of Congress.

SECTION 3. Whenever the President transmits to the President pro tempore of the Senate and the Speaker of the House of Representatives his written declaration that he is unable to discharge the powers and duties of his office, and until he transmits to them a written declaration to the contrary, such powers and duties shall be discharged by the Vice President as Acting President.

SECTION 4. When the Vice President and a majority of either the principal officers of the executive departments or of such other body as Congress may by law provide, transmit to the President pro tempore of the Senate and the Speaker of the House of Representatives their written declaration that the President is unable to discharge the powers and duties of his office, the Vice President shall immediately assume the powers and duties of the office as Acting President.

Thereafter, when the President transmits to the President pro tempore of the Senate and the Speaker of the House of Representatives his written declaration that no inability exists, he shall resume the powers and duties of his office unless the Vice President and a majority of either the principal officers of the executive department or of such other body as Congress may by law provide, transmit within four days to the President pro tempore of the Senate and the Speaker of the House of Representatives their written declaration that the President is unable to discharge the powers and duties of his office. Thereupon Congress shall decide the issue, assembling within forty-eight hours for that purpose if not in session. If the Congress, within twenty-one days after receipt of the latter written declaration, or, if Congress in not in session, within twenty-one days after Congress is required to assemble, determines by two-thirds vote of both Houses that the President is unable to discharge the powers and duties of his office, the Vice President shall continue to discharge the same as Acting President; otherwise, the President shall resume the powers and duties of his office.

ABOUT THE CONTRIBUTORS

BIRCH BAYH served three terms as a United States Senator from Indiana (1963–81) and, as a member of Congress, was widely acknowledged as one of the foremost experts in the area of constitutional law. As Chairman of the Subcommittee on the Constitution, he wrote and sponsored two amendments to the Constitution, the Twenty-Fifth (dealing with presidential disability) and the Twenty-Sixth (dealing with lowering the voting age). No other lawmaker since the Founding Fathers has written two amendments to the United States Constitution. Senator Bayh holds a law degree from Indiana University School of Law and is now a senior partner in the law firm of Oppenheimer Wolff, Donnelly and Bayh LLP in Washington, D.C.

JOHN D. FEERICK, L.L.B. Fordham, has served as Dean of the Fordham University School of Law since 1982. Among his numerous publications are two books that deal with the issue of presidential disability: *The Twenty-Fifth Amendment* and *From Failing Hands*, both published by Fordham University Press. Dean Feerick is currently Chairman of the Board of the American Arbitration Association. He has served as a special New York State Attorney General (1987–90) and as President of the Association of the Bar of the City of New York. He has received the Federal Bar Council's Public Service Award, the Law and Society Award from the New York Lawyers for the Public Interest, the 1999 Citizen Achievement Award from the New York State League of Women Voters, and the Dean of the Year Award from the National Association of Public Interest Law.

ROBERT E. GILBERT, Ph.D. University of Massachusetts, Amherst, is Professor of Political Science at Northeastern University. The second edition of his book *The Mortal Presidency: Illness and Anguish in the White House* (Fordham University Press), was designated by *Choice* as one of 1998's Outstanding Academic Books. In addition to an earlier book *Television and Presidential Politics*, he has published articles in such journals as *Political Psychology, Presidential Studies Quarterly, Congress and the Presidency, Il Politico,* and *Politics and the Life Sciences.* Professor Gilbert is a John F. Kennedy Foundation grantee and a grantee of the Center for the Study of the Presidency. A former chair of Northeastern's Political Science Department, he is also a University Excellence in Teaching Award winner.

JOEL K. GOLDSTEIN, J.D. Harvard University, D. Phil. in Politics, Oxford University, is Professor of Law at St. Louis University School of Law. Among his publications are two books *The Modern Vice Presidency* and *Understanding Constitutional Law* (2nd edition). He has contributed to the *Encyclopedia of the American Presidency* and to the *Encyclopedia of the American Constitution* and has published articles on American government and law in various journals and books. Professor Goldstein was a Rhodes Scholar and a Wexner Heritage Scholar and in 1996–97 was designated Faculty Member of the Year at St. Louis University School of Law. He is currently Casenote Editor for the *Journal of Maritime Law and Commerce.*

ROBERT J. JOYNT, M.D., Ph.D., is Distinguished University Professor of Neurology, Neurobiology, and Anatomy at the University of Rochester. His medical and graduate degrees are both from the University of Iowa, and he attended Cambridge University in England as a Fulbright Scholar. A former department chair and former Dean of the University of Rochester School of Medicine, he has authored numerous publications, including articles in such journals as *Archives of Neurology, Neurology, Journal of the American Medical Association, Clinical Neurology,* and *Clinical Neuropsychology.* Among his many awards are the Kaiser Medal, the Jacoby Award, the Williams Foundation Award, the Scripps Society Medal, and the Lifetime Achievement Award of the Arthritis Foundation. He is a member of the Institute of Medicine of the National Academy of Science.

E. CONNIE MARIANO, M.D., F.A.C.P. (Uniformed Services University of the Health Sciences) became, in 1992, the first military woman to be selected as a White House Physician. In February 1994, she was named Director of the White House Medical Unit and personal physician to President Clinton. As Director of the White House Medical Unit, Dr. Mariano oversees a tri-service health care team responsible for providing worldwide comprehensive medical care and protective medical support to the President, Vice President, and their families. In addition, she is an Assistant Professor of Medicine at the Uniformed Services University of the Health Sciences. Dr. Mariano is a Fellow of the American College of Physicians and a Captain in the United States Navy Medical Corps.

LAWRENCE C. MOHR, M.D., F.A.C.P., F.C.C.P., is Professor of Medicine and Director of the Environmental Biosciences Program at the Medical University of South Carolina. From 1987 to 1993, he served as White House Physician to Presidents Reagan, Bush, and Clinton. Dr. Mohr received his M.D. degree from the University of North Carolina School of Medicine. Among his publications are two edited books: *International Case Studies in Risk Assessment* and *Management and Biomarkers: Medical and Workplace Applications*. His awards include the Outstanding Medical Resident Award and the Erskine Award at Walter Reed Army Hospital. Dr. Mohr has served as U.S. Representative to the International Conference on Medical Assistance to Central and Eastern Europe and is a member of the Board of Directors of the International Lung Association.

JERROLD M. POST, M.D. Yale University, is Professor of Psychiatry and Director of the Political Psychology Program at The George Washington University. He is co-author of *Political Paranoia: The Psychopolitics of Hatred* and *When Illness Strikes the Leader*, both published by Yale University Press and has written numerous articles. Dr. Post is a founding member and former Vice President of the International Society for Political Psychology. He played the lead role in developing the Camp David profiles of Menachem Begin and Anwar Sadat for President Carter. In 1979, he received a Civilian Medal of Merit in recognition of his work with the U.S. government. He now chairs the Task Force for National and International Terrorism for the American Psychiatric Association and serves on its Council of International Affairs.

ROBERT S. ROBINS, Ph. D. Duke University, is Professor of Political Science at Tulane University. His most recent books are the co-authored *Political Paranoia: The Psychopolitics of Hatred* and *When Illness Strikes the Leader*. His articles have appeared in such journals as *Psychohistory Review*, *Perspectives in Biology and Medicine*, and *Political Psychology*. Dr. Robins has served as Deputy Provost at Tulane and as Chairman of its Political Science Department. He has been a Canadian Government Grantee, a Japan Foundation Grantee, a Faculty Fellow of The Government of Quebec and is an Academic Associate of the Atlantic Council. He has also served as a consultant to the Carnegie Commission on Higher Education. During 1998–99, he was a Visiting Scholar at Simon Fraser University in Vancouver, British Columbia.

KENNETH W. THOMPSON, Ph. D. University of Chicago, served as Director of the Miller Center at the University of Virginia from 1978 until his retirement in 1998. He also served as Commonwealth Professor and then as White Burkett Miller Professor of Government and Foreign Affairs at the University of Virginia. Earlier, he was Vice President of the Rockefeller Foundation. His numerous books include *Schools of International Thought, Fathers of International Thought, Traditions and Values in Politics and Diplomacy, The President and the Public Philosophy, Winston Churchill's World View*, and *Morality and Foreign Policy*. In 1981, Dr. Thompson was named Virginia Laureate and, three years later, received the Virginia Phi Beta Kappa Prize and the College Stores Prize for his book on Winston Churchill.

JAMES F. TOOLE, M.D. Cornell, L.L.B. Lasalle, is Teagle Professor of Neurology and Professor of Public Health Sciences at the Bowman Gray School of Medicine at Wake Forest University. He has authored more than 600 publications in the fields of cerebrovascular disease, medical ethics, and medical history. A former chair of the Department of Neurology at Bowman Gray, Dr. Toole has served as President of the American Neurological Association, the International Stroke Society, and the American Society of Neuroimaging and is currently President of the World Federation of Neurology. He is co-editor of *World Neurology* and former editor of *Journal of Neurological Sciences*. Included in *The Best Doctors in America*, Dr. Toole served as Co-Chair, with Arthur Link, of the Working Group on Presidential Disability.

TOM WICKER was a prominent journalist for *The New York Times* for twenty-five years until his retirement in 1991. In addition to his writing, he served as Washington Bureau Chief for *The New York Times*, 1964–68, and then became its Associate Editor. Earlier, he had been Associate Editor of the *Nashville Tennesseean* and a Nieman Fellow at Harvard University. He has written ten novels and six books of non-fiction: *Kennedy Without Tears*; *JFK and LBJ: The Influence of Personality upon Politics* ; *One of Us: Richard Nixon and the American Dream*; *A Time to Die*; *On Press*; and *Tragic Failure: Racial Integration in America*. He also is the author of a chapter on Richard Nixon in *Character Above All* and of the text accompanying a book of photographs by Fred Maroon: *The Nixon Years: 1969–1974*.

JAMES M. YOUNG, M.D., F.A.C.P., served as White House Physician to Presidents Kennedy and Johnson (1963–66). He holds the M.D. degree from Duke University and has published in such journals as *Archives of Surgery*, *Journal of the National Cancer Institute*, *Transplantation Bulletin*, and *International Journal of Technology Assessment in Health Care*. Also, he has authored reports for both the U.S. Office of Technology Assessment and for the Massachusetts Department of Public Health. From 1969 to 1974, Dr. Young was Chief of Medicine at the Boston Naval Hospital; then, from 1975 to 1987, Vice President of Blue Cross-Blue Shield of Massachusetts and, later, of the Greenery Rehabilitation Group. From 1992 to 1995, he served as Chief of Medicine and Associate Medical Director, New England Rehabilitation Hospital.

INDEX